중학 내신 완벽 대비 종합서

능률 중학 영어

중2

능률중학영어 중2

지은이	NE능률 영어교육연구소
선임 연구원	김지현
연구원	윤인아 박효빈 남휘영 이희진
영문 교열	August Niederhaus Nathaniel Galletta Patrick Ferraro
디자인	안훈정 김연주
내지 일러스트	박응식 최은미 김동현 정경호
내지 사진	www.shutterstock.com
맥편집	김미진
영업	한기영 이경구 박인규 정철교 김남준 이우현
마케팅	박혜선 남경진 이지원 김여진

43rd SINCE1980
Let's grow together
NE능률이
미래를
창조합니다.
건강한 배움의 고객가치를 제공하겠다는 꿈을 실현하기 위해
40년이 넘는 시간 동안 열심히 달려왔습니다.
앞으로도 끊임없는 연구와 노력을 통해
당연한 것을 멈추지 않고
고객, 기업, 직원 모두가 함께 성장하는 NE능률이 되겠습니다.
NE 능률

"Success is not the key to happiness.
Happiness is the key to success.
If you love what you are doing, you will be successful."

성공은 행복을 얻는 비결이 아닙니다. 행복이 성공을 얻는 비결입니다.
여러분이 하는 일을 사랑한다면, 여러분은 성공할 것입니다.

- Albert Schweitzer -

Structures & Features

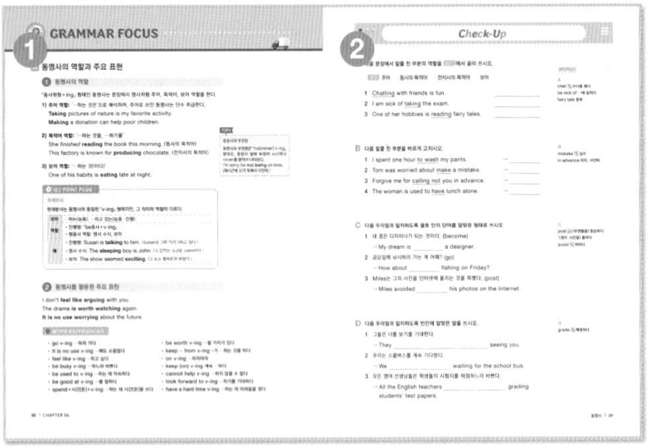

❶ GRAMMAR FOCUS

2015년 개정 교육과정을 분석하여 중학교 2학년에서 알아야 할 필수 문법을 체계적으로 정리했습니다. 시험에 자주 출제되는 내용은 내신 POINT PLUS로, 주의해야 할 문법 사항은 TIPS로 정리하여 쉽게 학습할 수 있습니다.

❷ Check-Up

GRAMMAR FOCUS에서 배운 내용을 간단한 유형의 연습 문제를 통해 확인해 볼 수 있습니다.

❸ Grammar Practice

앞서 배운 문법 사항을 통합하여 Check-Up보다 심화된 문제를 제공하여 이해도를 더 확실하게 점검할 수 있습니다.

❹ 내신 완성 Grammar Practice

학교 시험과 유사한 문제로 구성하여 실전에 대비할 수 있습니다.

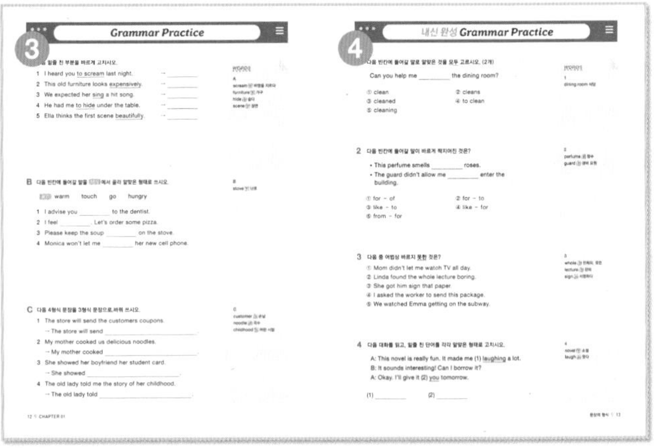

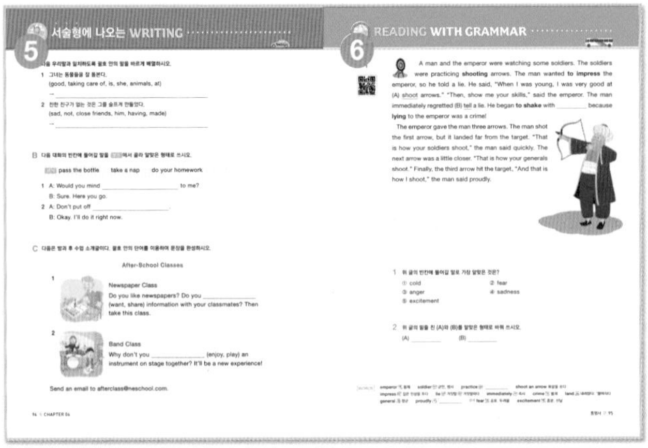

❺ 서술형에 나오는 WRITING

다양한 서술형 문제를 통해 GRAMMAR FOCUS를 반복 학습할 수 있고, 쓰기는 물론 학교 내신 시험의 서술형 주관식 문항 대비도 완벽하게 할 수 있습니다.

❻ READING WITH GRAMMAR

해당 문법 항목이 녹아 있는 흥미로운 내용의 지문을 통해 문법 연습은 물론 독해 실력도 동시에 높일 수 있습니다.

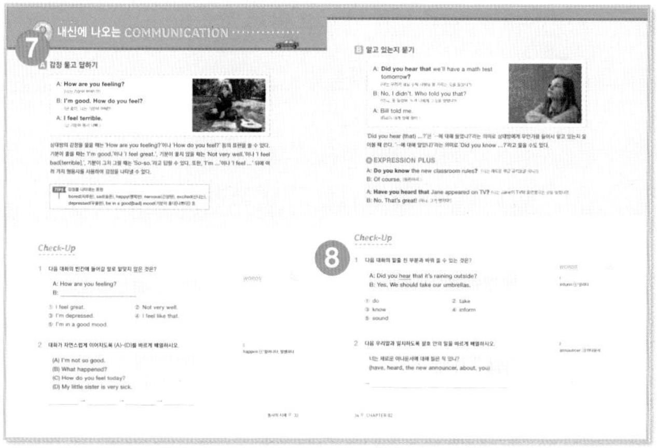

⑦ 내신에 나오는 COMMUNICATION

중학교 2학년 과정의 필수 의사소통 기능을 생생한 대화문을 통해 학습할 수 있습니다. 각 의사소통 기능과 관련된 다른 표현들도 추가로 학습할 수 있습니다.

⑧ Check-Up

학교 시험과 유사한 문제 유형을 통해 학습한 내용을 확인하고 내신에 대비할 수 있습니다.

⑨ FINAL TEST

어휘, 의사소통 기능, 문법 등 앞에서 학습한 내용을 종합적으로 확인해 볼 수 있습니다. 학교 내신 시험과 유사한 난이도의 다양한 문제를 풀어보며 실전에 대비하고 실력도 점검해 볼 수 있습니다.

⑩ 내신 완성 서술형

내신에 자주 출제되는 서술형 주관식 문제를 풀며 서술형 주관식에 대한 자신감을 높일 수 있습니다.

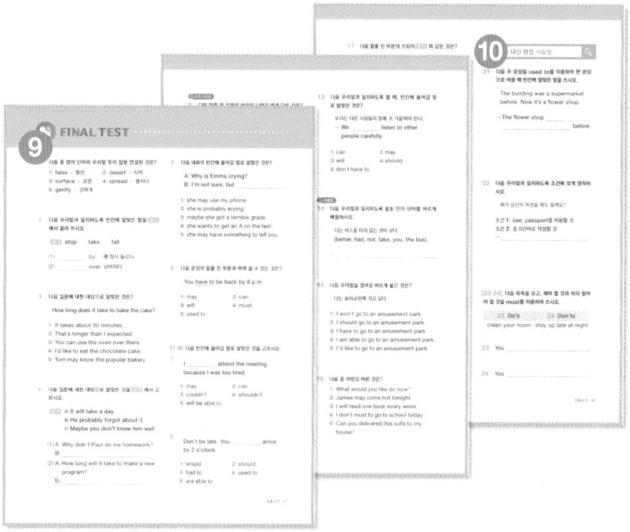

⑪ WORD LIST

해당 과에서 쓰인 어휘 중 핵심 어휘만을 별도로 학습할 수 있습니다. 어휘를 학습하며 한 과를 마무리할 수 있습니다.

Contents

CHAPTER 01

문장의 형식

GET READY

This sauce **tastes** sweet.
(이 소스는 단맛이 난다.)

She **gave** her son a birthday gift.
(그녀는 그녀의 아들에게 생일 선물을 주었다.)

The beautiful weather **makes** me happy.
(아름다운 날씨는 나를 행복하게 만든다.)

영어 문장에서는 동사의 종류에 따라 뒤에 오는 말이 달라져요. 감각동사 뒤에는 주격 보어 역할을 하는 형용사가 오고, 수여동사 뒤에는 두 개의 목적어가 와요. 또 어떤 동사들은 목적어의 성질이나 상태 등을 설명해 주는 목적격 보어를 필요로 해요.

GRAMMAR FOCUS

A 감각동사와 수여동사

1 「감각동사+형용사」 (2형식)

감각동사는 '보이다, 맛이 나다, 느끼다' 등 사람의 감각을 표현하는 동사이다. 감각동사 뒤에 형용사가 쓰여 주어의 성질이나 상태를 보충 설명하는 주격 보어의 역할을 한다. 주격 보어로 형용사 대신 부사를 쓰지 않도록 주의한다.

예 look, sound, smell, taste, feel 등

「감각동사+형용사」	예
「look+형용사」: …해 보이다	The patients **look good** today.
「sound+형용사」: …하게 들리다	His idea **sounds great**.
「smell+형용사」: …한 냄새가 나다	The coffee **smells nice**.
「taste+형용사」: …한 맛이 나다	The milk **tastes sour**.
「feel+형용사」: …하게 느끼다	Fred's family **felt tired**.

TIPS

「감각동사+like+명사(구)」
감각동사 뒤에 「like+명사(구)」를 써서 '…처럼 ~하다'를 나타낼 수 있다. 이때 like는 '…처럼'을 의미하는 전치사이다.
The painting **looked like** *a real photo*. (그 그림은 진짜 사진처럼 보였다.)

2 「수여동사+간접목적어+직접목적어」 (4형식)

수여동사는 두 개의 목적어가 필요한 동사이다. 수여동사가 쓰인 문장은 '…에게(간접목적어) ~를(직접목적어) …(해)주다'로 해석한다.

예 give, bring, send, tell, teach, show, lend, make, buy, cook 등
I **bought** my sister some ice cream.
The clerk **showed** us new clothes.

내신 POINT PLUS

4형식의 3형식 전환
4형식 문장은 간접목적어와 직접목적어의 순서를 바꾸고 간접목적어 앞에 전치사 to, for, of 등을 붙여 3형식 문장으로 전환할 수 있다.

1 to를 쓰는 동사: give, send, show, teach, tell 등
I **sent** John a Christmas card. (4형식) ⇨ I **sent** a Christmas card **to** John. (3형식)
(나는 John에게 크리스마스카드를 보냈다.)

2 for를 쓰는 동사: buy, make, cook 등
He **made** me a cup of coffee. (4형식) ⇨ He **made** a cup of coffee **for** me. (3형식)
(그는 내게 커피 한 잔을 만들어 주었다.)

Check-Up

A 다음 괄호 안에서 알맞은 말을 고르시오.

1 The noise (sounded / sounded like) thunder.

2 The flowers in the garden smell (good / well).

3 Ashley bought some toys (for / to) her children.

4 I feel (nervous / nervously) in front of many people.

WORDS

A
thunder 명 천둥
nervous 형 불안해하는

B 다음 밑줄 친 부분을 바르게 고치시오.

1 The music sounds wonderfully. → ________

2 The company sent the bill of us. → ________

3 Your new necklace looks greatly. → ________

4 Somebody gave a chocolate cake Anne. → ________

B
wonderfully 부 아주; 놀랍도록
bill 명 계산서
necklace 명 목걸이

C 다음 두 문장이 같은 뜻이 되도록 빈칸에 알맞은 말을 쓰시오.

1 My mom made me a scarf.
→ My mom made a scarf ________ ________.

2 Long ago, Wendy told them her secret.
→ Long ago, Wendy told her secret ________ ________.

3 His older brother teaches us Korean history.
→ His older brother teaches Korean history ________ ________.

C
secret 명 비밀
history 명 역사

D 다음 우리말과 일치하도록 괄호 안의 말을 이용하여 문장을 완성하시오.

1 이 수프는 매운맛이 난다. (soup, spicy)
→ This ________ ________ ________.

2 그는 나에게 얼마의 돈을 빌려주었다. (lend, some money)
→ He ________ ________ ________ ________.

3 Paul은 그녀에게 지도를 보여 주었다. (show, the map)
→ Paul ________ ________ ________ ________.

D
lend 동 빌려주다
(lent - lent)

B 목적격 보어를 가지는 동사

1 「동사+목적어+목적격 보어」 (5형식)

일부 동사들은 목적어 뒤에 목적어의 성질이나 상태를 보충 설명하는 목적격 보어가 필요하다.

2 목적격 보어의 형태

동사에 따라 뒤에 오는 목적격 보어가 명사, 형용사, to부정사로 달라진다.

1) 명사(구)를 목적격 보어로 취하는 동사 예 call, make, name 등

They **named** their cat "**Mimi**."

The TV show **made** the boy **a star**.

2) 형용사(구)를 목적격 보어로 취하는 동사 예 make, keep, find, think 등

I **kept** the door **open**.

Eric **found** the movie **boring**.

3) to부정사(구)를 목적격 보어로 취하는 동사 예 want, allow, expect, tell, advise, ask, persuade 등

Do you **want** me **to help** you?

Mom **allowed** us **to play** computer games.

3 사역동사와 지각동사

1) 「사역동사+목적어+동사원형」

사역동사는 주어가 목적어에게 어떤 동작을 하도록 시킬 때 쓰는 동사이다. 사역동사가 쓰인 문장은 '(목적어)가 …하게 하다'라고 해석한다.

예 let, have, make 등

Please **let** me **borrow** your textbook.

Her father **made** her **go** to bed early.

TIPS

1 help는 목적격 보어로 to부정사와 동사원형을 모두 쓸 수 있다.
I **helped** him (**to**) **move** a sofa. (나는 그가 소파를 옮기는 것을 도왔다.)

2 get은 사역의 의미지만 목적격 보어로 to부정사를 쓴다.
My sister **got** me **to see** a doctor. (나의 언니는 내가 진찰을 받도록 했다.)

2) 「지각동사+목적어+동사원형/현재분사」

지각동사가 쓰인 문장은 '(목적어)가 …하는 것을 보다/듣다/느끼다'라고 해석한다. 동작이 진행 중임을 강조할 때는 목적격 보어로 현재분사를 쓴다.

예 see, watch, hear, feel 등

We **felt** the ground **shake**.

Jessica **heard** someone **crying**.

Check-Up

A 다음 괄호 안에서 알맞은 말을 고르시오.

1 I saw the girl (waving / to wave) at me.
2 Ron told his classmate (be / to be) quiet.
3 Fiona had me (listen / to listen) to the song.
4 His rude behavior made us (angry / angrily).

B 다음 밑줄 친 부분을 바르게 고치시오.

1 People want the suspect <u>tell</u> the truth. → ________
2 We watched the dog <u>to run</u> in the yard. → ________
3 My dad made me <u>picking</u> up the trash. → ________
4 Keep your hands <u>cleanly</u> before you eat. → ________

C 다음 괄호 안의 단어를 빈칸에 알맞은 형태로 쓰시오.

1 I thought the test ________. (easy)
2 She felt her legs ________. (tremble)
3 You always ask me ________ milkshakes. (make)
4 Amanda allowed her sister ________ her pants. (wear)

D 다음 우리말과 일치하도록 괄호 안의 단어를 이용하여 문장을 완성하시오.

1 나는 어제 개가 시끄럽게 짖는 것을 들었다. (bark)
→ I heard a dog ________ loudly yesterday.
2 우리는 그들이 경기에서 이길 거라 예상했다. (expect, win)
→ We ________ them ________ ________ the game.
3 그의 친구들은 그를 천재라고 부른다. (call, a genius)
→ His friends ________ ________ ________ ________.

WORDS

A
wave 동 (손을) 흔들다
behavior 명 행동

B
suspect 명 용의자
yard 명 마당
trash 명 쓰레기

C
tremble 동 떨다; *떨리다

D
bark 동 (개가) 짖다
win 동 이기다
genius 명 천재

Grammar Practice

A 다음 밑줄 친 부분을 바르게 고치시오.

1 I heard you <u>to scream</u> last night. → ________
2 This old furniture looks <u>expensively</u>. → ________
3 We expected her <u>sing</u> a hit song. → ________
4 He had me <u>to hide</u> under the table. → ________
5 Ella thinks the first scene <u>beautifully</u>. → ________

WORDS

A
scream 동 비명을 지르다
furniture 명 가구
hide 동 숨다
scene 명 장면

B 다음 빈칸에 들어갈 말을 보기 에서 골라 알맞은 형태로 쓰시오.

보기 warm touch go hungry

1 I advise you ________ to the dentist.
2 I feel ________. Let's order some pizza.
3 Please keep the soup ________ on the stove.
4 Monica won't let me ________ her new cell phone.

B
stove 명 난로

C 다음 4형식 문장을 3형식 문장으로 바꿔 쓰시오.

1 The store will send the customers coupons.
→ The store will send ________________.
2 My mother cooked us delicious noodles.
→ My mother cooked ________________.
3 She showed her boyfriend her student card.
→ She showed ________________.
4 The old lady told me the story of her childhood.
→ The old lady told ________________.

C
customer 명 손님
noodle 명 국수
childhood 명 어린 시절

내신 완성 Grammar Practice

1 다음 빈칸에 들어갈 말로 알맞은 것을 모두 고르시오. (2개)

Can you help me ________ the dining room?

① clean ② cleans
③ cleaned ④ to clean
⑤ cleaning

2 다음 빈칸에 들어갈 말이 바르게 짝지어진 것은?

• This perfume smells ________ roses.
• The guard didn't allow me ________ enter the building.

① for – of ② for – to
③ like – to ④ like – for
⑤ from – for

3 다음 중 어법상 바르지 못한 것은?

① Mom didn't let me watch TV all day.
② Linda found the whole lecture boring.
③ She got him sign that paper.
④ I asked the worker to send this package.
⑤ We watched Emma getting on the subway.

4 다음 대화를 읽고, 밑줄 친 단어를 각각 알맞은 형태로 고치시오.

A: This novel is really fun. It made me (1) laughing a lot.
B: It sounds interesting! Can I borrow it?
A: Okay. I'll give it (2) you tomorrow.

(1) ________ (2) ________

WORDS

1
dining room 식당

2
perfume 명 향수
guard 명 경비 요원

3
whole 형 전체의, 모든
lecture 명 강의
sign 동 서명하다

4
novel 명 소설
laugh 동 웃다

서술형에 나오는 WRITING

A 다음 우리말과 일치하도록 괄호 안의 말을 바르게 배열하시오.

1 이 인도 카레는 맛있다.
(Indian curry, good, this, tastes)
→ ______________________

2 제게 수건 좀 가져다줄래요?
(you, a towel, me, would, bring)
→ ______________________

3 그는 그의 엄마에게 그의 용돈을 올려달라고 설득했다.
(persuaded, raise, he, his mom, his allowance, to)
→ ______________________

B 다음 우리말과 일치하도록 괄호 안의 단어를 이용하여 문장을 완성하시오.

1 그들은 그를 영웅이라고 부른다. (call, a hero)
→ ______________________

2 그 아이디어는 창의적이게 들린다. (the idea, creative)
→ ______________________

3 Min은 나에게 중국어를 가르쳐 주었다. (teach, Chinese)
→ ______________________

C 다음 광고문을 보고, 괄호 안의 말을 바르게 배열하여 문장을 완성하시오.

Emily's Flower Shop

Do you want to **1** ______________________ (happy, your parents, make)? We have lots of beautiful flowers. **2** ______________________ (smell, fresh and sweet, they). Your parents will love them!

1

You want to borrow your neighbor's bicycle for a day. But you're afraid she will say no. What should you do? Ask to borrow it for a month! This may sound (A) [strange / strangely], but it's actually an effective way to persuade people. It's called the "door-in-the-face technique."

(①) Imagine the following situation: You knock on your neighbor's door and ask her (B) [lend / to lend] you her bicycle for a month. (②) Of course, she says no, but she **feels sorry** for you. (③) You are disappointed, but instead, you ask to borrow it for just one day. (④) With the door-in-the-face technique, you can **persuade** her **to lend** you her bicycle for a day. (⑤)

1 글의 흐름으로 보아 주어진 문장이 들어갈 위치로 가장 적절한 곳은?

Your neighbor is relieved, so she happily agrees and gives her bicycle to you.

① ② ③ ④ ⑤

2 위 글의 (A)와 (B)의 각 네모 안에서 어법에 맞는 표현을 골라 쓰시오.

(A) ____________ (B) ____________

WORDS borrow 동 빌리다 neighbor 명 이웃 actually 부 실제로, 사실은 effective 형 [1] ____________ persuade 동 설득하다 technique 명 기법, 기술 imagine 동 [2] ____________ situation 명 상황 disappointed 형 실망한 instead 부 대신에

2

May's Blog

It's winter here in Beijing. People in this city are wearing masks. Do you know why? This is because of the dirty air. Air pollution gets worse in winter because people burn coal to heat their houses. This produces harmful gases, and the gases form *fine dust.

Some may think this is not a big deal, but it affects our daily lives. First of all, fine dust in the air reduces *visibility. For this reason, many airports were closed last week. Also, when people breathe, the fine dust can enter the lungs and **make** them **ill**. I wanted to go jogging this evening, but my parents didn't let me ________ outside. They said the government has **advised** people **to stay** indoors for their health. When will the sky be clear again?

*fine dust: 미세먼지 (지름이 10㎛ 이하인 먼지)
*visibility: 가시성 (눈에 잘 보이는 정도)

1 **What is the passage mainly about?**

① How fine dust is formed
② Weather changes in Beijing
③ Useful health advice in winter
④ Causes and effects of fine dust
⑤ What fine dust and visibility are

2 **Which is the best choice for the blank?**

① went ② go
③ going ④ to go
⑤ gone

WORDS
pollution 명 오염 **burn** 동 태우다 **coal** 명 석탄 **heat** 동 뜨겁게[따뜻하게] 만들다 **produce** 동 [1] ________ **harmful** 형 [2] ________ **form** 동 형성시키다 **a big deal** 대단한 것, 중대한 것 **affect** 동 영향을 미치다 **lung** 명 폐 **ill** 형 아픈 **government** 명 정부 **indoors** 부 실내에서 문제 **cause** 명 원인 **effect** 명 영향; 결과

A 안부 묻고 답하기

A: Hi! Long time no see!
(안녕! 오랜만이구나!)

B: **How have you been?**
(어떻게 지내셨어요?)

A: **I've been fine**, thanks.
(잘 지냈어, 고마워.)

한동안 보지 못했던 상대방에게 그동안의 안부를 물을 때는 'How have you been?'이라고 말할 수 있다. 대답할 때는 'I've been fine.', 'Not bad.' 등의 표현을 쓸 수 있다.

EXPRESSION PLUS

1 안부 묻기
- How are you doing? (어떻게 지내니?)
- How's it going? (어떻게 지내니?)

2 안부 답하기
- (Pretty) Good. / Very well. (잘 지내.)
- Not bad. (나쁘지 않아.) / So-so. (그저 그래.)
- Not (so) good. (잘 지내지 못해.)

Check-Up

1 다음 대화의 빈칸에 들어갈 말로 알맞지 않은 것은?

A: How are you doing?
B: ____________

① Not bad.
② Just so-so.
③ Pretty good.
④ I'm fine, thanks.
⑤ That's all right.

WORDS
1
pretty 부 꽤

2 다음 괄호 안의 단어를 이용하여 대화를 완성하시오.

A: ________ ________ ________ ________?
(have, be)
B: I've been good, thanks.

B 경험 묻고 답하기

A: **Have you ever been** to Paris**?**
(너는 파리에 가 본 적이 있니?)

B: **Yes, I have. I've been** there **twice**.
What about you?
(응, 있어. 나는 그곳에 두 번 가 봤어. 너는 어때?)

A: **I've never been** there.
(나는 그곳에 가 본 적이 없어.)

상대방의 경험에 대해 물을 때는 'Have you ever v-ed ...?'로 표현할 수 있다. 이에 대한 대답으로 경험한 적이 있을 때는 'Yes, I have.', 경험한 적이 없을 때는 'No, I haven't.'라고 말할 수 있다.

EXPRESSION PLUS

A: **Have you ever played** tennis**?** (너는 테니스를 쳐 본 적이 있니?)
B: **No, I haven't.** (아니, 없어.)

TIPS 경험을 묻고 답할 때는 ever, before, never, once, twice 등의 부사를 함께 쓰는 경우가 많다.
I have eaten at that restaurant **before**. (나는 전에 그 식당에서 먹어 본 적이 있어.)

Check-Up

1 다음 질문에 대한 알맞은 응답을 찾아 연결하시오.

(1) Have you ever had a pet? •
(2) Have you ever seen an actor in person? •
(3) Have you ever played the guitar? •

• ⓐ Yes, I had one once.
• ⓑ No, I've never played it before.
• ⓒ Yes. I've seen Charlie Andrews before.

WORDS
1
pet 명 애완동물
actor 명 배우
in person 직접

2 다음 대화의 빈칸에 들어갈 말로 알맞은 것은?

A: ____________________
B: Yes, I've been there once.

① How have you been?
② Where do you come from?
③ When will you go to Busan?
④ Have you ever been to Busan?
⑤ How did you get to Busan last summer?

FINAL TEST

1 다음 중 영어 단어와 우리말 뜻이 잘못 연결된 것은?

① win - 이기다 ② whole - 전체의
③ novel - 소설 ④ instead - 대신에
⑤ customer - 점원

2 다음 빈칸에 들어갈 말을 보기 에서 골라 쓰시오.

보기 wave hide heat form

(1) ________ a frying pan and add some oil.

(2) He wanted to ________ behind the tree.

3 다음 대화의 빈칸에 들어갈 말로 알맞은 것은?

A: Hi! I haven't seen you for a while.
B: Hi. ____________________
A: Not good. I've been pretty busy these days.

① What's the matter?
② How are you doing?
③ Why did you do that?
④ How did you know that?
⑤ What are you going to do?

4 대화가 자연스럽게 이어지도록 (A)~(D)를 바르게 배열하시오.

(A) Oh! How was it?
(B) Yes, I've eaten *kimchi*.
(C) Have you ever tried Korean food?
(D) It was a little spicy but tasted great!

______ → ______ → ______ → ______

5 다음 중 짝지어진 대화가 어색한 것은?

① A: Have you ever skated?
B: No, I haven't.
② A: How have you been?
B: So-so. I have been sick.
③ A: Have you ever worked part-time?
B: I've been fine, thanks.
④ A: Have you ever been to Thailand?
B: Yes, I've been there twice.
⑤ A: How is it going?
B: Very well. How about you?

[6-7] 다음 빈칸에 들어갈 말로 알맞은 것을 고르시오.

6 I expected him ________ a home run.

① hit ② hits
③ was hit ④ to hit
⑤ hitting

7 Mom let me ________ for a week.

① travel ② travels
③ traveled ④ to travel
⑤ traveling

자주 나와요

8 다음 빈칸에 들어갈 말이 바르게 짝지어진 것은?

- Ann bought a necktie ________.
- They want you ________ on your studies.

① me - focus ② to me - focus
③ to me - to focus ④ for me - focus
⑤ for me - to focus

[9-10] 다음 빈칸에 들어갈 말로 알맞지 않은 것을 고르시오.

9 Why does Paulina look ________ today?

① tired ② excited
③ happy ④ sadly
⑤ depressed

10 Our group members found English ________.

① fun ② easy
③ boring ④ interest
⑤ difficult

11 다음 빈칸에 공통으로 들어갈 말을 쓰시오.

- He told surprising news ________ his son.
- We showed our collection of paintings ________ them.

12 다음 우리말을 영어로 바르게 옮긴 것은?

나는 그가 해변에 누워 있는 것을 보았다.

① I see him lie on the beach.
② I saw he lying on the beach.
③ I saw him lied on the beach.
④ I saw him lying on the beach.
⑤ I saw him to lie on the beach.

서술형

[13-14] 다음 우리말과 일치하도록 괄호 안의 말을 바르게 배열하시오.

13 그 발명품은 그녀를 백만장자로 만들었다.
(made, a millionaire, her, the invention)

→ ________________________________
____

14 우리 아빠는 내가 내 교복을 세탁하기를 원하셨다.
(my school uniform, me, wanted, wash, to, my dad)

→ ________________________________
____

15 다음 중 어법상 바르지 못한 것은?

① This tea smells well.
② I allowed him to sit next to me.
③ You must keep your desk clean.
④ He thought her behavior strange.
⑤ Matt taught the rules of baseball to me.

16 다음 중 어법상 바른 것은?

① I expect her apologize to me.
② Sally asked him keep his promise.
③ He heard someone to sing a song.
④ Mom cooked chicken soup for me.
⑤ They feel nervously about the test tomorrow.

어려워요

17 다음 밑줄 친 부분 중 어법상 바르지 못한 것은?

Jenny got a bad cold. So her brother got her ① going to the hospital. The doctor had her ② take a deep breath. He advised her ③ to take some medicine and ④ to drink enough water. He said that it would keep her ⑤ healthy.

자주 나와요

18 다음 문장을 3형식 문장으로 바르게 고친 것은?

Robin bought me a movie ticket.

① Robin bought a movie ticket me.
② Robin bought to me a movie ticket.
③ Robin bought me for a movie ticket.
④ Robin bought a movie ticket to me.
⑤ Robin bought a movie ticket for me.

[19-20] 다음 우리말과 일치하도록 괄호 안의 말을 이용하여 문장을 완성하시오.

19 우리는 이 인형을 Amber라 부른다.
(call, doll)

→ We ________ ________ ________ ________.

20 선생님은 그녀에게 몇 가지 충고를 해 주었다.
(give, some advice)

→ The teacher ________ ________ ________ ________.

내신 완성 서술형

21 다음 두 문장을 5형식 문장으로 바꿔 쓰시오.

Baker cleaned his studio. Lisa helped him.

→ Lisa helped ________ ________ ________ ________.

22 다음 우리말과 일치하도록 조건에 맞게 영작하시오.

그는 무언가가 그를 향해 날아오는 것을 느꼈다.

조건 1: something, fly toward를 이용할 것
조건 2: 총 6단어로 작성할 것

→ ________________________________

[23-24] 다음 글에서 밑줄 친 부분을 바르게 고치시오.

There was a watermelon at the market. It looked a soccer ball. The clerk allowed me have a slice of it.

23 looked → ________________

24 have → ________________

WORD LIST

Grammar

□ thunder	명 천둥
□ nervous	형 불안해하는
□ bill	명 계산서
□ secret	명 비밀
□ history	명 역사
□ lend	동 빌려주다
□ wave	동 (손을) 흔들다
□ behavior	명 행동
□ yard	명 마당
□ trash	명 쓰레기
□ bark	동 (개가) 짖다
□ win	동 이기다
□ genius	명 천재
□ furniture	명 가구
□ hide	동 숨다
□ scene	명 장면
□ customer	명 손님
□ childhood	명 어린 시절
□ perfume	명 향수
□ guard	명 경비 요원
□ whole	형 전체의, 모든
□ lecture	명 강의
□ sign	동 서명하다
□ novel	명 소설
□ laugh	동 웃다

Reading

□ borrow	동 빌리다
□ neighbor	명 이웃
□ actually	부 실제로, 사실은
□ effective	형 효과적인
□ persuade	동 설득하다
□ imagine	동 상상하다
□ situation	명 상황
□ disappointed	형 실망한
□ instead	부 대신에
□ pollution	명 오염
□ burn	동 태우다
□ heat	동 뜨겁게[따뜻하게] 만들다
□ produce	동 생산하다
□ harmful	형 해로운
□ form	동 형성시키다
□ a big deal	대단한 것, 중대한 것
□ affect	동 영향을 미치다
□ lung	명 폐
□ ill	형 아픈
□ government	명 정부
□ indoors	부 실내에서
□ cause	명 원인

Communication

□ pretty	부 꽤
□ pet	명 애완동물
□ actor	명 배우

Final Test

□ focus on	…에 주력하다, 초점을 맞추다
□ depressed	형 우울한
□ collection	명 수집품
□ invention	명 발명품
□ rule	명 규칙
□ apologize	동 사과하다
□ promise	명 약속
□ clerk	명 점원

CHAPTER 02

동사의 시제

GET READY

I **ride** a bike every day.
(나는 매일 자전거를 탄다.)

I **rode** a bike yesterday.
(나는 어제 자전거를 탔다.)

I **will ride** a bike tomorrow.
(나는 내일 자전거를 탈 것이다.)

I **have** just **ridden** a bike.
(나는 방금 자전거를 탔다.)

어떤 일이 일어난 시간을 표현하는 것을 시제라고 해요. '자전거를 탄다', '자전거를 탔다', '자전거를 탈 것이다', '방금 자전거를 탔다' 등과 같이 동사를 변화시켜 다양하게 시제를 표현해요.

GRAMMAR FOCUS

A 단순시제와 진행형

1 현재시제

현재시제는 현재의 사실이나 상태, 습관, 반복되는 일, 또는 변하지 않는 진리를 나타낼 때 쓴다.

I **have** dinner at six in the evening.

Earth **moves** around the sun.

2 과거시제

과거시제는 과거의 특정 시점에 일어났던 일이나 상태를 나타낼 때 쓴다.

Daniel **bought** a used car yesterday.

Rachel **was** very sick last night.

TIPS

과거시제와 자주 함께 쓰이는 부사(구)

- last night(어젯밤)
- yesterday(어제)
- then/at that time(그때)
- a week/month/year ago (일주일/한 달/일 년 전에)
- in+과거 년도(…년에)

3 미래시제

미래시제는 미래에 일어날 일을 예측하거나 미래의 계획을 나타낼 때 쓴다.

1) 「**will+동사원형**」**:** 미래에 대한 예측이나 주어의 의지를 나타내며, '…할 것이다'로 해석한다.

Dad **will arrive** home at 8 p.m. as usual.

I **will not**[**won't**] **give** up on the travel plan.

2) 「**be going to+동사원형**」**:** 미래에 대한 예측이나 이미 예정된 계획을 나타내며, '…할 것이다, …할 예정이다'로 해석한다.

It'**s going to snow**[**will snow**] next weekend.

I **am not going to invite** my friends to my house tonight.

⊕ 내신 POINT PLUS

미래를 나타내는 현재시제와 현재진행형

가까운 미래의 확정된 일이나 계획은 현재시제 또는 현재진행형으로 나타낼 수 있다.

The exams **start** next Tuesday. (시험은 다음 주 화요일에 시작할 것이다.)

He **is moving** to Seoul tomorrow. (그는 내일 서울로 이사 갈 것이다.)

4 진행형

1) 현재진행형: 「be동사의 현재형+v-ing」의 형태로, '(지금) …하고 있다'의 의미이다.

Lucas **is washing** his dog in the bathroom.

They **are preparing** a surprise party for Sam.

2) 과거진행형: 「be동사의 과거형+v-ing」의 형태로, '(과거에) …하고 있었다'의 의미이다.

They **were looking** at each other.

My sister **was talking** to her friends when I saw her.

TIPS

like, hate, want, know, own, have(가지다) 등 감정이나 지각, 소유를 나타내는 동사는 진행형으로 쓰지 않는다.

Check-Up

A 다음 괄호 안에서 알맞은 말을 고르시오.

1 We (eat / ate) lunch together a week ago.
2 I (called / will call) Seojin, but he didn't pick up.
3 Lena (goes / is going) for a walk for 30 minutes every morning.
4 Dan (is reading / was reading) a book when I opened the door.

WORDS

A
pick up 전화를 받다

B 다음 밑줄 친 부분을 바르게 고치시오.

1 There were 24 hours in a day. → __________
2 Yuna is knowing how to play chess. → __________
3 The children are swim in the pool right now. → __________
4 She's going to traveling to Europe next month. → __________

B
chess 명 체스
travel 동 여행하다

C 다음 빈칸에 들어갈 말을 보기 에서 골라 쓰시오.

보기 now yesterday tomorrow every day

1 He lives in Hong Kong alone __________.
2 Amy takes the same bus __________.
3 They will arrive at Jeju-do at 11 a.m. __________.
4 I didn't bring my homework to school __________.

C
alone 부 혼자
same 형 같은, 동일한

D 다음 괄호 안의 단어를 빈칸에 알맞은 형태로 쓰시오.

1 Paul is __________ a seat right now. (book)
2 Her brother __________ a middle school student now. (be)
3 Emily __________ a skirt online last month. (order)
4 My family __________ __________ a barbecue party next weekend. (have)

D
book 동 예약하다
order 동 주문하다
have a party 파티를 열다

GRAMMAR FOCUS

B 현재완료

1 현재완료의 의미와 형태

현재완료는 과거의 일이나 상태가 현재까지 영향을 미칠 때 쓴다.

1) 긍정문: 「have[has]+v-ed」
Tom and his wife **have waited** for their son all day long.

2) 부정문: 「have[has]+not+v-ed」로, not 대신 never를 쓸 수도 있다.
I **have not**[**haven't**] **tried** this recipe before.

3) 의문문: 「Have[Has]+주어+v-ed ...?」
A: **Have** you **been** to London**?** B: **Yes**, I **have**. / **No**, I **haven't**.

TIPS

1 현재완료와 함께 쓰이지 않는 표현
현재완료는 과거의 특정 시점을 나타내는 표현(yesterday, ago, when 등)과 함께 쓰지 않는다.
I have seen this movie yesterday. (x)

2 주의해야 할 동사의 불규칙 변형
- have-had-had • meet-met-met • read-read-read • see-saw-seen
- go-went-gone • wear-wore-worn • know-knew-known • take-took-taken

2 현재완료의 용법

1) 완료: '(지금) 막 …했다'의 뜻으로, 과거에 시작된 동작이 지금 막 완료되었음을 나타낸다.
자주 함께 쓰이는 표현 예 already(이미, 벌써), just(막, 방금), yet(아직) 등
We'**ve** *just* **sold** our old items.
The subway **has not arrived** at the station *yet*.

2) 경험: '…해 본 적이 있다'의 뜻으로, 과거부터 현재까지의 경험을 나타낸다.
자주 함께 쓰이는 표현 예 ever(한 번이라도), never(절대, 한 번도 … 않다), before(전에), once(한 번) 등
Have you *ever* **seen** a rainbow**?**
I **have** *never* **lied** to you.

3) 계속: '…해 왔다'의 뜻으로, 과거에 시작된 동작이나 상태가 현재까지 계속되고 있음을 나타낸다.
자주 함께 쓰이는 표현 예 since(… 이후, …부터), for(… 동안) 등
She **has had** cats *since* she was fifteen.
Charlie **has studied** Korean *for* six months.

4) 결과: '…해 버렸다 (그래서 지금 …하다)'의 뜻으로, 과거에 일어난 일의 결과가 현재까지 영향을 미치고 있음을 나타낸다.
I **have lost** my wallet. (→ So I don't have any money now.)
I **have forgotten** my email password. (→ So I can't log in to my email now.)

Check-Up

A 다음 괄호 안에서 알맞은 말을 고르시오.

1 Have you ever (hear / heard) this story?

2 Julie (taken / has taken) violin lessons for two years.

3 She (finished / has finished) the work three hours ago.

4 It (has been / was) two years since you graduated from elementary school.

WORDS

A

graduate from …를 졸업하다

elementary school 초등학교

B 다음 밑줄 친 현재완료의 용법으로 알맞은 것을 보기 에서 골라 쓰시오.

보기 경험 결과 계속

1 Sam has been to South America five times. ________

2 My father has worked at a bank for ten years. ________

3 They have moved to Canada. So they don't live here. ________

C 다음 밑줄 친 부분을 바르게 고치시오.

1 Did they already had lunch? → ________

2 I have read comic books last night. → ________

3 She has never be to the top floor. → ________

4 Mina donated money since she got her job. → ________

C

donate 동 기부하다

job 명 일, 직장

D 다음 우리말과 일치하도록 괄호 안의 단어를 이용하여 문장을 완성하시오.

1 그 비행기는 아직 출발하지 않았다. (depart)

→ The flight ________ ________ ________ yet.

2 Jack은 그 기계를 방금 수리했다. (just, repair)

→ Jack ________ ________ ________ the machine.

3 나는 어렸을 때부터 안경을 썼다. (wear)

→ I ________ ________ glasses since I was a child.

D

depart 동 출발하다

repair 동 수리하다

Grammar Practice

A 다음 밑줄 친 부분을 바르게 고치시오.

1 How were you today? → ________
2 I will going jogging after work. → ________
3 A man has delivered a package yesterday. → ________
4 Josh played the cello since he was young. → ________
5 When I came back home, my brother is doing the dishes. → ________

B 다음 괄호 안의 단어를 빈칸에 알맞은 형태로 쓰시오.

1 He ________ his class last Monday. (cancel)
2 She ________ ________ old coins for the last three years. (collect)
3 My aunt ________ ________ cookies in the kitchen right now. (bake)
4 I ________ never ________ her, but I saw her in a picture. (meet)
5 I ________ ________ ________ ________ my cat to the vet tomorrow. (take)

C 다음 우리말과 일치하도록 괄호 안의 말을 이용하여 문장을 완성하시오.

1 그 대전행 버스는 항상 정시에 출발한다. (leave)
→ The bus to Daejeon always ________ on time.
2 Tom은 2년 동안 군대에서 복무해 왔다. (serve in the army)
→ Tom ________ ________ ________ ________ ________ for two years.
3 나는 3일 전에 뮤지컬 모차르트를 관람했다. (see the musical)
→ I ________ ________ ________ *Mozart* three days ago.
4 넌 7시에 무엇을 하고 있었니? (do)
→ What ________ ________ ________ at 7 o'clock?

WORDS

A
deliver 동 배달하다
do the dishes 설거지하다

B
cancel 동 취소하다
coin 명 동전
collect 동 수집하다
vet 명 수의사

C
serve 동 근무[복무]하다
army 명 군대

내신 완성 Grammar Practice

1 다음 중 어법상 바르지 <u>못한</u> 것은?

① Mike will visit the office next Friday.
② Jenny has talked with Mira for an hour.
③ Daniel has been a pilot for seven years.
④ Pandas mainly live in the mountains of China.
⑤ She is going to rides a horse in the field.

2 다음 빈칸에 들어갈 말로 알맞지 <u>않은</u> 것은?

Tina broke the world record ______________.

① in 2017
② last week
③ yesterday
④ since last year
⑤ a few days ago

3 다음 밑줄 친 부분의 쓰임이 보기와 같은 것은?

보기 Ron <u>has stayed</u> up since yesterday.

① I <u>have met</u> the U.S. president before.
② I <u>have</u> just <u>turned</u> on my cell phone.
③ <u>Have</u> you already <u>made</u> a decision?
④ Jessica <u>has taught</u> yoga for three years.
⑤ My father <u>has visited</u> France several times.

4 다음 두 문장을 보기처럼 한 문장으로 바꿀 때 빈칸에 알맞은 말을 쓰시오. (현재완료로 작성할 것)

보기 Marie lost her ring a week ago. She doesn't have it now.
→ Marie <u>has not had</u> her ring for a week.

I bought the backpack last month. I am still using it.
→ I ______________ the backpack since last month.

WORDS

1
pilot 명 조종사, 비행사
mainly 부 주로

2
break a record 기록을 깨다

3
stay up 안 자다[깨어 있다]
decision 명 결정
several times 몇 번

4
backpack 명 배낭

서술형에 나오는 WRITING

A 다음 우리말과 일치하도록 괄호 안의 말을 바르게 배열하시오.

1 그 팀은 5년 전에 이 게임을 개발했다.
(developed, this game, ago, five years)
→ The team ______________________________.

2 Sue는 아직 아무것도 먹지 않았다.
(not, has, anything, eaten, Sue)
→ ______________________________ yet.

3 나는 저녁 식사 후에 개를 산책시킬 것이다.
(walk the dog, am, to, after, going, dinner)
→ I ______________________________.

B 다음 괄호 안의 말을 이용하여 문장을 완성하시오.

1 __________ you ever ______________? (see a ghost)

2 The World Cup ______________ every four years. (take place)

3 __________ she ______________ last month? (pass the exam)

4 Yoonho ______________ in the garden right now. (pick fruit)

C 다음은 Rosa의 계획표이다. 표를 보고, 보기 처럼 문장을 완성하시오.

Days	Plans
Tuesday	study science with Aaron
Wednesday right now	volunteer at a nursing home
Thursday	go to the library to borrow a book
Friday	play badminton at a park

보기 Rosa will go to the library to borrow a book tomorrow.

1 Rosa ______________________________ on Tuesday.

2 Rosa ______________________________ right now.

3 Rosa ______________________________ this Friday.

1

Have you ever **seen** a river with five different colors**?** I **have**! On my last vacation, I **went** to Colombia and **visited** Cano Cristales. It **is** one of the most beautiful rivers in the world. Local people **call** it the "Liquid Rainbow" due to its colors. The red **comes** from an underwater plant called *Macarenia clavigera*. The blue **is** created by the water itself. And the other colors **come** from *algae, the rocks at the bottom of the river, and shiny yellow sand.

If you **are going to visit** Cano Cristales, the best time **is** in the summer. That**'s** when I **went**! The hot weather **makes** the *Macarenia clavigera* turn bright red! 나는 더 멋진 장소에 가 본 적이 없어!

*algae: 조류(물속에 사는 식물)

1 위 글의 제목으로 가장 알맞은 것은?

① The World's Deepest River
② Colorful Fish in Cano Cristales
③ Colombia's Most Popular Color
④ A River of Five Colors in Colombia
⑤ Underwater Tourism in Cano Cristales

서술형

2 위 글의 밑줄 친 우리말과 일치하도록 괄호 안의 말을 바르게 배열하시오.

→ ______________________ a more amazing place!
(I, never been, have, to)

WORDS vacation 명 방학 local 형 지역의, 현지의 liquid 명 액체 due to … 때문에 underwater 형 물속의, 수중의 create 동 창조하다; *만들어 내다, …를 야기하다 rock 명 암석 shiny 형 빛나는 sand 명 모래 bright 형 ¹__________
문제 colorful 형 (색이) 다채로운 tourism 명 관광업

2

Times Square **is** a famous intersection in Manhattan, the center of New York City. It **has** many tourist attractions, such as well-known buildings, street performances, and its New Year's Eve celebration. However, it (A) look very different in the past.

In the 1800s, it **was** called Long Acre Square, and there **were** only a few houses there. At that time, it **was** a center for the *carriage-making industry. Later, in the 1890s, it **was** developed into an area with large theaters and fancy restaurants. In 1904, Times Square **got** its name when the famous newspaper *The New York Times* **moved** to new offices nearby. Although the company **moved** to a different place in 1913, the name "Times Square" (B) stay the same since that time.

*carriage: 마차

1 **Which is NOT true about Times Square?**

① A New Year's Eve celebration is held there.
② It had a different name in the past.
③ Large theaters appeared there in the 19th century.
④ It got its name from a newspaper.
⑤ Since 1913, its name has changed several times.

2 **Choose the grammatically correct forms for (A) and (B).**

	(A)		(B)
①	looks	-	stay
②	looked	-	stayed
③	looked	-	has stayed
④	has looked	-	stayed
⑤	has looked	-	has stayed

WORDS **intersection** 명 교차로 **attraction** 명 매력; *명소[명물] **performance** 명 [1] ________ **celebration** 명 기념[축하] 행사 **only a few** 다만 몇 안 되는 **industry** 명 산업, 공업 **develop** 동 발달하다; *개발하다 **area** 명 [2] ________ **fancy** 형 화려한; *일류의, 고급의 **although** 접 비록 …이긴 하지만

A 감정 묻고 답하기

A: **How are you feeling?**
(너는 기분이 어떠니?)

B: **I'm good. How do you feel?**
(난 좋아. 너는 기분이 어때?)

A: **I feel terrible.**
(난 기분이 몹시 나빠.)

상대방의 감정을 물을 때는 'How are you feeling?'이나 'How do you feel?' 등의 표현을 쓸 수 있다. 기분이 좋을 때는 'I'm good.'이나 'I feel great.', 기분이 좋지 않을 때는 'Not very well.'이나 'I feel bad[terrible].', 기분이 그저 그럴 때는 'So-so.'라고 답할 수 있다. 또한, 'I'm ...'이나 'I feel ...' 뒤에 여러 가지 형용사를 사용하여 감정을 나타낼 수 있다.

TIPS 감정을 나타내는 표현
bored(지루한), sad(슬픈), happy(행복한), nervous(긴장된), excited(신나는), depressed(우울한), be in a good[bad] mood(기분이 좋다[나쁘다]) 등

Check-Up

1 다음 대화의 빈칸에 들어갈 말로 알맞지 않은 것은?

A: How are you feeling?
B: ____________________

① I feel great.
② Not very well.
③ I'm depressed.
④ I feel like that.
⑤ I'm in a good mood.

2 대화가 자연스럽게 이어지도록 (A)~(D)를 바르게 배열하시오.

(A) I'm not so good.
(B) What happened?
(C) How do you feel today?
(D) My little sister is very sick.

________ → ________ → ________ → ________

WORDS

2
happen 동 일어나다, 발생하다

B 알고 있는지 묻기

A: **Did you hear that** we'll have a math test tomorrow**?**
(너는 우리가 내일 수학 시험을 볼 거라는 것을 들었니?)

B: No, I didn't. Who told you that?
(아니, 못 들었어. 누가 너에게 그것을 말했니?)

A: Bill told me.
(Bill이 내게 말해 줬어.)

'Did you hear (that) ...?'은 '…에 대해 들었니?'라는 의미로 상대방에게 무언가를 들어서 알고 있는지 물어볼 때 쓴다. '…에 대해 알았니?'라는 의미로 'Did you know ...?'라고 물을 수도 있다.

EXPRESSION PLUS

A: **Do you know** the new classroom rules**?** (너는 새로운 학급 규칙들을 아니?)
B: Of course. (물론이지.)

A: **Have you heard that** Jane appeared on TV**?** (너는 Jane이 TV에 출연했다는 것을 들었니?)
B: No. That's great! (아니. 그거 멋지다!)

Check-Up

1 다음 대화의 밑줄 친 부분과 바꿔 쓸 수 있는 것은?

A: Did you <u>hear</u> that it's raining outside?
B: Yes. We should take our umbrellas.

① do ② take
③ know ④ inform
⑤ sound

2 다음 우리말과 일치하도록 괄호 안의 말을 바르게 배열하시오.

너는 새로운 아나운서에 대해 들은 적 있니?
(have, heard, the new announcer, about, you)

→ ____________________

WORDS

1
inform 동 알리다

2
announcer 명 아나운서

FINAL TEST

1 다음 빈칸에 들어갈 말을 보기 에서 골라 쓰시오.

보기 happen book deliver

(1) A postman will __________ his letter soon.
(2) Did you __________ your hotel in Bali?

2 다음 우리말과 일치하도록 빈칸에 알맞은 말을 쓰시오.

그는 그의 악기들을 기부하고 싶어 한다.

→ He wants to __________ his musical instruments.

3 자연스러운 대화가 되도록 빈칸에 알맞은 말을 보기 에서 고르시오.

보기 ⓐ When is it?
ⓑ How do you feel about that?
ⓒ Did you hear that we'll have a school festival?

A: (1) ______________
B: No. (2) ______________
A: Next Friday. I will host the talent show.
B: Really? That sounds fun!

4 다음 괄호 안의 말을 이용하여 대화를 완성하시오.

A: How are you feeling? You look good today.
B: __________ __________ __________ __________ __________ __________.
(a good mood)

5 다음 중 짝지어진 대화가 어색한 것은?

① A: How do you feel?
B: I feel depressed.
② A: How are you feeling today?
B: Not good. I failed the exam.
③ A: Do you know Van Gogh's works?
B: Yes, I do. I love his paintings.
④ A: Have you heard about the concert tomorrow?
B: No. Who is playing?
⑤ A: Did you know that Tim broke the cup?
B: No. I didn't do that.

! 자주 나와요

[6-8] 다음 빈칸에 들어갈 말로 알맞은 것을 고르시오.

6 George heard a loud noise when he __________ TV.

① watches ② is watching
③ was watching ④ will watch
⑤ has watched

7 I __________ my grandparents last weekend.

① visit ② visited
③ am visiting ④ will visit
⑤ have visited

8 Flowers and trees __________ plants.

① are ② were
③ have been ④ were being
⑤ will be

[9-10] 다음 빈칸에 들어갈 말로 알맞지 않은 것을 고르시오.

9

Bob will go to the hospital to see his friend ________.

① tomorrow
② this Friday
③ next month
④ yesterday
⑤ this weekend

! 자주 나와요

10

I have worked at a nursing home ________.

① before
② once
③ since 2015
④ three years ago
⑤ for a long time

11 다음 우리말과 일치하도록 괄호 안의 단어를 이용하여 문장을 완성하시오.

우리 팀은 5년 동안 경기에서 진 적이 없다.
(lose)

→ Our team ________ ________ ________ a game for five years.

12 다음 밑줄 친 부분 중 어법상 바르지 못한 것은?

① The store is open on Sunday.
② Sam has taught English for 10 years.
③ I usually take a bus to school.
④ Jina is buying a gift for her friend right now.
⑤ My mom is liking to sing late at night.

! 어려워요

13 다음 밑줄 친 부분의 쓰임이 보기 와 같은 것은?

보기 I have finished reading the novel.

① The plane has just left for Busan.
② I have eaten Thai food twice before.
③ Sarah has gone to Canada to study.
④ Jenny has been in China for two years.
⑤ I haven't visited the art gallery in town.

! 서술형

14 다음 우리말과 일치하도록 괄호 안의 단어를 바르게 배열하시오.

그녀는 많은 돈을 쓰지 않을 것이다.
(to, is, she, going, much money, not, spend)

→ ________________________

[15-16] 다음 우리말을 영어로 바르게 옮긴 것을 고르시오.

15

Jim은 인터넷 서핑을 하고 있다.

① Jim surfed the Internet.
② Jim will surf the Internet.
③ Jim is surfing the Internet.
④ Jim doesn't surf the Internet.
⑤ Jim is not surfing the Internet.

16

우리는 어제 캠핑장에서 만났다.

① We met at the campsite yesterday.
② We meet at the campsite yesterday.
③ We'll meet at the campsite yesterday.
④ We have met at the campsite yesterday.
⑤ We're meeting at the campsite yesterday.

17 다음 빈칸에 들어갈 말로 알맞지 않은 것은?

A: When will you go back to your country?
B: ____________________

① I'm going back soon.
② I go back next weekend.
③ I'll go back there this winter.
④ I have gone back next Monday.
⑤ I'm going to go back next month.

18 다음 중 어법상 바른 것은?

① Lauren will sign up at the gym.
② Kate is having her own room.
③ I didn't see John since last Friday.
④ He is running a race last month.
⑤ I'm going to join a study club a year ago.

19 다음 빈칸에 들어갈 말이 바르게 짝지어진 것은?

• The train hasn't arrived ________.
• Jade has ________ gotten on the bus.

① just – yet ② yet – already
③ yet – before ④ already – never
⑤ never – yet

어려워요

20 다음 문장을 괄호 안의 지시대로 바꿔 쓰시오.

The singer changed his mind.
(현재완료 의문문으로)

→ ____________________

내신 완성 서술형

21 다음 두 문장을 현재완료와 since를 이용하여 한 문장으로 바꿔 쓰시오.

It started to rain yesterday. It still rains.

→ ____________________

22 다음 우리말과 일치하도록 조건에 맞게 영작하시오.

그녀는 그들에 관한 기사를 쓰고 있었다.

조건 1: an article about을 이용할 것
조건 2: 총 7단어로 작성할 것
→ ____________________
____

[23-24] 다음은 Jia의 계획표이다. 표의 내용과 일치하도록 대화를 완성하시오.

Days	Plans	Done
Thursday	finish my report	X
Saturday	finish my report	
Sunday	plant some flowers	

Dan: Finally, it's Friday! What are you going to do tomorrow?

Jia: **23** I ________ ________ ________ ________ on Thursday. So I will do it on Saturday.

Dan: Then what will you do on Sunday?

Jia: **24** I ________ ________ ________ ________ on Sunday.

WORD LIST

Grammar

□ pick up	전화를 받다
□ travel	동 여행하다
□ book	동 예약하다
□ have a party	파티를 열다
□ graduate from	…를 졸업하다
□ elementary school	초등학교
□ donate	동 기부하다
□ job	명 일, 직장
□ depart	동 출발하다
□ repair	동 수리하다
□ deliver	동 배달하다
□ do the dishes	설거지하다
□ cancel	동 취소하다
□ coin	명 동전
□ serve	동 근무[복무]하다
□ army	명 군대
□ pilot	명 조종사, 비행사
□ mainly	부 주로
□ break a record	기록을 깨다
□ stay up	안 자다[깨어 있다]
□ decision	명 결정
□ several times	몇 번
□ backpack	명 배낭

Reading

□ vacation	명 방학
□ local	형 지역의, 현지의
□ liquid	명 액체
□ due to	… 때문에
□ underwater	형 물속의, 수중의
□ rock	명 암석
□ shiny	형 빛나는
□ sand	명 모래
□ bright	형 밝은
□ intersection	명 교차로, 교차 지점
□ attraction	명 매력; 명소[명물]
□ performance	명 공연
□ celebration	명 기념[축하] 행사
□ only a few	다만 몇 안 되는
□ industry	명 산업, 공업
□ develop	동 발달하다; 개발하다
□ area	명 지역; 구역
□ fancy	형 화려한; 일류의, 고급의
□ although	접 비록 …이긴 하지만

Communication

□ happen	동 일어나다, 발생하다
□ announcer	명 아나운서

Final Test

□ host	동 (행사를) 주최하다; 사회를 맡다
□ fail	동 실패하다; (시험에) 떨어지다
□ noise	명 소리, 소음
□ surf	동 파도타기를 하다; 인터넷을 서핑하다
□ own	형 … 자신의
□ get on	…에 타다
□ still	부 아직도
□ article	명 기사
□ environment	명 (자연) 환경

CHAPTER 03

수동태

GET READY

Alice **waters** the flowers.
(Alice는 그 꽃들에 물을 준다.)

The flowers **are watered by** Alice.
(그 꽃들은 Alice에 의해 물이 주어진다.)

A big tree **blocked** the road.
(큰 나무가 그 길을 가로막았다.)

The road **was blocked by** a big tree.
(그 길은 큰 나무에 의해 가로막혔다.)

주어가 동작의 영향을 받거나 어떤 행동을 당하는 것을 표현하기 위해서 동사의 형태를 변화시킨 것을 수동태라고 해요. 수동태를 이용하여 '물을 주다'를 '물이 주어지다'로, '가로막았다'를 '가로막혔다'로 표현할 수 있어요.

A 수동태의 의미와 형태

1 능동태와 수동태

주어가 동작을 직접 행할 때는 능동태로, 주어가 동작의 영향을 받거나 행동을 당할 때는 수동태로 쓴다.
수동태 「be동사+v-ed(+by+행위자)」는 '(~에 의해) …되다[받다/당하다]'로 해석한다.

Many people	love	the song. (능동태)
주어	동사	목적어
The song	is loved	by many people. (수동태)
주어	be동사+v-ed	by+행위자

TIPS

수동태에서 행위자가 분명하지 않거나 중요하지 않을 때, 막연한 일반인일 때 「by+행위자」를 생략할 수 있다.
English **is spoken** in many countries.
(영어는 많은 나라에서 말해진다.)

2 수동태의 시제

1) 과거시제: 「be동사의 과거형+v-ed」, '…되었다'

Grayson **discovered** the old boxes.
→ The old boxes **were discovered** by Grayson.

2) 미래시제: 「will be+v-ed」, '…될 것이다'

The students **will clean** the classroom.
→ The classroom **will be cleaned** by the students.

3) 진행형: 「be동사+being+v-ed」, '…되고 있다/있었다'

Technology **is changing** our lives.
→ Our lives **are being changed** by technology.
They **were painting** the room.
→ The room **was being painted** by them.

3 수동태의 부정문과 의문문

1) 부정문: 「주어+be동사+not+v-ed ...」

Hailey **didn't set** the alarm yesterday.
→ The alarm **wasn't set** by Hailey yesterday.

2) 의문문: 「be동사+주어+v-ed ...?」

Did he **take** these pictures**?**
→ **Were** these pictures **taken** by him**?**

TIPS

미래시제 수동태의 부정문과 의문문
1 부정문: 「주어+will not be+v-ed ...」
The food **will not be served** by her. (음식은 그녀에 의해 제공되지 않을 것이다.)
2 의문문: 「Will+주어+be동사+v-ed ...?」
Will the old man **be guided** by you? (그 노인은 당신에 의해 안내받을 건가요?)

Check-Up

A 다음 괄호 안에서 알맞은 말을 고르시오.

1 Is the TV show (enjoy / enjoyed) by teenagers?

2 The problem will (solve / be solved) by them.

3 The lost child (found / was found) by a security guard.

4 The actor is still (remembered / remembering) by many people.

5 The song (didn't write / wasn't written) by a famous composer.

WORDS

A
solve 동 해결하다
security guard 경비원
composer 명 작곡가

B 다음 밑줄 친 부분을 바르게 고치시오.

1 The plan is being review by the experts. → ________

2 Did the error corrected by your teacher? → ________

3 The curtains in the hall was closed by me. → ________

4 Some apple trees will planted in the garden. → ________

B
expert 명 전문가
error 명 오류
correct 동 바로잡다
hall 명 복도

C 다음 괄호 안의 단어를 바르게 배열하여 문장을 완성하시오.

1 The wall ________________ Dylan.
(will, decorated, be, by)

2 The walnut pie ________________ my friend.
(not, by, was, baked)

3 The hotel room ________________ the staff.
(was, by, prepared, being)

C
decorate 동 장식하다, 꾸미다
walnut 명 호두
staff 명 직원

D 다음 우리말과 일치하도록 괄호 안의 단어를 이용하여 문장을 완성하시오.

1 그 보고서는 너에 의해 마무리되었니? (finish)
→ ________ the report ________ ________ you?

2 그 시장은 많은 관광객들에 의해 방문된다. (visit)
→ The market ________ ________ ________ many tourists.

3 그 질병은 새들에 의해 확산되고 있다. (spread)
→ The disease ________ ________ ________ ________ birds.

D
tourist 명 관광객
spread 동 퍼뜨리다, 확산시키다
(spread - spread)
disease 명 질병, 병

B 주의해야 할 수동태

1 수동태로 쓰지 않는 동사

1) 목적어가 필요 없는 동사 예 arrive, happen, appear, disappear 등

The earthquake **happened** last night.
The earthquake was happened last night. (x)

Big letters **appeared** on the screen.
Big letters were appeared on the screen. (x)

2) 소유나 상태를 나타내는 동사 예 have(가지고 있다), exist(존재하다), resemble(닮다) 등

Jina **has** a lot of ski equipment.
A lot of ski equipment is had by Jina. (x)

The baby **resembles** George.
George is resembled by the baby. (x)

2 by 이외의 전치사를 쓰는 수동태

수동태의 행위자는 보통 by를 써서 나타내지만 with, at, in 등의 다른 전치사를 쓰는 경우도 있다.
I **was surprised at** the news.
The department store **is filled with** people.

MORE EXPRESSIONS

- be surprised at …에 놀라다
- be known to …에게 알려져 있다
- be known as …로 알려져 있다
- be made of …로 만들어지다 (물리적 변화)
- be made from …로 만들어지다 (화학적 변화)
- be filled with …로 가득 차다
- be covered with/in …로 덮여 있다
- be pleased with …로 즐거워하다
- be satisfied with …에 만족하다
- be interested in …에 관심이 있다

3 동사구의 수동태

「동사+전치사」 또는 「동사+부사」 등의 동사구가 쓰인 문장을 수동태로 바꿀 때는 동사구를 하나의 단어처럼 취급한다.

Nancy's family **took care of** my dog.
→ My dog **was taken care of** by Nancy's family.

TIPS

여러 가지 동사구

- bring up …를 기르다[양육하다]
- laugh at …를 비웃다
- run over (차가) …를 치다
- put off …를 연기하다[미루다]
- look after …를 돌보다
- look up to …를 존경하다
- ask for …를 요청하다
- throw away …를 버리다
- look down on …를 얕보다

Check-Up

A 다음 괄호 안에서 알맞은 말을 고르시오.

1 Butter is made (by / from) milk.
2 A deer was (run / run over) by a car.
3 Was she (brought / brought up) by her aunt?
4 Andrew (disappeared / was disappeared) suddenly.
5 All the houses in this village (resemble / are resembled) each other.

WORDS

A
suddenly 부 갑자기
village 명 마을
resemble 동 닮다

B 다음 밑줄 친 부분을 바르게 고치시오.

1 The school bus was arrived on time. → ____________
2 The man is known as everyone in the city. → ____________
3 Those damaged goods will thrown be away. → ____________
4 We were had one hour to shop at the mall. → ____________

B
damaged 형 손상된
goods 명 상품

C 다음 빈칸에 들어갈 말을 보기 에서 골라 쓰시오.

보기 at of with in to

1 I was satisfied ________ my test scores.
2 Julia is very interested ________ sports.
3 Megan was laughed ________ by her friends.
4 The chair and the desk are made ________ wood.

C
score 명 점수
wood 명 나무, 목재

D 다음 우리말과 일치하도록 괄호 안의 말을 이용하여 문장을 완성하시오.

1 달이 구름 뒤에서부터 나타났다. (appear)
→ The moon ________________ from behind the clouds.
2 그 영화에서는, 지구에 외계인들이 존재한다. (exist)
→ In the movie, aliens ________________ on Earth.
3 그 아기는 그녀의 할머니에 의해 돌봐질 것이다. (look after)
→ The baby ________________ by her grandmother.

D
alien 명 외계인

Grammar Practice

A 다음 밑줄 친 부분을 바르게 고치시오.

1 Were you be bitten by a dog? → ______________

2 I didn't invited to her birthday party. → ______________

3 The singer will be appeared on the stage. → ______________

4 Most of the customers were satisfied by the service. → ______________

WORDS

A
bite 동 물다
(bit - bitten)
customer 명 손님, 고객

B 다음 빈칸에 들어갈 말을 보기에서 골라 알맞은 형태로 쓰시오. (한 번씩만 쓸 것)

보기 break test have speak laugh at

1 Mike __________ beautiful blond hair now.

2 The cup was not __________ by my sister.

3 Her strange clothes were __________ by other students.

4 The new medicine will be __________ by the researchers.

5 Spanish is __________ in many countries in South America.

B
blond hair 금발 머리
researcher 명 연구원

C 다음 문장을 수동태로 바꿀 때 빈칸에 알맞은 말을 쓰시오.

1 Did Wilson change this design?
→ __________ this design ______________ Wilson?

2 The baseball players respect the coach.
→ The coach __________________________ the baseball players.

3 The mechanic was repairing the truck.
→ The truck __________________________ the mechanic.

4 The company will employ five workers.
→ Five workers __________________________ the company.

5 The rude boy looked down on poor people.
→ Poor people __________________________ the rude boy.

C
respect 동 존경하다
mechanic 명 정비공
employ 동 고용하다

내신 완성 Grammar Practice

1 다음 빈칸에 들어갈 말로 알맞은 것은?

The first computer mouse ________ in the 1960s.

① creates ② created
③ to create ④ was created
⑤ was creating

2 다음 빈칸에 들어갈 말이 바르게 짝지어진 것은?

- The children are pleased ________ their new toys.
- They were surprised ________ the loud sound outside.

① by - as ② by - with
③ with - at ④ with - to
⑤ as - from

3 다음 중 어법상 바르지 <u>못한</u> 것은?

① Was this party hosted by Frank?
② The photo is being print on paper.
③ The show will be finished by 4 o'clock.
④ The movie was directed by my uncle.
⑤ The school bus is covered with snow.

4 다음 대화를 읽고, 밑줄 친 단어를 각각 알맞은 형태로 고치시오.

A: What are you doing?
B: I'm reading news about a car accident.
A: Really? What (1) <u>happen</u>?
B: A man (2) <u>hit</u> by a car yesterday.
A: Oh, that's terrible.

(1) ________ (2) ________

WORDS

1
create 동 창조하다

3
host 동 (행사를) 주최하다
direct 동 감독[연출]하다

4
accident 명 사고
hit 동 치다
(hit - hit)

서술형에 나오는 WRITING

A **다음 우리말과 일치하도록 괄호 안의 말을 바르게 배열하시오.**

1 그 관람객들은 예술에 관심이 있다.
(in, is, the audience, art, interested)
→ ______________________________

2 Jeff는 그들에 의해 키워지지 않았다.
(raised, not, them, by, Jeff, was)
→ ______________________________

3 지하철역이 기사들에 의해 지어지고 있다.
(being, the engineers, a subway station, built, is, by)
→ ______________________________

B **다음 우리말과 일치하도록 괄호 안의 단어를 이용하여 문장을 완성하시오.**

1 그 음악은 오케스트라에 의해 연주되었다. (play, the orchestra)
→ The music ______________________________.

2 그 크리스마스트리는 아이들에 의해 옮겨지고 있니? (move, the children)
→ __________ the Christmas tree ______________________________?

3 그 시험은 컴퓨터에 의해 채점될 것이다. (grade, computer)
→ The exam ______________________________.

C **다음 그림을 보고, 괄호 안의 단어를 이용하여 문장을 완성하시오. (현재시제로 작성할 것)**

1

(cover, leaves)
The street ______________________________.

2

(fill, water)
The cups ______________________________.

1

People around the world love chili peppers, but usually they ①aren't considered a health food. ___(A)___, they have hidden health benefits! Some types of chili peppers ②contain more vitamin C than oranges. And the ancient Mayans used chili peppers as a cure for stomachaches.

In fact, chili peppers ③are using as a kind of medicine even today. You don't eat them, though—instead, you rub them on your skin. Have you ever touched your eyes after cooking with chili peppers? If you have, you know that they ④create a burning feeling. ___(B)___, chili peppers **are** commonly **found** in creams for body aches. They ⑤are added to create a feeling of heat in your muscles.

1 위 글의 빈칸 (A)와 (B)에 들어갈 말이 바르게 짝지어진 것은?

(A)		(B)
① In addition	–	Instead
② For example	–	In other words
③ However	–	For this reason
④ Nonetheless	–	Otherwise
⑤ Therefore	–	As a result

2 위 글의 밑줄 친 ①~⑤ 중 어법상 틀린 것은?

① ② ③ ④ ⑤

WORDS
chili pepper 고추 consider 동 고려하다; *여기다 benefit 명 [1]__________ contain 동 …이 들어[함유되어] 있다
ancient 형 [2]__________ cure 명 치유법 stomachache 명 복통 rub 동 문지르다, 바르다 burning 형 불타는; *화끈거리는
commonly 부 흔히 ache 명 아픔 muscle 명 근육

2

Susan B. Anthony **was born** in the U.S. in 1820, before *voting rights ① were given to women. At that time, only men had the right to vote. However, she ② believed that this was unfair. She decided to visit towns across the U.S. to give lectures about it. Many women ③ were moved by Anthony's speeches. In 1872, she even tried voting! **Was** her vote **counted?** No. Instead, she ④ sent to jail. But Anthony **wasn't stopped** by these difficulties. She kept working to improve women's rights.

She died in 1906, fourteen years before women ⑤ gained the right to vote. Today Anthony **is** still **being praised** for her efforts, and an image of her is on the U.S. one-dollar coin.

*voting rights: 선거권, 투표권

1 **Which is the best title for the passage?**

① Social Problems in the U.S.
② Famous People on U.S. Coins
③ The Importance of a Free and Fair Vote
④ Susan B. Anthony's Difficult Childhood
⑤ Susan B. Anthony's Efforts for Women's Rights

2 **Which is NOT grammatically correct?**

① ② ③ ④ ⑤

WORDS right 명 권리 vote 동 투표하다 명 표, 투표 unfair 형 부당한, 불공평한 give a lecture 강연하다 move 동 움직이다; *감동시키다 speech 명 연설, 담화 jail 명 [1]__________ difficulty 명 어려움, 곤경 improve 동 개선하다, 향상시키다 gain 동 얻다 praise 동 칭찬하다 effort 명 수고, 노력 문제 social 형 사회의, 사회적인 fair 형 공정한, 공평한

내신에 나오는 COMMUNICATION

A 확인 요청하기

A: Hey, look at those girls. They are cute.
(얘, 저 여자아이들 좀 봐. 그들은 귀여워.)

B: **Do you mean** the girls with glasses**?**
(안경 쓴 여자아이들 말이니?)

A: Yes, that's right.
(그래, 맞아.)

상대방이 한 말을 다시 확인할 때는 'Do you mean ...?'이라고 말할 수 있다. 이와 유사한 표현으로는 'Are you saying ...?'(…라는 말이니?), 'Did you say ...?'(…라고 말했니?), 'You mean ..., right?'(…라는 말이지, 그렇지?) 등이 있다.

EXPRESSION PLUS

- **Are you saying that** you want to go home now**?** (너는 지금 집에 가고 싶다는 말이니?)
- **Did you say** you missed the bus this morning**?** (너는 오늘 아침에 버스를 놓쳤다고 말했니?)

Check-Up

1 다음 대화의 빈칸에 들어갈 말로 알맞은 것은?

A: Let's go to the bakery together.
B: ______________________
A: No, I mean the one in front of the post office.

① Do you go to the bakery often?
② Do you think that the bakery is good?
③ Do you mean the one on the corner?
④ Do you want to go to the bakery, too?
⑤ Do you go to the bakery in front of the post office?

WORDS

1
corner 명 모퉁이

2 다음 우리말과 일치하도록 괄호 안의 단어를 바르게 배열하시오.

너는 샐러드를 먹었다고 말했니?
(ate, you, did, salad, say, you)

→ ______________________

B 빈도 묻고 답하기

A: David, **how often** do you jog**?**
(David, 너는 얼마나 자주 조깅을 하니?)

B: I jog **every day**.
(난 매일 조깅해.)

A: Wow, you're really diligent!
(와, 너 정말 부지런하구나!)

'How often ...?'은 '얼마나 자주 ⋯하니?'의 의미로 빈도를 물을 때 쓰는 표현이다. 대답할 때는 always, never 등의 빈도부사나 every day, once a week 등 빈도를 나타내는 부사구를 써서 말할 수 있다.

⊕ EXPRESSION PLUS

A: **How many times a week** do you walk your dog**?** (너는 일주일에 몇 번 네 강아지를 산책시키니?)
B: I walk my dog **three times a week.** (나는 일주일에 세 번 강아지를 산책시켜.)

TIPS 빈도를 나타내는 표현
always(항상), usually(보통, 대개), often(자주), sometimes(때때로), never(한 번도 ⋯않다),
once a week(일주일에 한 번), twice a month(한 달에 두 번), every other day(하루걸러, 이틀에 한 번) 등

Check-Up

1 다음 대화의 빈칸에 알맞은 말을 쓰시오.

A: ________ ________ ________ a day do you drink coffee, Dad?
B: I rarely drink it.

WORDS

1
rarely 부 드물게, 좀처럼 ⋯하지 않는

2 대화가 자연스럽게 이어지도록 (A)~(D)를 바르게 배열하시오.

(A) That's right.
(B) I play tennis every other day.
(C) How often do you play tennis?
(D) Are you saying that you practice every two days?

________ → ________ → ________ → ________

FINAL TEST

1 다음 영영 풀이에 해당하는 단어로 알맞은 것은?

to make something right

① bite ② vote
③ correct ④ respect
⑤ consider

[2-3] 다음 우리말과 일치하도록 빈칸에 알맞은 말을 보기 에서 골라 쓰시오.

보기 create move employ contain

2 그들은 사람들을 더 고용할 예정이다.

→ They will ________ more people.

3 그의 노래는 관중들을 감동시켰나요?

→ Did his song ________ the audience?

4 다음 빈칸에 들어갈 말이 바르게 짝지어진 것은?

- ______ does your family eat out?
(너의 가족은 얼마나 자주 외식을 하니?)
- ______ you need to stop by the shop?
(너는 가게에 들러야 한다고 말했니?)

① How long - Do you think
② How long - Did you say
③ How long - Do you mean
④ How often - Do you think
⑤ How often - Did you say

5 다음 대화의 빈칸에 들어갈 말로 알맞은 것은?

A: You look tired. What happened?
B: I cleaned my room.
A: How many times a week do you clean your room?
B: ____________

① Not at all. ② Don't worry.
③ It's very clean. ④ For two hours.
⑤ Once or twice.

6 대화가 자연스럽게 이어지도록 (A)~(D)를 바르게 배열하시오.

(A) Okay. What about that one?
(B) Can you help me choose a shirt?
(C) Do you mean the shirt with blue stripes?
(D) Right. That is our best-selling shirt.

______ → ______ → ______ → ______

[7-9] 다음 빈칸에 들어갈 말로 알맞은 것을 고르시오.

7 The house ________ by the hurricane this summer.

① destroys ② destroying
③ destroyed ④ was destroyed
⑤ was destroying

8 The boxes ________ onto a truck now.

① loads ② have loaded
③ be loading ④ be loaded
⑤ are being loaded

9 The two boys ________ each other.

① resemble ② resembling
③ are resembled ④ are resembling
⑤ will be resembled

10 다음 우리말과 일치하도록 괄호 안의 말을 이용하여 문장을 완성하시오.

그 교수는 많은 연구자들에게 존경받는다.
(look up to)

→ The professor ____________ many researchers.

자주 나와요

11 다음 빈칸에 들어갈 말이 바르게 짝지어진 것은?

- They are pleased ________ my gift.
- Cheese is made ________ milk.

① at - to ② at - with
③ with - of ④ with - from
⑤ from - at

12 다음 밑줄 친 부분 중 생략할 수 있는 것은?

① The memo was written by Terry.
② This pig was fed by my aunt.
③ Jay is liked by my cousin, Sarah.
④ A bike was left by someone in the street.
⑤ This machine was invented by Edison.

[13-14] 다음 우리말을 영어로 바르게 옮긴 것을 고르시오.

13 그의 그림은 오늘 전시되지 않는다.

① His paintings display today.
② His paintings displayed today.
③ His paintings aren't display today.
④ His paintings don't displayed today.
⑤ His paintings aren't displayed today.

14 이 창문은 Daniel에 의해 깨졌나요?

① Did this window broken by Daniel?
② Was this window break by Daniel?
③ Was this window broken by Daniel?
④ Were this window broken by Daniel?
⑤ Did this window was broken by Daniel?

서술형

15 다음 문장을 바르게 고쳐 쓰시오.

The festival will hold this weekend.

→ ______________________

16 다음 밑줄 친 부분 중 어법상 바르지 못한 것은?

① We are interested in sports.
② The bridge is made by steel.
③ She wasn't satisfied with her job.
④ The rumor is known to everyone.
⑤ The baby was looked after by Luke.

17 다음 문장을 수동태로 바르게 바꾼 것은?

He will not finish the work soon.

① The work not finished by him soon.
② The work will not finish by him soon.
③ The work not be finished by him soon.
④ The work will not finished by him soon.
⑤ The work will not be finished by him soon.

! 어려워요

18 다음 중 수동태로 바꿀 수 없는 문장은?

① He kicked the ball into a net.
② Susan cut the rope with a knife.
③ Eric's friends laughed at his effort.
④ They didn't accept my suggestion.
⑤ The ship disappeared into the water.

! 서술형

19 다음 우리말과 일치하도록 괄호 안의 말을 바르게 배열하시오.

그녀의 눈이 눈물로 가득 차 있었다.
(with, her eyes, tears, filled, were)

→ ________________

20 다음 중 어법상 바른 것은?

① The problem didn't solved.
② Two brothers are had by me.
③ Was the broken cell phone repair?
④ The man was run over a speeding car.
⑤ My new shoes were delivered last Tuesday.

내신 완성 서술형

[21-22] 다음 문장을 수동태로 바꿔 쓰시오.

21 The police officer was checking a man's bag.

→ ________________
____

22 Andy will throw away the old books.

→ ________________
____

23 다음 우리말과 일치하도록 조건에 맞게 영작하시오.

그 파티는 그들에 의해 준비되었니?

조건 1: the party, prepare를 이용할 것
조건 2: 총 6단어로 작성할 것

→ ________________

24 다음 그림을 보고, 괄호 안의 말을 이용하여 문장을 완성하시오. (진행형으로 작성할 것)

→ The cat ________________ ________ now.
(take care of, the vet)

WORD LIST

Grammar

□ solve	동 해결하다
□ security guard	경비원
□ composer	명 작곡가
□ correct	동 바로잡다
□ hall	명 복도
□ staff	명 직원
□ tourist	명 관광객
□ suddenly	부 갑자기
□ village	명 마을
□ damaged	형 손상된
□ goods	명 상품
□ bite	동 물다
□ customer	명 손님, 고객
□ researcher	명 연구원
□ respect	동 존경하다
□ mechanic	명 정비공
□ employ	동 고용하다
□ create	동 창조하다
□ host	동 (행사를) 주최하다
□ direct	동 감독[연출]하다
□ accident	명 사고

Reading

□ consider	동 고려하다; 여기다
□ benefit	명 혜택, 이득
□ contain	동 …이 들어[함유되어] 있다
□ ancient	형 고대의
□ cure	명 치유법
□ rub	동 문지르다, 바르다
□ commonly	부 흔히
□ ache	명 아픔
□ muscle	명 근육
□ right	명 권리
□ vote	동 투표하다 명 표, 투표
□ unfair	형 부당한, 불공평한
□ give a lecture	강연하다
□ move	동 움직이다; 감동시키다
□ speech	명 연설, 담화
□ jail	명 감옥
□ difficulty	명 어려움, 곤경
□ effort	명 수고, 노력

Communication

□ corner	명 모퉁이
□ rarely	부 드물게, 좀처럼 …하지 않는

Final Test

□ audience	명 관중
□ stop by	(…에) 잠시 들르다
□ choose	동 선택하다, 고르다
□ stripe	명 줄무늬
□ destroy	동 파괴하다
□ load	동 싣다
□ cousin	명 사촌
□ display	동 전시하다
□ kick	동 (발로) 차다
□ accept	동 받아들이다
□ suggestion	명 제안, 제의
□ tear	명 눈물

CHAPTER 04

조동사

GET READY

He **can** speak Chinese.
(그는 중국어로 말할 수 있다.)

I **will** go there by 10 a.m.
(나는 오전 10시까지 거기에 갈 것이다.)

She **may** call you tonight.
(그녀는 너에게 오늘 밤 전화할지도 모른다.)

You **must** change your password.
(너는 비밀번호를 바꿔야 한다.)

조동사는 뒤에 오는 동사만으로 나타낼 수 없는 여러 가지 의미를 보충하는 역할을 해요. 조동사가 더해 주는 의미로는 능력, 허가, 요청, 예정, 의무, 추측 등이 있어요.

GRAMMAR FOCUS

A 조동사 can, may, will

1 can

1) 능력 · 가능: '…할 수 있다'의 의미이며, be able to로 바꿔 쓸 수 있다.

My little brother **can**[**is able to**] swim.

I **can't**[**am not able to**] sing well like her.

TIPS

can의 과거형과 미래형

can이 능력이나 가능을 나타낼 때 과거는 could 또는 was/were able to로, 미래는 will be able to로 쓴다.

I **couldn't**[**wasn't able to**] find my glasses. (나는 안경을 찾을 수 없었다.)

The baby **will be able to** walk soon. (그 아기는 곧 걸을 수 있을 것이다.)

2) 허가: '…해도 된다'

You **can** use my hair dryer. I've already used it.

Can I exchange this skirt for a new one**?**

3) 요청: '…해 주시겠어요?'

Can[**Could**] you bring some water to me please**?**

2 may

1) 불확실한 추측: '…일지도 모른다'의 의미이며, might는 may보다 더 불확실한 추측을 나타낸다.

Mr. Parker **may** be in the office on the weekend.

The store **may not** open tomorrow.

He **might** have a problem with his friends.

2) 허가: '…해도 좋다, …해도 된다'의 의미이며, can보다 더 정중하게 표현할 때 쓴다.

You **may** join the book club anytime.

May I enter the building without an ID card**?**

3 will

1) 예측 · 의지: '…할 것이다'

My grandmother **will** be 80 years old next year.

I **will not**[**won't**] bother you anymore.

2) 요청: '…해 주시겠어요?'

Will[**Would**] you turn off the air conditioner**?**

TIPS

could와 would는 can이나 will보다 더 정중하게 요청하는 표현으로 사용된다.

Could[**Would**] you close the window? (창문을 닫아 주시겠어요?)

Check-Up

A 다음 괄호 안에서 알맞은 말을 고르시오.

1 I will (send / sending) you the box by post.

2 I (can / be able to) go to Jason's concert with you.

3 Dan talks too fast, so they (can't / may) understand him.

4 Aaron isn't in his room. He (may / is able to) be watering the grass now.

WORDS

A
by post 우편으로

B 다음 문장에서 밑줄 친 조동사의 의미를 보기 에서 골라 쓰시오.

보기 능력 허가 요청 추측

1 You may bring your pet if you want. __________

2 Joshua can run 100 meters in 14 seconds. __________

3 Will you help me with my math homework? __________

B
second 명 (시간 단위) 초

C 다음 밑줄 친 부분을 바르게 고치시오.

1 The news about her may is false. → __________

2 Sophia is able pay for the buffet. → __________

3 You will can learn about painting next time. → __________

4 Bruce's computer was broken, so he could use not it. → __________

C
false 형 틀린, 사실이 아닌
pay 동 지불하다
buffet 명 뷔페

D 다음 우리말과 일치하도록 빈칸에 알맞은 말을 쓰시오.

1 우리는 서둘러야 한다. 비행기가 곧 이륙할 것이다.
→ We need to hurry. The airplane __________ take off soon.

2 이 책이 네가 역사를 공부하는 데 도움이 될지도 모른다.
→ This book __________ help you study history.

3 나는 지난번 경기에 참가할 수 없었다.
→ I __________ __________ __________ __________ participate in the last game.

D
take off 이륙하다
participate in …에 참가[참여]하다

B 조동사 must, should

1 must

1) 강한 의무: '…해야 한다'의 의미이며, have to로 바꿔 쓸 수 있다. 과거형은 had to, 미래형은 will have to로 나타낸다.

We **must**(= **have to**) be quiet in the theater.
I **had to** stop my car suddenly.
We **will have to** pay a higher bus fare from next week.

2) 강한 추측: '…임이 틀림없다'의 의미이며, 부정의 의미인 '…일 리가 없다'는 can't로 나타낸다.

William **must** be surprised at your lie.
Jenny **can't** be her sister. They do not look alike.

내신 POINT PLUS

must와 have to의 부정형

1 must not: …해서는 안 된다 (금지)
You **must not** touch the pictures. (너는 그림들을 만지면 안 된다.)

2 don't have to: …할 필요가 없다 (불필요)
I **don't have to** go to school on Sunday. (나는 일요일에 학교에 갈 필요가 없다.)

2 should

'…하는 것이 좋다, …해야 한다'의 의미이며, must보다는 약한 정도의 의무, 충고를 나타낸다.

We **should** wear knee pads when we skate.
You **should not** judge people by their appearance.

C 다양한 조동사 표현

1) would like to: '…하고 싶다'

I **would**[**I'd**] **like to** invite many people to my birthday party.
Would you **like to** exercise at the park**?**

2) had better: '…하는 것이 낫다[좋겠다]' (충고·경고)

She looks tired. She **had better** go to bed early.
You **had**[You'**d**] **better not** go now. It's raining heavily.

3) used to: '…하곤 했다' (과거의 습관), '(예전에는) …였다' (과거의 상태)

I **used to** eat chicken every Friday.
This restaurant **used to** be a church.

TIPS

1 had better는 약간의 명령조가 섞인 표현으로 모르는 사람이나 손윗사람에게 쓰면 무례할 수 있다.

2 used to가 과거의 습관을 나타낼 때는 would로 바꿔 쓸 수도 있다.
I **used to**(= **would**) eat eggs every day.
(나는 매일 계란을 먹곤 했다.)

Check-Up

A 다음 괄호 안에서 알맞은 말을 고르시오.

1 This shoe store (used to / have to) be a pharmacy.

2 You (should / used to) take this medicine now.

3 The ticket is free today, so you (must not / don't have to) pay.

4 The students (must / had better) be excited about their field trip.

WORDS

A
pharmacy 명 약국
field trip 현장 학습

B 다음 밑줄 친 부분을 바르게 고치시오.

1 I would like to having breakfast at the bakery. → ________

2 If you fail the test, you will must take it again. → ________

3 I use to go for walks with my grandfather on Saturdays. → ________

4 The bag is too expensive. You had not better buy it. → ________

B
expensive 형 비싼

C 다음 우리말과 일치하도록 빈칸에 알맞은 말을 쓰시오.

1 그들은 줄을 서서 기다릴 필요가 없다.
→ They ________ ________ ________ wait in line.

2 땀이 많이 났구나. 너는 샤워하는 게 낫겠다.
→ You are sweaty. You ________ ________ take a shower.

3 우리는 면허 없이 운전을 해서는 안 된다.
→ We ________ ________ drive without a license.

4 저는 햄버거와 감자튀김을 주문하고 싶어요.
→ I ________ ________ ________ order a hamburger and french fries.

5 그가 어렸을 때, 그는 겨울마다 스키를 타러 가곤 했다.
→ When he was young, he ________ ________ go skiing every winter.

C
sweaty 형 땀에 젖은

Grammar Practice

A 다음 빈칸에 들어갈 말을 보기 에서 골라 쓰시오. (한 번씩만 쓸 것)

보기 can used to should had better not

1 You ________ warm up before you swim.
2 You ________ go out in this stormy weather.
3 ________ you carry these books for me for a minute?
4 Susan ________ be a member of the ice hockey team in the past.

WORDS
A
warm up 준비 운동을 하다
stormy 형 폭풍우가 몰아치는

B 다음 밑줄 친 부분을 바르게 고치시오.

1 All the players must follows the rules. → ________
2 He has better accept his coach's offer. → ________
3 You not must cross the street at a red light. → ________
4 I missed the bus last night, so I have to get a taxi. → ________

B
accept 동 받아들이다
offer 명 제안, 제의

C 다음 우리말과 일치하도록 괄호 안의 말을 이용하여 문장을 완성하시오.

1 너는 이 구획에서 아무 데나 앉아도 된다. (sit)
→ You ________ ________ anywhere in this section.

2 당신은 저희 샴푸를 쓰고 싶으세요? (use)
→ ________ ________ ________ ________ ________ our shampoo?

3 나는 내일 너희 집에 잠시 들를 것이다. (stop by)
→ I ________ ________ ________ your house tomorrow.

4 우리는 미래에 언젠가 화성에서 살 수 있을 것이다. (live)
→ We ________ ________ ________ ________ ________ on Mars someday in the future.

C
anywhere 부 아무 데나
section 명 부분, 구획
stop by …에 잠시 들르다

내신 완성 Grammar Practice

1 다음 빈칸에 들어갈 말로 알맞은 것은?

Amelia and Olivia __________ be at home. The lights are turned on now.

① will　② may
③ used to　④ must not
⑤ had better

WORDS

2 다음 중 어법상 바르지 못한 것은?

① May I borrow your laptop computer?
② We would like to go on a trip to the desert.
③ I couldn't sleep because of the terrible noise.
④ You had better say you're sorry to your brother.
⑤ Tom must works on Saturdays from January.

2
desert 명 사막

3 다음 밑줄 친 부분의 쓰임이 보기 와 같은 것은?

보기 He must be our neighbor. I've seen him before.

① I must reply to the email today.
② It's very late. You must go to bed now.
③ You must hand in your homework now.
④ She must be angry. She doesn't talk to me.
⑤ You must be careful when you swim in the ocean.

3
neighbor 명 이웃
reply 동 답장[답신]을 보내다
hand in 제출하다

4 다음 빈칸에 들어갈 말이 바르게 짝지어진 것은?

If you visit Seattle, you __________ ride a tour bus. On a tour bus, you __________ see the city's tourist spots.

① should – can　② used to – can
③ should – don't have to　④ used to – don't have to
⑤ should – would like to

4
tourist spot 관광 명소

A 다음 우리말과 일치하도록 괄호 안의 말을 바르게 배열하시오.

1 그녀는 첼로를 연주할 수 있니?
(able, she, play, to, is, the cello)
→ ______________________________

2 나는 두꺼운 옷을 입을 필요가 없다.
(don't, to, I, wear, have, thick clothes)
→ ______________________________

3 이 공장은 환경을 해칠지도 모른다.
(may, the environment, this factory, harm)
→ ______________________________

B 상자 (A)와 (B)에서 알맞은 조동사와 표현을 하나씩 골라 다음 문장을 완성하시오.

(A)	(B)
used to	ask
had better	be thin
would like to	recycle

1 Mia ______________________ when she was young.
2 You ______________________ those bottles from now on.
3 I ______________________ you a favor. Can you move this table?

C 다음 그림을 보고, must와 괄호 안의 말을 이용하여 문장을 완성하시오.

1

(speak)
You ______________ loudly in the library.

2

(throw away)
You ______________ garbage in a trash can.

READING WITH GRAMMAR

1

Would you **like to** make something delicious for lunch**?** Then you **should** try this omelet recipe! You **will** need five eggs, 200 grams of mushrooms, an onion, and some salt. Also, you can add some meat, such as ham or bacon.

Start by mixing the eggs, salt, and onion together, and then fry the mushrooms in a pan for a few minutes. Pour the egg mixture over the mushrooms. Gently push the mixture toward the center of the pan so that the uncooked parts **can** reach the hot surface. When the omelet starts to turn brown, you **should** flip it. Fry it some more, and then put it on a plate. It is big enough for two people, so you **had better** share it with a friend!

1 위 글을 쓴 목적으로 알맞은 것은?

① 오믈렛의 기원을 소개하기 위해
② 오믈렛 조리법을 설명하기 위해
③ 유명 오믈렛 식당을 홍보하기 위해
④ 다양한 음식 축제를 안내하기 위해
⑤ 오믈렛의 영양 정보를 알려 주기 위해

2 위 글의 밑줄 친 can과 쓰임이 같은 것은?

① Eagles can fly very high.
② You can call me anytime.
③ Can he speak a foreign language?
④ I can finish my homework by tomorrow.
⑤ Can you recommend a good restaurant?

WORDS
recipe 명 조리법 **mushroom** 명 버섯 **onion** 명 양파 **fry** 동 (기름에) 굽다[부치다]; 볶다 **pour** 동 [1] ________ **mixture** 명 혼합물 **gently** 부 부드럽게 **toward** 전 [2] ________ **reach** 동 …에 이르다[닿다] **surface** 명 표면 **flip** 동 홱 뒤집다 **plate** 명 접시, 그릇

2

Ostriches **cannot** fly, but their wings have other important jobs. For example, ostriches use their wings to balance when they **have to** run fast. The birds spread their wings to keep from falling over. Furthermore, ostriches use their wings as *rudders when (have to, directions, change, they) quickly.

(①) Ostriches use their wings for protection, too. (②) The birds mainly live in Africa, where the sun is extremely strong. (③) Ostriches **can** use their wings to block the sunshine from hurting their babies. (④) If it's cold outside, the wings cover their naked upper legs. (⑤) In contrast, if it's too hot outside, the birds expose the naked skin to cool themselves off.

*rudder: (배의) 키

1 Where would the following sentence best fit?

The feathers of their wings also control their body temperature.

① ② ③ ④ ⑤

서술형

2 Unscramble the words in brackets.

→ ______________________________

(have to, directions, change, they)

WORDS
job 명 직장; *일 spread 동 펼치다 fall over 넘어지다 direction 명 방향 protection 명 [1] __________
extremely 부 극도로, 극히 block 동 막다, 차단하다 naked 형 벌거벗은 in contrast 반대로, 그에 반해
expose 동 [2] __________ cool off 서늘하게 하다, 식히다 문제 feather 명 털, 깃털 temperature 명 온도, 기온; *체온

내신에 나오는 COMMUNICATION

A 소요 시간 묻고 답하기

A: Bob, how do you get to school?
(Bob, 너는 학교에 어떻게 가니?)

B: I ride my bike to school.
(나는 자전거를 타고 학교에 가.)

A: **How long does it take to** get there**?**
(거기까지 가는 데 시간이 얼마나 걸리니?)

B: **It takes** 10 minutes.
(10분 걸려.)

'How long does it take to ...?'는 '…하는 데 (시간이) 얼마나 걸리니?'라는 의미로 소요 시간을 묻는 표현이다. 시간이 얼마나 걸리는지 답할 때는 'It takes+시간'이라고 말할 수 있다.

EXPRESSION PLUS

A: **How long did it take to** cook a sausage**?** (소시지를 조리하는 데 시간이 얼마나 걸렸니?)
B: **It took** 15 minutes. (15분 걸렸어.)

A: **How long will it take to** fix my computer**?** (제 컴퓨터를 고치는 데 시간이 얼마나 걸릴까요?)
B: **It will take** about an hour. (약 1시간 정도 걸릴 겁니다.)

Check-Up

1 다음 대화의 빈칸에 들어갈 말로 알맞은 것은?

A: How long will it take to finish the report?
B: ______________________

① That is quite a long time.
② I think the report is terrible.
③ I had to do some research.
④ It took a long time to write.
⑤ It will take about four hours.

WORDS
1
quite 부 꽤, 상당히
research 명 연구, 조사

2 다음 우리말과 일치하도록 괄호 안의 말을 이용하여 영작하시오.

정상에 오르는 데 시간이 얼마나 걸렸니? (reach the top)

→ ______________________

B 추측 표현하기

A: Amy is absent from school today.
(Amy는 오늘 학교에 결석했어.)

B: Do you know why?
(너는 왜인지 아니?)

A: Well, **maybe** she is sick.
(음, 어쩌면 그녀는 아픈지도 몰라.)

어떤 일이나 상태에 대한 불확실한 추측을 표현할 때는 '아마, 어쩌면'의 의미인 부사 maybe나 probably를 써서 말할 수 있다. 또한, 'I guess ...'나 조동사 may를 사용하여 추측을 표현할 수도 있다.

⊕ EXPRESSION PLUS

A: Will you go to see a movie? (너 영화 보러 갈 거니?)
B: **Probably**, but I'm not sure. (아마도, 하지만 확실하지는 않아.)

A: Do you know Jimmy's phone number? (너는 Jimmy의 전화번호를 아니?)
B: No, I don't. But Cathy **may** know. (아니, 난 몰라. 하지만 Cathy는 알지도 몰라.)

Check-Up

1 다음 질문에 대한 알맞은 응답을 찾아 연결하시오.

(1) When will she come home? •
(2) Where is Jake from? •
(3) Liam didn't pick up the phone. Do you know why? •

• ⓐ Well, maybe he is sleeping.
• ⓑ He's probably Canadian.
• ⓒ She may come soon.

2 다음 대화의 밑줄 친 문장과 바꿔 쓸 수 있는 것을 모두 고르시오. (2개)

A: Your little sister is really good at singing.
B: Yeah. Maybe she will become a singer in the future.

① She may become a singer in the future.
② She must become a singer in the future.
③ She wants to become a singer in the future.
④ She will probably become a singer in the future.
⑤ She will certainly become a singer in the future.

WORDS

1
pick up 전화를 받다

2
be good at …를 잘하다
certainly 부 틀림없이

FINAL TEST

1 다음 중 영어 단어와 우리말 뜻이 잘못 연결된 것은?

① false - 틀린　② desert - 사막
③ surface - 표면　④ spread - 펼치다
⑤ gently - 강하게

2 다음 우리말과 일치하도록 빈칸에 알맞은 말을 보기에서 골라 쓰시오.

보기 stop　take　fall

(1) ________ by: …에 잠시 들르다
(2) ________ over: 넘어지다

3 다음 질문에 대한 대답으로 알맞은 것은?

How long does it take to bake the cake?

① It takes about 30 minutes.
② That's longer than I expected.
③ You can use the oven over there.
④ I'd like to eat the chocolate cake.
⑤ Tom may know the popular bakery.

4 다음 질문에 대한 대답으로 알맞은 것을 보기에서 고르시오.

보기 ⓐ It will take a day.
ⓑ He probably forgot about it.
ⓒ Maybe you don't know him well.

(1) A: Why didn't Paul do his homework?
B: ____________________
(2) A: How long will it take to make a new program?
B: ____________________

5 다음 대화의 빈칸에 들어갈 말로 알맞은 것은?

A: Why is Emma crying?
B: I'm not sure, but ____________.

① she may use my phone
② she is probably crying
③ maybe she got a terrible grade
④ she wants to get an A on the test
⑤ she may have something to tell you

6 다음 문장의 밑줄 친 부분과 바꿔 쓸 수 있는 것은?

You have to be back by 8 p.m.

① may　② can
③ will　④ must
⑤ used to

[7-8] 다음 빈칸에 들어갈 말로 알맞은 것을 고르시오.

7
I ________ attend the meeting because I was too tired.

① may　② can
③ couldn't　④ shouldn't
⑤ will be able to

8
Don't be late. You ________ arrive by 2 o'clock.

① would　② should
③ had to　④ used to
⑤ are able to

! 자주 나와요

9 다음 밑줄 친 부분의 쓰임이 나머지 넷과 다른 것은?

① Max may not be very busy.
② This laptop may be broken.
③ You may use my pen if you want.
④ Ben and Tom may be in the gym.
⑤ The teacher may not give the students homework.

10 다음 빈칸에 공통으로 들어갈 말로 알맞은 것은?

- I ________ to cancel my order for the book.
- You ________ better keep your promise.

① may ② had ③ must
④ would ⑤ should

11 다음 빈칸에 들어갈 말이 바르게 짝지어진 것은?

- I ________ travel to Taiwan this vacation.
- We ________ play together when we were young.

① will – can ② will – used to
③ may – will ④ must – can
⑤ used to – should

12 다음 우리말과 일치하도록 괄호 안의 단어를 이용하여 문장을 완성하시오.

너는 오늘 이 일정을 따를 필요가 없다.
(have, follow)

→ You ________________ this schedule today.

13 다음 우리말과 일치하도록 할 때, 빈칸에 들어갈 말로 알맞은 것은?

우리는 다른 사람들의 말에 귀 기울여야 한다.
→ We ________ listen to other people carefully.

① can ② may
③ will ④ should
⑤ don't have to

! 서술형

14 다음 우리말과 일치하도록 괄호 안의 단어를 바르게 배열하시오.

너는 버스를 타지 않는 것이 낫다.
(better, had, not, take, you, the bus)

→ ____________________________

15 다음 우리말을 영어로 바르게 옮긴 것은?

나는 놀이공원에 가고 싶다.

① I won't go to an amusement park.
② I should go to an amusement park.
③ I have to go to an amusement park.
④ I am able to go to an amusement park.
⑤ I'd like to go to an amusement park.

16 다음 중 어법상 바른 것은?

① What would you like do now?
② James may come not tonight.
③ I will read one book every week.
④ I don't must to go to school today.
⑤ Can you delivered this sofa to my house?

17 다음 밑줄 친 부분의 쓰임이 보기 와 같은 것은?

보기 I can teach you how to fix this machine.

① Can I turn on the radio?
② He can translate English to Korean.
③ You can park your car here now.
④ Can you pick me up at the station?
⑤ Customers can use the computer for free.

18 다음 두 문장이 같은 뜻이 되도록 빈칸에 알맞은 말을 쓰시오.

Sarah could drive when she was twenty.

→ Sarah ________ ________ ________ ________ when she was twenty.

19 다음 밑줄 친 부분 중 어법상 바르지 못한 것은?

This is the weather forecast for tomorrow. It ① will ② be very cold in the morning. You ③ should ④ wear warm clothes. However, you will ⑤ can enjoy a sunny afternoon.

! 어려워요

20 다음 중 어법상 바르지 못한 것은?

① He can't eat this spicy curry.
② You have to not call me back.
③ I would like to run a marathon.
④ I will buy a desk calendar tomorrow.
⑤ The ticket is sold out, so we can't see the show.

내신 완성 서술형

21 다음 두 문장을 used to를 이용하여 한 문장으로 바꿀 때 빈칸에 알맞은 말을 쓰시오.

The building was a supermarket before. Now it's a flower shop.

→ The flower shop ________________ ________________ before.

22 다음 우리말과 일치하도록 조건에 맞게 영작하시오.

제가 당신의 여권을 봐도 될까요?

조건 1: see, passport를 이용할 것
조건 2: 총 5단어로 작성할 것
→ ________________________

[23-24] 다음 목록을 보고, 해야 할 것과 하지 말아야 할 것을 must를 이용하여 쓰시오.

23 Do's	24 Don'ts
clean your room	stay up late at night

23 You ________________________.

24 You ________________________.

WORD LIST

Grammar

□ by post	우편으로
□ second	명 (시간 단위) 초
□ false	형 틀린, 사실이 아닌
□ pay	동 지불하다
□ take off	이륙하다
□ participate in	…에 참가[참여]하다
□ pharmacy	명 약국
□ field trip	현장 학습
□ expensive	형 비싼
□ sweaty	형 땀에 젖은
□ warm up	준비운동을 하다
□ stormy	형 폭풍우가 몰아치는
□ accept	동 받아들이다
□ offer	명 제안, 제의
□ anywhere	부 아무 데나
□ section	명 부분, 구획
□ stop by	…에 잠시 들르다
□ desert	명 사막
□ reply	동 답장[답신]을 보내다
□ hand in	제출하다
□ tourist spot	관광 명소

Reading

□ recipe	명 조리법
□ mushroom	명 버섯
□ onion	명 양파
□ pour	동 붓다[따르다]
□ mixture	명 혼합물
□ gently	부 부드럽게
□ toward	전 …쪽으로
□ reach	동 …에 이르다[닿다]
□ surface	명 표면
□ plate	명 접시, 그릇
□ spread	동 펼치다
□ fall over	넘어지다
□ direction	명 방향
□ protection	명 보호
□ block	동 막다, 차단하다
□ in contrast	반대로, 그에 반해
□ expose	동 드러내다
□ feather	명 털, 깃털
□ temperature	명 온도, 기온; 체온

Communication

□ quite	부 꽤, 상당히
□ research	명 연구, 조사
□ pick up	전화를 받다
□ be good at	…를 잘하다
□ certainly	부 틀림없이

Final Test

□ probably	부 아마
□ cancel	동 취소하다
□ schedule	명 일정, 스케줄
□ translate	동 번역하다
□ park	동 주차하다
□ weather forecast	일기예보

CHAPTER 05

to부정사

GET READY

To build a snowman is fun.
(눈사람을 만드는 것은 재미있다.)

We need something **to eat**.
(우리는 먹을 것이 필요하다.)

A group of people ran **to catch** the bus.
(한 무리의 사람들이 버스를 잡기 위해 달렸다.)

「to+동사원형」의 형태인 to부정사는 문장에서 다양한 역할을 해요. to부정사는 명사처럼 주어, 목적어, 보어로 사용될 수도 있고, 형용사처럼 명사를 수식하거나, 부사처럼 동사나 형용사를 수식할 수도 있어요.

A to부정사의 용법

1 명사적 용법

「to+동사원형」 형태인 to부정사는 명사처럼 문장에서 주어, 목적어, 보어 역할을 한다.

1) 주어 역할: '…하는 것은'으로 해석하며, 주어로 쓰인 to부정사는 단수 취급한다.

To learn the history of Rome is fun.

To listen to classical music relaxes me.

2) 목적어 역할: '…하는 것을, …하기를'

Gerald wants **to get** a high score on the test.

She forgot **to turn** off the air conditioner.

3) 보어 역할: '…하는 것(이다)'

My plan is **to go** to the festival this weekend.

His dream is **to be** an astronaut.

TIPS

to부정사의 부정형

to부정사의 부정형은 「not[never] to-v」 형태로, to부정사 앞에 not이나 never를 붙여서 나타낸다.

I hope **not to make** a mistake. (나는 실수하지 않기를 바란다.)

2 형용사적 용법

to부정사는 형용사처럼 앞의 명사를 수식하며, '…할, …하는'으로 해석한다.

I have something **to tell** you.

Can you show me the way **to get** to the temple?

3 부사적 용법

to부정사는 부사처럼 동사나 형용사를 수식하며, 목적, 결과, 감정의 원인 등 다양한 의미를 나타낸다.

1) 목적: '…하기 위해서'

I have to go to the post office **to send** a package.

2) 결과: '(…해서) ~하다'

My grandmother lived **to be** 90 years old.

3) 감정의 원인: '…해서, …하게 되어'

Mary was happy **to meet** her favorite actor.

4) 판단의 근거: '…하다니, …하는 것을 보니'

He is very rude **to talk** like that.

5) 형용사 수식: '…하기에'

Your phone number is easy **to remember**.

TIPS

「in order to-v」

to부정사의 부사적 용법 중 목적을 나타내는 to부정사는 그 의미를 더 분명히 하기 위해서 「in order to-v」로 바꿔 쓸 수 있다.

He came to Japan **in order to make** money. (그는 돈을 벌기 위해 일본에 왔다.)

Check-Up

A 다음 문장에서 밑줄 친 부분의 역할을 보기 에서 골라 쓰시오.

보기 주어 목적어 보어

1 We decided <u>to travel</u> around Europe. ________
2 <u>To deal</u> with social problems is difficult. ________
3 His goal is <u>to be</u> a successful businessman. ________

WORDS

A
deal with …를 다루다, 처리하다
social 형 사회의, 사회적인
businessman 명 사업가

B 자연스러운 문장이 되도록 다음을 연결하시오.

1 I was sad • • ⓐ to play with.
2 Sam grew up • • ⓑ to be a great model.
3 This toy is safe • • ⓒ to say goodbye to him.
4 I need a new shirt • • ⓓ to wear on the field trip.

C 다음 밑줄 친 부분을 바르게 고치시오.

1 Will you go to the airport <u>see</u> Mary off? → ________
2 To take care of babies <u>are</u> Yuri's job. → ________
3 Let's get something <u>drinking</u> before class. → ________
4 Sally planned <u>to joins</u> the drama club at school. → ________

C
see off 배웅하다

D 다음 우리말과 일치하도록 괄호 안의 말을 이용하여 문장을 완성하시오.

1 나는 살 집을 찾고 있다. (live in)
→ I'm looking for a house ________ ________ ________.
2 액션 영화를 보는 것은 매우 흥미롭다. (watch)
→ ________ ________ action movies is very interesting.
3 그 학교에 다니다니 그들은 똑똑한 것이 틀림없다. (attend)
→ They must be smart ________ ________ that school.
4 Kevin은 약속을 취소하지 않겠다고 약속했다. (cancel)
→ Kevin promised ________ ________ ________ the appointment.

D
attend 동 참석하다; *…에 다니다
smart 형 똑똑한, 영리한
appointment 명 약속

B 가주어와 의미상의 주어

1 가주어(it)와 진주어(to-v)

to부정사(구)가 주어로 쓰일 때 보통 주어 자리에 가주어 it을 쓰고 to부정사(구)는 뒤로 보내 「it(가주어) ... to-v(진주어)」의 형태로 쓴다. 이때 가주어 it을 '그것'으로 해석하지 않는다.

To get the tickets for the final game was hard.

→ **It** was hard **to get** the tickets for the final game.

2 의미상의 주어

to부정사가 나타내는 동작이나 상태의 주체가 문장의 주어와 다를 때, to부정사 앞에 「for / of + 목적격」을 써서 의미상의 주어를 나타낸다.

1) 「for + 목적격」: 대부분의 의미상의 주어는 「for + 목적격」의 형태로 쓴다.

The article was boring *for me* **to read**.

It is difficult *for us* **to understand** Picasso's paintings.

2) 「of + 목적격」: 사람의 성격이나 태도를 나타내는 형용사(예 kind, nice, smart, wise, rude, careless 등) 뒤에는 「of + 목적격」을 쓴다.

It is *kind of you* **to help** the people in need.

It was *careless of her* **to break** the cup again.

C to부정사를 활용한 중요 표현

1) 「too + 형용사 / 부사 + to-v」: '…하기에는 너무 ~한, 너무 …해서 ~할 수 없는'의 의미이며, 「so ... that + 주어 + cannot[can't]」으로 바꿔 쓸 수 있다.

Owen was **too tired to get** up early.

= Owen was **so tired that he couldn't get** up early.

2) 「형용사 / 부사 + enough + to-v」: '~할 만큼 충분히 …한'의 의미이며, 「so ... that + 주어 + can」으로 바꿔 쓸 수 있다. 부정형은 형용사나 부사 앞에 not을 붙여서 나타낸다.

She is **strong enough to carry** these heavy boxes.

= She is **so strong that she can carry** these heavy boxes.

This bag is **not big enough to hold** the books.

TIPS

「의문사+to-v」

「의문사+to-v」는 문장에서 주어, 목적어, 보어로 사용되며, 대개 「의문사+주어+should+동사원형」으로 바꿔 쓸 수 있다.

- what to-v 무엇을 …할지
- where to-v 어디서[어디로] …할지
- who(m) to-v 누가(누구를) …할지
- when to-v 언제 …할지
- how to-v 어떻게 …할지, …하는 방법

I don't know **what to do** first. (나는 무엇을 먼저 할지 모르겠다.)

= I don't know **what I should do** first.

Check-Up

A 다음 괄호 안에서 알맞은 말을 고르시오.

1 (It / That) is illegal to park your car here.
2 We are (so / too) hungry to walk anymore.
3 This game is easy (too / enough) for beginners to play.
4 I haven't decided where (go / to go) for summer vacation.

B 다음 빈칸에 for, of 중 알맞은 것을 골라 쓰시오.

1 It was difficult ________ her to pass the exam.
2 It is foolish ________ you to believe his lies again.
3 This homework is too much ________ me to finish today.

C 다음 밑줄 친 부분을 바르게 고치시오.

1 It is impossible of him to understand French. → ________
2 It is a good idea for book a table in advance. → ________
3 The water is enough warm to take a shower. → ________
4 These jeans are too big that I can't wear them. → ________

D 다음 우리말과 일치하도록 괄호 안의 단어를 이용하여 문장을 완성하시오.

1 매일 자외선 차단제를 바르는 것이 중요하다. (important, wear)
→ It is ________ ________ ________ sunblock every day.
2 너는 바이올린을 어떻게 연주하는지 아니? (how, play)
→ Do you know ________ ________ ________ the violin?
3 그 수프는 내가 먹기에 너무 뜨거웠다. (hot)
→ The soup was ________ ________ for me ________ eat.
4 그는 운전을 할 만큼 충분히 나이 들지 않았다. (old)
→ He is ________ ________ ________ ________ drive.

WORDS

A
illegal 형 불법적인
park 동 주차하다
beginner 명 초보자

B
foolish 형 어리석은

C
impossible 형 불가능한
book 동 예약하다
in advance 미리

D
sunblock 명 자외선 차단제

Grammar Practice

A 다음 밑줄 친 부분을 바르게 고치시오.

1 It is enough clean to drink. → __________

2 We don't have time take a nap. → __________

3 It was brave for him to catch the thief. → __________

4 The letters on the paper were so small for me to read. → __________

WORDS

A
take a nap 낮잠을 자다
thief 명 도둑

B 다음 두 문장을 to부정사를 이용하여 한 문장으로 바꿔 쓰시오.

1 Regina wants to become a photographer. It is her dream.
→ Regina's dream is ____________________.

2 Sue will help her mom. She will wash the dishes.
→ Sue will wash the dishes ____________________.

3 Hugo won first prize. He was very proud.
→ Hugo was very proud ____________________.

B
photographer 명 사진작가

C 다음 우리말과 일치하도록 괄호 안의 단어를 이용하여 문장을 완성하시오.

1 복도에서 뛰지 않는 것이 규칙들 중 하나이다. (run)
→ ______ ______ ______ in the halls is one of the rules.

2 너는 비상시에 무엇을 할지 알아야 한다. (do)
→ You should know ______ ______ ______ in emergencies.

3 그 선반이 너무 높아서 나는 그것에 닿을 수 없다. (high, reach)
→ The shelf is ______ ______ that ______ ______ ______ it.

4 우리가 그 산을 오르는 것은 매우 힘들었다. (us, climb)
→ ______ was very hard ______ ______ ______ ______ the mountain.

C
hall 명 복도
emergency 명 비상(사태)
reach 동 …에 이르다; *(손이) 닿다

내신 완성 Grammar Practice

1 다음 빈칸에 공통으로 들어갈 말로 알맞은 것은?

- It was easy ________ me to make pancakes.
- It is bad ________ you to eat junk food every night.

① to ② of ③ for ④ with ⑤ on

2 다음 밑줄 친 부분의 쓰임이 보기와 같은 것은?

보기 I finally got a chance <u>to see</u> the painting.

① Ann likes <u>to dance</u> during her free time.
② There are many places <u>to visit</u> in Korea.
③ My father's job is <u>to write</u> children's books.
④ The director's movies are difficult <u>to understand</u>.
⑤ The actors sold their clothes <u>to raise</u> money for the poor.

3 다음 중 어법상 바르지 <u>못한</u> 것은?

① My wish is to travel into space someday.
② It is difficult to master a foreign language.
③ Jessica ran very fast enough winning the race.
④ We only have 20 minutes to have breakfast this morning.
⑤ Let's go to the bookstore to buy a fashion magazine.

4 다음 문장을 가주어와 진주어가 포함된 문장으로 바꿔 쓰시오.

To use the machine can be dangerous for kids.

→ ________ can be dangerous for ________________.

WORDS

2
director 명 감독
raise 동 들어올리다; *(돈을) 모으다

3
space 명 공간; *우주
foreign 형 외국의

4
machine 명 기계
dangerous 형 위험한

서술형에 나오는 WRITING

A 다음 우리말과 일치하도록 괄호 안의 말을 바르게 배열하시오.

1 우리의 계획을 변경할 이유가 없다.
(is, our plans, there, change, to, no reason)
→ ______________________________

2 Henry와 친구가 되는 것은 쉬웠다.
(with, to, easy, become friends, Henry, it, was)
→ ______________________________

3 그들은 어떻게 수학을 가르칠지에 대해 이야기했다.
(how, talked about, teach, to, they, math)
→ ______________________________

B 다음 우리말과 일치하도록 괄호 안의 단어를 이용하여 문장을 완성하시오.

1 Clara는 자전거를 타기 위해 공원에 갈 것이다. (ride, a bicycle)
→ Clara will go to the park ______________.

2 제가 이 책들을 언제 반납할지 말씀해 주시겠어요? (return)
→ Can you tell me ______________ these books?

3 그것을 매일 하다니 너는 축구를 좋아하는 것이 틀림없다. (play)
→ You must like soccer ______________ it every day.

C 다음 그림을 보고, 괄호 안의 단어를 이용하여 문장을 완성하시오.

1 

(want, be)
Julie ______________ a judge someday.

2 

(close, enough, see)
I am sitting ______________ the opera singer on the stage.

1

In Oamaru, New Zealand, *little blue penguins leave the sea and walk to their nests every evening. In the past, they had to cross a road **to get** to their home. 불행하게도, 그 길은 펭귄들이 안전하게 건너기에는 너무 붐빈다. There were many accidents because the lights of the cars blinded the penguins. Now, however, they have a better way **to walk** to their nests.

To keep the penguins safe, the town decided **to build** a 25-meter-long tunnel under the road. The tunnel opened in 2016. It includes lights **in order to help** the penguins see. **To monitor** the penguins' use of the tunnel, there are cameras as well. These cameras also give people the opportunity **to watch** videos of the penguins online.

*little blue penguin: 쇠푸른펭귄

1 위 글에서 펭귄 터널에 대한 내용으로 언급되지 않은 것은?

① 펭귄이 바다에서 둥지로 돌아갈 때 이용한다.
② 눈을 다친 펭귄을 위한 전용 터널이다.
③ 도로 아래에 25미터 길이로 설치되었다.
④ 2016년에 개통되었다.
⑤ 터널 내부에는 카메라가 있다.

서술형

2 위 글의 밑줄 친 우리말과 일치하도록 괄호 안의 단어를 바르게 배열하시오.

→ Unfortunately, ______________________________
safely.
(too, the penguins, busy, is, cross, the road, to, for)

WORDS nest 명 둥지 light 명 빛, 전등 blind 동 눈을 멀게 만들다 include 동 [1] __________ monitor 동 관찰하다, 감시하다
opportunity 명 기회 문제 unfortunately 부 불행하게도 busy 형 바쁜; *붐비는 cross 동 (가로질러) 건너다

2

One Friday, a woman parked her car in City Hall's parking lot. Her plan was **to visit** the eighth floor quickly. She got into the elevator, and it began **to move** as usual. Then suddenly it stopped between two floors. She shouted and pressed the emergency button, but nobody answered. (①)

On Monday, workers came, found her, and helped her **to escape**. (②) But when she was leaving the parking lot, a worker didn't believe her story and made her pay over $300 for parking! (③) The woman went to court ________. (④) The court declared that it was wrong for the worker **to charge** her. (⑤) Furthermore, City Hall had to pay her $1,000. From that day forward, City Hall let her use the parking lot for free anytime she wanted.

1 Where would the following sentence best fit?

She had to stay in the elevator all weekend.

① ② ③ ④ ⑤

2 Which is the best choice for the blank?

① complain
② complained
③ to complaining
④ to complain
⑤ to be complained

WORDS parking lot 주차장 as usual 평상시처럼 shout 동 ¹________ press 동 누르다 escape 동 탈출하다 court 명 법정, 법원 declare 동 선언하다 charge 동 (요금을) 청구하다 forward 부 (시간·공간상) 앞으로 for free 무료로 문제 complain 동 불평[항의]하다

내신에 나오는 COMMUNICATION

A 여가 활동 묻고 답하기

A: **What do you usually do in your free time?**
(너는 여가 시간에 주로 무엇을 하니?)

B: **I usually** sing pop songs.
(나는 주로 팝송을 불러.)

A: Oh, **I like to** sing pop songs, too.
(오, 나도 팝송 부르는 것을 좋아해.)

여가 시간에 하는 활동에 대해 물을 때는 'What do you usually do in your free time?'이라고 말할 수 있다. 대답할 때는 'I usually ...'를 사용해 주로 무엇을 하는지 말할 수 있다.

EXPRESSION PLUS

A: **What do you usually do when you have free time?** (너는 여가 시간이 있을 때 주로 무엇을 하니?)
B: I usually watch TV **when I have free time.** (나는 여가 시간이 있을 때 주로 TV를 봐.)

A: **What do you like to do when you're free?** (너는 한가할 때 무엇을 하는 걸 좋아하니?)
B: I like to play computer games. (나는 컴퓨터 게임 하는 것을 좋아해.)

Check-Up

1 다음 대화의 빈칸에 들어갈 말로 알맞은 것은?

A: What do you like to do when you're free?
B: ____________________

① I work for a bank.
② I'm not free today.
③ I like to play dominoes.
④ I'd like to have some pizza.
⑤ I read comic books yesterday.

2 다음 괄호 안의 단어를 이용하여 대화를 완성하시오.

A: ________ ________ ________ ________
________ in your free time? (do, usually)
B: I usually do my shopping on the Internet.

WORDS

1
domino 명 도미노 게임
comic book 만화책

2
on the Internet 인터넷에서

B 허락 요청하고 답하기

A: It's really hot. **Can I** open the window**?**
(너무 더워. 내가 창문을 열어도 될까?)

B: **Of course.** You can open it.
(물론이지. 너는 그것을 열어도 돼.)

A: Okay.
(알겠어.)

'Can I ...?'는 '내가 …해도 될까?'의 의미로 상대방의 허락을 구할 때 쓰는 표현이다. 좀 더 격식을 갖추고 물어볼 때는 'May I ...?'를 쓴다. 상대방의 요청을 허락하는 경우에는 'Yes, you can[may].', 허락하지 않는 경우에는 'No, you can't[may not].'라고 대답할 수 있다.

⊕ EXPRESSION PLUS

1 허락 요청하기
- Can I see the picture? (내가 그 사진을 봐도 될까?)
- May I use your cup? (제가 당신의 컵을 사용해도 될까요?)

2 허락 또는 거절하기
- Yes, you can[may]. (응, 그래도 돼.)
- Of course. / Sure. / No problem. / Why not? (물론이지.)
- No, you can't[may not]. (아니, 안 돼.) / I'm afraid not. (유감이지만 안 돼.)

Check-Up

1 다음 대화의 빈칸에 들어갈 말로 알맞지 않은 것은?

A: Can I get a refill?
B: ____________________

① No problem.
② Sounds great.
③ Yes, you can.
④ Sorry, you can't.
⑤ I'm afraid not.

2 대화가 자연스럽게 이어지도록 (A)~(D)를 바르게 배열하시오.

(A) Why not?
(B) I like to jog along the river.
(C) Can I join you next time?
(D) What do you like to do when you have free time?

________ → ________ → ________ → ________

WORDS

1
refill 명 한 잔 더, 리필

2
jog 동 조깅하다
join 동 함께 하다

FINAL TEST

1 다음 빈칸에 들어갈 말이 바르게 짝지어진 것은?

- deal ________ : …를 다루다, 처리하다
- ________ advance: 미리

① for - in ② for - with
③ with - in ④ with - for
⑤ with - off

2 다음 우리말과 일치하도록 빈칸에 알맞은 말을 쓰시오.

우리는 배달 요금을 청구하지 않습니다.

→ We don't ________ for delivery.

3 다음 질문에 대한 대답으로 알맞지 않은 것은?

May I try on this T-shirt?

① Of course. ② No problem.
③ Yes, you may. ④ I'm afraid not.
⑤ I agree with you.

4 다음 대화의 빈칸에 들어갈 말로 알맞은 것은?

A: ____________________
B: I like to write poems.

① What are you doing?
② What did you do yesterday?
③ Why don't you write a poem?
④ Why do you like to write poems?
⑤ What do you like to do when you're free?

5 다음 문장이 들어갈 위치로 가장 알맞은 곳은?

Can I borrow yours?

A: What do you usually do in your free time?
B: I usually play tennis. (①)
A: Really? I want to learn tennis. (②)
B: Then I can teach you. (③)
A: But I don't have a tennis racket. (④)
B: Of course. (⑤)

[6-7] 다음 빈칸에 들어갈 말로 알맞은 것을 고르시오.

6 Dave grew up ________ an architect.

① be ② was
③ to be ④ to being
⑤ has been

7 I don't know ________ to give her for her birthday gift.

① how ② who
③ what ④ when
⑤ where

8 다음 빈칸에 들어갈 말이 바르게 짝지어진 것은?

- It is fun ________ me to plan trips.
- It was silly ________ you to trust him.

① of - of ② of - for
③ of - to ④ for - of
⑤ for - to

서술형

9 다음 우리말과 일치하도록 괄호 안의 말을 바르게 배열하시오.

내 지갑은 내 주머니에 넣기에는 너무 크다.
(big, put, is, my wallet, to, too, in my pocket)

→ ________________

[10-11] 다음 두 문장이 같은 뜻이 되도록 빈칸에 알맞은 말을 쓰시오.

10 Susan didn't tell me when I should call her back.

→ Susan didn't tell me ________ ________ ________ her back.

11 Charlie is so rich that he can buy all those diamonds.

→ Charlie is ________ ________ ________ ________ all those diamonds.

어려워요

12 다음 중 어법상 바른 것은?

① I need someone help with my work.
② It was kind for him to carry my bag.
③ This lake is so deep for us to swim in.
④ She went to the bank to pay taxes.
⑤ My goal is play for the national soccer team.

자주 나와요

13 다음 밑줄 친 부분의 쓰임이 나머지 넷과 다른 것은?

① This essay is boring to read.
② I was sad to part with my old friends.
③ Eric must be angry to behave like that.
④ We have some old things to throw away.
⑤ Be careful not to cut yourself when you have a knife.

[14-15] 다음 우리말과 일치하도록 to부정사와 괄호 안의 말을 이용하여 문장을 완성하시오.

14 우리는 오늘 외출하지 않기로 결정했다.
(go out)

→ We decided ________________ today.

15 그 나라는 여행하기에 안전하다.
(safe, travel around)

→ The country is ________________.

16 다음 우리말을 영어로 바르게 옮긴 것은?

나는 너무 바빠서 너와 쇼핑을 갈 수 없어.

① I'm so busy to go shopping with you.
② I'm not busy to go shopping with you.
③ I'm busy so I can go shopping with you.
④ I'm not busy, so I'll go shopping with you.
⑤ I'm so busy that I can't go shopping with you.

17 다음 중 어법상 바르지 못한 것은?

① Her ability to jump is amazing.
② It is interesting to make new friends.
③ He showed me how bake cupcakes.
④ It is too hot to play baseball outside.
⑤ Katie likes to go bowling with her family.

! 자주 나와요

18 다음 밑줄 친 부분의 쓰임이 보기 와 같은 것은?

보기 My class planned to have a class meeting.

① I forgot to empty the recycle bin.
② This sentence is hard to translate.
③ I visited Lily to discuss the problem.
④ My mom was upset to see my dirty room.
⑤ He didn't have the energy to work at that time.

19 다음 밑줄 친 부분 중 어법상 바르지 못한 것은?

Our restaurant will hold an event ①to celebrate our twenty-year anniversary on March 3. We will ②give all guests a free drink on that day. ③It will also be free ④for you to take a photo with our mascot, Bambi! We are very glad ⑤in order to serve you.

내신 완성 서술형

20 다음 두 문장을 보기 처럼 한 문장으로 바꿔 쓰시오.

보기 She is standing on one foot. It is easy.
→ It is easy for her to stand on one foot.

I found her house. It was difficult.
→ ______________________

21 다음 우리말과 일치하도록 조건에 맞게 영작하시오.

Josh는 그녀를 다시 보게 되어 신이 났다.

조건 1: excited, see, again을 이용할 것
조건 2: 총 7단어로 작성할 것
→ ______________________

[22-23] 다음 학생들의 인터넷 사용에 대한 그래프를 보고, to부정사를 이용하여 문장을 완성하시오.

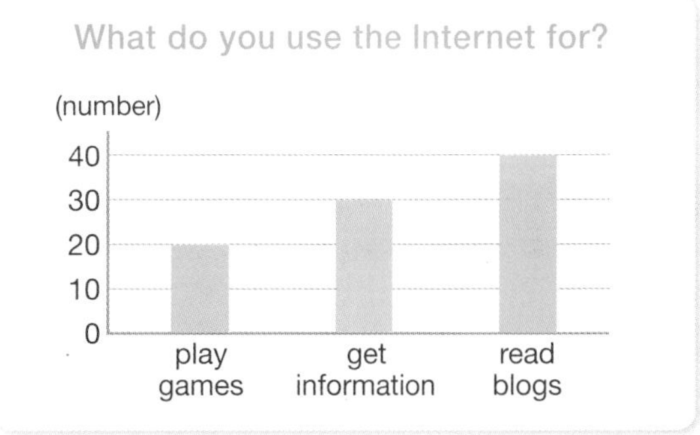

22 Forty students use the Internet ______________________.

23 Thirty students use the Internet ______________________.

WORD LIST

Grammar

☐ deal with	…를 다루다, 처리하다
☐ see off	배웅하다
☐ attend	동 참석하다; …에 다니다
☐ illegal	형 불법적인
☐ park	동 주차하다
☐ beginner	명 초보자
☐ foolish	형 어리석은
☐ impossible	형 불가능한
☐ book	동 예약하다
☐ in advance	미리
☐ take a nap	낮잠을 자다
☐ thief	명 도둑
☐ photographer	명 사진작가
☐ hall	명 복도
☐ emergency	명 비상(사태)
☐ reach	동 …에 이르다; (손이) 닿다
☐ director	명 감독
☐ raise	동 들어올리다; (돈을) 모으다
☐ space	명 공간; 우주
☐ foreign	형 외국의
☐ machine	명 기계
☐ dangerous	형 위험한

Reading

☐ nest	명 둥지
☐ light	명 빛, 전등
☐ blind	동 눈을 멀게 만들다
☐ include	동 포함하다
☐ opportunity	명 기회
☐ unfortunately	부 불행하게도
☐ busy	형 바쁜; 붐비는
☐ as usual	평상시처럼
☐ shout	동 소리치다
☐ press	동 누르다
☐ escape	동 탈출하다
☐ court	명 법정, 법원
☐ declare	동 선언하다
☐ charge	동 (요금을) 청구하다
☐ forward	부 (시간·공간상) 앞으로
☐ for free	무료로
☐ complain	동 불평[항의]하다

Communication

☐ comic book	만화책
☐ join	동 함께 하다

Final Test

☐ delivery	명 배달
☐ architect	명 건축가
☐ silly	형 어리석은
☐ trust	동 신뢰하다
☐ lake	명 호수
☐ deep	형 깊은
☐ national	형 국가의
☐ ability	명 능력
☐ empty	동 비우다
☐ discuss	동 의논하다
☐ celebrate	동 기념하다, 축하하다
☐ anniversary	명 기념일
☐ information	명 정보

CHAPTER 06

동명사

GET READY

Drinking too much soda is unhealthy.
(탄산음료를 너무 많이 마시는 것은 건강에 해롭다.)

I like **hiking** in the mountains.
(나는 산에서 하이킹하는 것을 좋아한다.)

Lucy's hobby is **making** cookies.
(Lucy의 취미는 쿠키를 만드는 것이다.)

동사원형에 -ing를 붙인 형태를 동명사라고 해요. 동명사는 문장에서 주어, 목적어, 보어 역할을 해요.

GRAMMAR FOCUS

A 동명사의 역할과 주요 표현

1 동명사의 역할

「동사원형+ing」 형태인 동명사는 문장에서 명사처럼 주어, 목적어, 보어 역할을 한다.

1) 주어 역할: '…하는 것은'으로 해석하며, 주어로 쓰인 동명사는 단수 취급한다.

Taking pictures of nature is my favorite activity.
Making a donation can help poor children.

2) 목적어 역할: '…하는 것을, …하기를'

She *finished* **reading** the book this morning. (동사의 목적어)
This factory is known *for* **producing** chocolate. (전치사의 목적어)

3) 보어 역할: '…하는 것(이다)'

One of his habits is **eating** late at night.

> **TIPS**
> 동명사의 부정형
> 동명사의 부정형은 「not[never] v-ing」 형태로, 동명사 앞에 부정어 not이나 never를 붙여서 나타낸다.
> I'm sorry for **not being** on time.
> (제시간에 오지 못해서 미안해.)

내신 POINT PLUS

현재분사

현재분사는 동명사와 동일한 「v-ing」 형태지만, 그 의미와 역할이 다르다.

의미	…하는(능동), …하고 있는(능동 · 진행)
역할	• 진행형: 「be동사+v-ing」 • 형용사 역할: 명사 수식, 보어
예	• 진행형: Susan is **talking** to him. (Susan은 그와 이야기하고 있다.) • 명사 수식: The **sleeping** boy is John. (그 잠자는 소년은 John이다.) • 보어: The show seemed **exciting**. (그 쇼는 흥미로워 보였다.)

2 동명사를 활용한 주요 표현

I don't **feel like arguing** with you.
The drama **is worth watching** again.
It is no use worrying about the future.

MORE EXPRESSIONS

- go v-ing …하러 가다
- It is no use v-ing …해도 소용없다
- feel like v-ing …하고 싶다
- be busy v-ing …하느라 바쁘다
- be used to v-ing …하는 데 익숙하다
- be good at v-ing …를 잘하다
- spend+시간[돈]+v-ing …하는 데 시간[돈]을 쓰다
- be worth v-ing …할 가치가 있다
- keep ~ from v-ing ~가 …하는 것을 막다
- on v-ing …하자마자
- keep (on) v-ing 계속 …하다
- cannot help v-ing …하지 않을 수 없다
- look forward to v-ing …하기를 기대하다
- have a hard time v-ing …하는 데 어려움을 겪다

Check-Up

A 다음 문장에서 밑줄 친 부분의 역할을 보기 에서 골라 쓰시오.

보기 주어 동사의 목적어 전치사의 목적어 보어

1 Chatting with friends is fun. ____________

2 I am sick of taking the exam. ____________

3 One of her hobbies is reading fairy tales. ____________

B 다음 밑줄 친 부분을 바르게 고치시오.

1 I spent one hour to wash my pants. → ____________

2 Tom was worried about make a mistake. → ____________

3 Forgive me for calling not you in advance. → ____________

4 The woman is used to have lunch alone. → ____________

C 다음 우리말과 일치하도록 괄호 안의 단어를 알맞은 형태로 쓰시오.

1 내 꿈은 디자이너가 되는 것이다. (become)

→ My dream is ____________ a designer.

2 금요일에 낚시하러 가는 게 어때? (go)

→ How about ____________ fishing on Friday?

3 Miles는 그의 사진을 인터넷에 올리는 것을 피했다. (post)

→ Miles avoided ____________ his photos on the Internet.

D 다음 우리말과 일치하도록 빈칸에 알맞은 말을 쓰시오.

1 그들은 너를 보기를 기대한다.

→ They ____________ ____________ ____________ seeing you.

2 우리는 스쿨버스를 계속 기다렸다.

→ We ____________ ____________ waiting for the school bus.

3 모든 영어 선생님들은 학생들의 시험지를 채점하느라 바쁘다.

→ All the English teachers ____________ ____________ grading students' test papers.

WORDS

A
chat 동 수다를 떨다
be sick of …에 질리다
fairy tale 동화

B
mistake 명 실수
in advance 미리, 사전에

C
post 동 (우편물을) 발송하다; *(정보·사진을) 올리다
avoid 동 피하다

D
grade 동 채점하다

B 동명사와 to부정사

동사에 따라 동명사나 to부정사 중 하나만을 목적어로 취하거나, 둘 다 목적어로 취한다.

1 동명사를 목적어로 취하는 동사

예 enjoy, finish, mind, keep, avoid, practice, quit, put off, give up 등
I **practice baking** cookies and bread on Mondays.
She **gave up solving** the math problem.

2 to부정사를 목적어로 취하는 동사

예 want, need, hope, wish, expect, choose, decide, plan, promise, learn 등
They **want to be** doctors in the future.
Michael **decided to change** his study habits.

3 동명사와 to부정사 둘 다 목적어로 취하는 동사

1) 의미 차이가 거의 없는 동사 예 like, love, hate, start, begin, continue 등
I **like drawing[to draw]** cartoons.
The flowers **start blooming[to bloom]** in the spring.

2) 의미 차이가 있는 동사 예 remember, forget, regret, try 등

① 「remember v-ing」: (과거에) …했던 것을 기억하다 / 「remember to-v」: (미래에) …할 것을 기억하다
I **remember having** a cat when I was a child.
Remember to bring your passport tomorrow.

② 「forget v-ing」: (과거에) …했던 것을 잊다 / 「forget to-v」: (미래에) …할 것을 잊다
She'll never **forget touching** the baby lions.
Don't **forget to clean** your room by this evening.

③ 「regret v-ing」: (과거에) …했던 것을 후회하다 / 「regret to-v」: (현재 · 미래에) …하게 되어 유감이다
Kelly **regretted buying** the white coat.
I **regret to disappoint** you.

④ 「try v-ing」: (시험 삼아) …하다 / 「try to-v」: …하려고 노력하다
I **tried putting** more salt in the soup.
He **tried to kill** the bug, but he couldn't.

TIPS

「stop v-ing」와 「stop to-v」
「stop v-ing」는 '…하는 것을 멈추다', 「stop to-v」는 '…하기 위해 멈추다'의 의미이다.
이때 to-v는 목적을 나타내는 부사적 용법의 to부정사이다.
He **stopped watching** the map. (그는 지도를 보는 것을 멈췄다.)
He **stopped to watch** the map. (그는 지도를 보기 위해 멈췄다.)

Check-Up

A 다음 괄호 안에서 알맞은 말을 고르시오.

1 Sophia gave up (teaching / to teach) Jeffrey.
2 My family wishes (going / to go) on a trip to Vietnam.
3 I enjoyed (playing / to play) basketball with my friends.
4 Some scientists expect (finding / to find) new planets in space.

WORDS

A
planet 명 행성

B 다음 밑줄 친 부분을 바르게 고치시오.

1 She plans leaving in a few days. → ________
2 Some people avoid to eat meat. → ________
3 I don't mind turn off the air conditioner. → ________
4 Remember sending me an email tomorrow. → ________
5 I tried to contacting him by calling him five times. → ________

B
by v-ing …함으로써

C 다음 괄호 안의 단어를 빈칸에 알맞은 형태로 쓰시오.

1 We hope ________ Paris someday. (visit)
2 The leaves began ________ color. (change)
3 The company stopped ________ the medicine because of its side effects. (sell)

C
side effect (약의) 부작용

D 다음 우리말과 일치하도록 괄호 안의 단어를 알맞은 형태로 쓰시오.

1 내 여동생은 알람 시계를 맞출 것을 잊었다. (set)
→ My sister forgot ________ her alarm clock.
2 그는 시험 삼아 그 종이에 선을 그었다. (draw)
→ He tried ________ a line on the paper.
3 나는 지난주에 운동장에서 그를 보았던 것을 기억한다. (see)
→ I remember ________ him at the playground last week.

Grammar Practice

A 다음 밑줄 친 부분을 바르게 고치시오.

1 We promised <u>keeping</u> in touch. → __________

2 Everyone started <u>laugh</u> at Jeremy. → __________

3 I had a hard time <u>get</u> to sleep last night. → __________

4 He looked forward to <u>continue</u> the conversation. → __________

B 다음 두 문장이 같은 뜻이 되도록 빈칸에 알맞은 말을 쓰시오.

1 I like to go to crowded places on weekends.
→ I enjoy __________ to crowded places on weekends.

2 He ran into his first love last week, and he can't forget it.
→ He can't forget __________ into his first love last week.

3 He stopped because he needed to ask for directions.
→ He stopped __________ for directions.

C 다음 빈칸에 들어갈 말을 보기 에서 골라 알맞은 형태로 쓰시오.

보기 win come play eat

1 I'm used to __________ spicy food.

2 Thank you for __________ to my birthday party.

3 My father loves __________ golf on sunny days.

4 His dream is __________ a gold medal in the Olympics.

D 다음 우리말과 일치하도록 괄호 안의 단어를 이용하여 문장을 완성하시오.

1 그 새로운 음식점은 시도해 볼 가치가 있었다. (worth, try)
→ The new restaurant ____________________.

2 나는 요즘 일하고 싶지 않다. (feel, work)
→ I don't ____________________ these days.

3 우리는 초대를 받아들이지 않을 수 없다. (help, accept)
→ We ____________________ the invitation.

WORDS

A
keep in touch 연락하고 지내다
get to sleep 잠이 들다
conversation 명 대화

B
crowded 형 붐비는
run into …를 우연히 만나다

D
invitation 명 초대

1 다음 빈칸에 들어갈 말로 알맞은 것은?

_________ things online is convenient.

① Buy ② Buys
③ Buying ④ Bought
⑤ Have bought

2 다음 밑줄 친 부분 중 어법상 바르지 못한 것은?

① I chose remain at home.
② Some students hate to study science.
③ Making money is not everything in life.
④ Where did you go swimming last weekend?
⑤ Their role is decorating cakes with chocolate.

3 다음 밑줄 친 부분의 쓰임이 나머지 넷과 다른 것은?

① It is no use crying now.
② Camping in a forest is enjoyable.
③ How about stopping by a convenience store?
④ On arriving at home, I opened the windows.
⑤ I was doing the dishes with my older brother at that time.

4 다음 빈칸에 들어갈 말이 바르게 짝지어진 것은?

Jackson broke his sister's headphones and forgot _________ her. When his sister found this out, she got very upset and kept on _________ at him.

① tell - yell ② to tell - to yell
③ to tell - yelling ④ telling - to yell
⑤ telling - yelling

WORDS

1
thing 명 물건, 용품
convenient 형 편리한

2
remain 동 남다
make money 돈을 벌다
decorate 동 장식하다

3
enjoyable 형 즐거운
convenience store 편의점

4
find out 알아내다[알게 되다]
yell 동 소리 지르다

A 다음 우리말과 일치하도록 괄호 안의 말을 바르게 배열하시오.

1 그녀는 동물들을 잘 돌본다.
(good, taking care of, is, she, animals, at)
→ ____________________

2 친한 친구가 없는 것은 그를 슬프게 만들었다.
(sad, not, close friends, him, having, made)
→ ____________________

B 다음 대화의 빈칸에 들어갈 말을 보기 에서 골라 알맞은 형태로 쓰시오.

보기 pass the bottle　take a nap　do your homework

1 A: Would you mind ____________ to me?
B: Sure. Here you go.

2 A: Don't put off ____________.
B: Okay. I'll do it right now.

C 다음은 방과 후 수업 소개글이다. 괄호 안의 단어를 이용하여 문장을 완성하시오.

After-School Classes

1

Newspaper Class
Do you like newspapers? Do you ____________ (want, share) information with your classmates? Then take this class.

2

Band Class
Why don't you ____________ (enjoy, play) an instrument on stage together? It'll be a new experience!

Send an email to afterclass@neschool.com.

1

A man and the emperor were watching some soldiers. The soldiers were practicing **shooting** arrows. The man wanted **to impress** the emperor, so he told a lie. He said, "When I was young, I was very good at (A) shoot arrows." "Then, show me your skills," said the emperor. The man immediately regretted (B) tell a lie. He began **to shake** with ________ because **lying** to the emperor was a crime!

The emperor gave the man three arrows. The man shot the first arrow, but it landed far from the target. "That is how your soldiers shoot," the man said quickly. The next arrow was a little closer. "That is how your generals shoot." Finally, the third arrow hit the target. "And that is how I shoot," the man said proudly.

1 위 글의 빈칸에 들어갈 말로 가장 알맞은 것은?

① cold
② fear
③ anger
④ sadness
⑤ excitement

2 위 글의 밑줄 친 (A)와 (B)를 알맞은 형태로 바꿔 쓰시오.

(A) ________ (B) ________

WORDS

emperor 명 황제 soldier 명 군인, 병사 practice 동 [1]________ shoot an arrow 화살을 쏘다
impress 동 깊은 인상을 주다 lie 명 거짓말 동 거짓말하다 immediately 부 즉시 crime 명 범죄 land 동 내려앉다; *떨어지다
general 명 장군 proudly 부 [2]________ 문제 fear 명 공포, 두려움 excitement 명 흥분, 신남

2

In 1841, the American artist John Rand invented the oil paint tube. Before this invention, artists had to grind their paints and mix them with oil. When they chose work outdoors, they had to pack the paints in breakable glass jars. On the other hand, paint tubes were easy to carry around.

One young artist, Claude Monet, was willing to spend a lot of money on paint tubes. Monet and his friend Renoir loved **painting** outdoors with paint tubes. They caught moments of light and color and expressed them on their canvases. This was a new way of **painting** called *Impressionism. Renoir said years later, "Without paint in tubes, there would be no Impressionism."

*Impressionism: 인상주의

1 Which is the best title for the passage?

① Characteristics of Monet's Paintings
② When Oil Paint Tubes Were Invented
③ The Bright Inventions of Two Young Artists
④ Influences of Paint Tubes on Impressionism
⑤ Monet vs. Renoir: Who Was the Greater Artist?

2 Correct the underlined word.

→ ______________

WORDS invent 동 발명하다 oil paint 유화 물감 grind 동 갈다 outdoors 부 야외에서 pack 동 (짐을) 싸다; *챙기다
breakable 형 깨지기 쉬운 jar 명 [1]__________ express 동 [2]__________ canvas 명 캔버스 천, 화폭
문제 characteristic 명 특징 bright 형 밝은; *영리한, 똑똑한 influence 명 영향

내신에 나오는 COMMUNICATION

A 관심에 대해 묻고 답하기

A: **What are you interested in?**
(너는 무엇에 관심이 있니?)

B: **I'm interested in** music. What about you?
(나는 음악에 관심이 있어. 너는 어떠니?)

A: **I'm interested in** sports.
(나는 운동에 관심이 있어.)

'What are you interested in?'은 상대방의 관심사를 물을 때 쓰는 표현이다. '너는 …에 관심이 있니?'라고 구체적으로 물을 때에는 'Are you interested in ...?'이라고 말할 수 있다. 대답할 때는 'I'm interested in ...'이라고 말할 수 있다.

EXPRESSION PLUS

1 관심에 대해 묻기
- **Do you have any interest in** traveling**?** (너는 여행에 관심이 있니?)
- **Do you find** English **interesting?** (너는 영어가 흥미롭다고 생각하니?)

2 관심에 대해 말하기
- **I'm into** sci-fi movies. (나는 공상 과학 영화에 빠져 있어.)
- **I find** webtoons **fun.** (나는 웹툰이 재미있다고 생각해.)
- **I have much interest in** Latin dance. (나는 라틴 댄스에 관심이 많아.)
- **I don't have any interest in** boxing. (나는 복싱에 전혀 관심이 없어.)

Check-Up

1 다음 대화의 밑줄 친 문장과 바꿔 쓸 수 있는 것은?

A: What are you interested in these days?
B: <u>I'm interested in decorating my room.</u>

① I never decorate my room.
② I'm into decorating my room.
③ I'm good at decorating my room.
④ I find decorating my room boring.
⑤ What about decorating my room?

WORDS
1
these days 요즘

2 다음 괄호 안의 단어를 바르게 배열하여 대화를 완성하시오.

A: Is your brother interested in space?
B: Yes, ______________________________.
(in, much, has, interest, he, space)

B 증상 묻고 답하기

A: You don't look good. **What's wrong?**
(너 안색이 안 좋아 보여. 무슨 일이니?)

B: **I have** a headache.
(저 두통이 있어요.)

A: Oh, that's too bad.
(저런, 안됐다.)

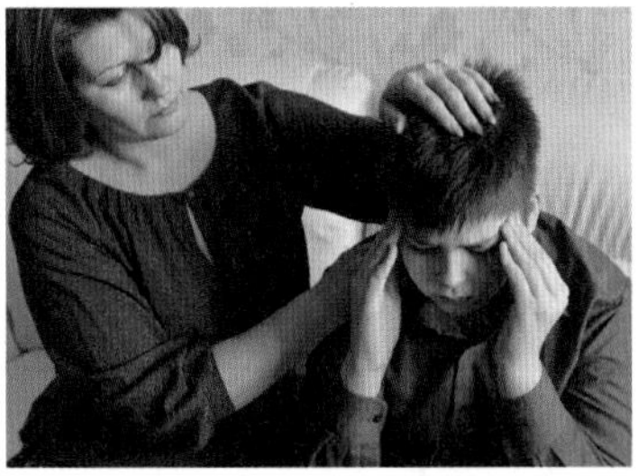

'What's wrong?', 'What's the matter?'는 상대방이 아파 보이거나 기분이 안 좋아 보일 때 그 원인을 묻는 표현이다. 대답할 때는 'I have ...', 'I feel ...'을 이용하여 자신이 겪고 있는 증상에 대해 표현할 수 있다.

TIPS 증상을 나타내는 여러 가지 표현
cold(감기), fever(열), runny nose(콧물), sore throat(인후염), toothache(치통), stomachache(복통) 등
I **feel[have] pain in** my back. (나는 허리에 통증이 느껴져.)
I **have a** terrible **sore throat**. (나는 목이 너무 아파.)

Check-Up

1 다음 대화의 빈칸에 들어갈 말로 알맞지 않은 것은?

A: You don't look good today. What's wrong?
B: ____________________

① I have a toothache.
② I have a runny nose.
③ I am sorry to hear that.
④ I feel pain in my finger.
⑤ I have pain in my stomach.

2 다음 대화의 밑줄 친 문장과 바꿔 쓸 수 있는 것은?

A: You look pale. What's wrong?
B: I have a fever.

① What do you think?
② What's the matter?
③ What's your opinion?
④ What are you doing?
⑤ What are you talking about?

WORDS

1
finger 명 손가락
stomach 명 위, 복부

2
pale 형 창백한
opinion 명 의견

FINAL TEST

1 다음 중 영어 단어와 우리말 뜻이 잘못 연결된 것은?

① yell - 소리 지르다 ② crime - 범죄
③ grade - 채점하다 ④ crowded - 한적한
⑤ breakable - 깨지기 쉬운

[2-3] 다음 우리말과 일치하도록 빈칸에 알맞은 말을 쓰시오.

2 나는 그 기계를 발명하기 위해 열심히 노력했다.

→ I worked hard to ________ the machine.

3 방학 중에 연락하고 지내자.

→ Let's ________ ________ ________ during the vacation.

4 다음 대화의 빈칸에 들어갈 말로 알맞은 것은?

A: You look sick. What's wrong?
B: ________________

① That's a pity.
② You're welcome.
③ It doesn't matter.
④ I have a bad cold.
⑤ I don't have time now.

5 다음 대화의 밑줄 친 문장과 바꿔 쓸 수 있는 것은?

A: Do you have any interest in volleyball?
B: Yes. I like to play it.

① Can you play volleyball?
② Do you want to play volleyball?
③ Are you interested in volleyball?
④ How often do you play volleyball?
⑤ Why do you find volleyball interesting?

6 다음 중 짝지어진 대화가 어색한 것은?

① A: What's the matter?
B: It couldn't be better.
② A: What's wrong?
B: I feel pain in my ankle.
③ A: What are you interested in?
B: I find playing the cello fun.
④ A: Are you interested in history?
B: No. I don't have much interest in history.
⑤ A: Is your father into cooking?
B: Yes, he's into it.

! 자주 나와요

[7-9] 다음 빈칸에 들어갈 말로 알맞은 것을 고르시오.

7 My mother practices ________ these days.

① drive ② drives
③ driving ④ to drive
⑤ driven

8 I know Peter. I remember ________ him at Jane's wedding.

① meet ② met
③ meeting ④ to meet
⑤ have met

9 Why did she decide ________ her job?

① change ② changed
③ changing ④ to change
⑤ have changed

10 다음 빈칸에 들어갈 말로 알맞지 않은 것은?

Emily ________ listening to classical music.

① loves ② hates
③ likes ④ hopes
⑤ enjoys

서술형

[11-12] 다음 문장을 바르게 고쳐 쓰시오.

11 I couldn't help laugh at his jokes.

→ ____________________

12 She gave up draw a picture of herself.

→ ____________________

13 다음 중 어법상 바른 것은?

① Her nose began to bleeding.
② I was afraid of going to the dentist.
③ Jina is looking forward to go skating.
④ Our goal is make customers happy.
⑤ Wearing not a helmet is dangerous.

자주 나와요

[14-15] 다음 우리말과 일치하도록 할 때, 빈칸에 들어갈 말로 알맞은 것을 고르시오.

14 뱀을 보자마자, 그는 빨리 도망갔다.
→ On ________ the snake, he ran away quickly.

① see ② sees
③ saw ④ seeing
⑤ to see

15 여러분께 미리 알려드리지 못해 죄송합니다.
→ I'm sorry for ________ you in advance.

① tell ② not tell
③ not telling ④ telling not
⑤ not to tell

어려워요

16 다음 밑줄 친 부분 중 어법상 바르지 못한 것은?

①Eating fast is a bad habit for your health. ②It makes you ③eat a lot because you don't feel full. It can ④cause stomach problems. From now on, try ⑤eat slowly.

[17-18] 다음 우리말을 영어로 바르게 옮긴 것을 고르시오.

17 나는 그를 돌보는 데 어려움을 겪었다.

① I had a hard time look after him.
② I had a hard time to look after him.
③ I had a hard time looking after him.
④ I had a hard time looked after him.
⑤ I had a hard time being looked after him.

18 그는 그의 가방을 찾으러 계속 두리번거렸다.

① He kept to look around for his bag.
② He kept look on around for his bag.
③ He kept on look around for his bag.
④ He kept to looking around for his bag.
⑤ He kept on looking around for his bag.

! 서술형

19 다음 우리말과 일치하도록 괄호 안의 말을 바르게 배열하시오.

나는 침대에서 잠을 자는 데 익숙하다.
(used, I, to, on a bed, am, sleeping)

→ ____________________

! 어려워요

20 다음 중 어법상 바르지 못한 것은?

① My hobby is writing for my blog.
② He is proud of winning a prize.
③ She promised keeping the secret.
④ Stop watching TV and clean your room.
⑤ Scott started to learn how to box at the gym.

21 다음 우리말과 일치하도록 괄호 안의 단어를 이용하여 문장을 완성하시오.

영화배우는 인터뷰에서 그 질문에 대답하는 것을 마쳤다. (finish, answer)

→ The actor ________ ________ the question in an interview.

내신 완성 서술형

22 다음 우리말과 일치하도록 조건에 맞게 영작하시오.

그 책은 살 가치가 없다.

조건 1: worth, buy를 이용할 것
조건 2: 총 6단어로 작성할 것

→ ____________________
____

[23-24] 다음은 금붕어를 키우는 방법에 대한 안내문이다. 안내문의 내용과 일치하도록 문장을 완성하시오.

How to Take Care of Goldfish

• change the water weekly
• feed the fish twice a day
• do not give too much food

If you want a pet goldfish, please follow these rules. Try to change the water weekly. 23 Don't forget ____________________.
24 Please avoid ____________ ________ to the fish.

WORD LIST

Grammar

- □ chat 동 수다를 떨다
- □ be sick of …에 질리다
- □ fairy tale 동화
- □ in advance 미리, 사전에
- □ avoid 동 피하다
- □ grade 동 채점하다
- □ planet 명 행성
- □ side effect (약의) 부작용
- □ keep in touch 연락하고 지내다
- □ get to sleep 잠이 들다
- □ crowded 형 붐비는
- □ run into …를 우연히 만나다
- □ convenient 형 편리한
- □ make money 돈을 벌다
- □ decorate 동 장식하다
- □ enjoyable 형 즐거운
- □ convenience store 편의점
- □ yell 동 소리 지르다

Reading

- □ emperor 명 황제
- □ soldier 명 군인, 병사
- □ practice 동 연습하다
- □ impress 동 깊은 인상을 주다
- □ immediately 부 즉시
- □ crime 명 범죄
- □ land 동 내려앉다; 떨어지다
- □ general 명 장군
- □ proudly 부 자랑스럽게
- □ fear 명 공포, 두려움
- □ excitement 명 흥분, 신남
- □ invent 동 발명하다
- □ outdoors 부 야외에서
- □ pack 동 (짐을) 싸다; 챙기다
- □ breakable 형 깨지기 쉬운
- □ jar 명 병
- □ express 동 나타내다, 표현하다
- □ characteristic 명 특징
- □ bright 형 밝은; 영리한, 똑똑한
- □ influence 명 영향

Communication

- □ these days 요즘
- □ finger 명 손가락
- □ stomach 명 위, 복부
- □ pale 형 창백한
- □ opinion 명 의견

Final Test

- □ volleyball 명 배구
- □ pain 명 고통
- □ history 명 역사
- □ wedding 명 결혼식
- □ laugh 동 웃다
- □ joke 명 우스갯소리, 농담
- □ goal 명 목표
- □ customer 명 손님, 고객
- □ run away 달아나다
- □ quickly 부 빠르게
- □ prize 명 상
- □ box 동 권투를 하다

CHAPTER 07

분사

GET READY

The boy **wearing** glasses is my cousin.
(안경을 쓰고 있는 소년은 나의 사촌이다.)

They seemed **shocked** at the tragic news.
(그들은 그 비극적인 소식에 충격을 받은 것 같았다.)

Smiling brightly, she looked at her son.
(밝게 웃으면서, 그녀는 그녀의 아들을 바라보았다.)

분사에는 현재분사(v-ing)와 과거분사(v-ed) 두 가지가 있어요. 분사는 형용사처럼 명사를 수식하거나 보어로 쓰일 수 있어요. 부사절을 간결하게 표현하기 위해서 쓰이는 분사구문은 문맥에 따라 다양한 의미를 나타내요.

GRAMMAR FOCUS

A 현재분사와 과거분사

분사에는 「동사원형+ing」 형태의 현재분사와 「동사원형+ed」 형태의 과거분사가 있다.
분사는 형용사처럼 명사를 수식하거나 주어나 목적어를 보충 설명하는 보어 역할을 한다.

1 현재분사와 과거분사

1) 현재분사 「v-ing」: 능동(…하는)이나 진행(…하고 있는)의 의미를 나타낸다.

a **surprising** story (능동)　　a **flying** bird (진행)

2) 과거분사 「v-ed」: 수동(…된)이나 완료(…해진)의 의미를 나타낸다.

an **ironed** shirt (수동)　　**fallen** leaves (완료)

TIPS

현재분사는 진행형(be+v-ing) 문장에, 과거분사는 수동태(be+v-ed)와 완료형(have+v-ed) 문장에도 쓰인다.
She is **crying**.
(그녀는 울고 있다.)
This ruler is **made** of plastic.
(이 자는 플라스틱으로 만들어져 있다.)

2 분사의 쓰임

1) 명사 수식: 분사가 단독으로 명사를 수식할 때는 명사 앞에 오고, 수식어구와 함께 쓰여 길어지면 명사 뒤에 온다.

The **screaming** man looks very angry.

I watched a play **called** *King Lear*.

2) 보어 역할: 분사는 주어나 목적어를 보충 설명하는 주격 보어, 목적격 보어의 역할을 한다.

Bentley seems **tired**. (주격 보어)

She kept me **waiting** for an hour. (목적격 보어)

TIPS

「지각동사/사역동사+목적어+목적격 보어(분사)」
분사가 지각동사나 사역동사의 목적격 보어로 쓰일 때는 목적어와의 관계에 따라 형태가 달라진다.
목적어와의 관계가 능동이면 현재분사, 수동이면 과거분사를 쓴다.
I **heard you singing**. (나는 네가 노래하는 것을 들었다.)
Daniel **had the computer fixed**. (Daniel은 컴퓨터가 고쳐지게 했다.)

3 감정을 나타내는 분사

주어 또는 분사의 수식을 받는 명사가 '…한 감정을 일으키는' 원인일 때는 현재분사를 쓰고, '…한 감정을 느끼는' 주체일 때는 과거분사를 쓴다.

My grade was **disappointing**. (실망스러운)

I was **disappointed** with my grade. (실망한)

MORE EXPRESSIONS

- amazing (놀라운) – amazed (놀란)
- boring (지루한) – bored (지루해하는)
- thrilling (황홀한) – thrilled (황홀해 하는)
- exciting (흥분하게 하는) – excited (흥분한)
- surprising (놀라운) – surprised (놀란)
- shocking (충격적인) – shocked (충격을 받은)
- interesting (흥미로운) – interested (흥미로워하는)
- confusing (혼란스러운) – confused (혼란스러워하는)

Check-Up

A 다음 괄호 안에서 알맞은 말을 고르시오.

1 Carl bought some (chopping / chopped) meat.
2 I know the man (living / lived) in this house.
3 The opera singer's voice is (amazing / amazed).
4 Everyone looks so (exciting / excited) about the game.

WORDS

A
chop 동 썰다, 다지다

B 다음 밑줄 친 부분을 바르게 고치시오.

1 This is a film make in the U.S. → ________
2 The slept baby looks like an angel. → ________
3 Who is that ballerina dance on the stage? → ________
4 The news about the earthquake was shocked. → ________

B
film 명 영화
earthquake 명 지진

C 다음 괄호 안의 단어를 빈칸에 알맞은 형태로 쓰시오.

1 Teddy feels ________ in art class. (bore)
2 The results of the experiment were ________. (interest)
3 There is no flight ________ for China this evening. (leave)
4 We are ________ with your decision to work with us. (please)

C
experiment 명 실험
flight 명 비행; *항공편
decision 명 결정

D 다음 우리말과 일치하도록 괄호 안의 단어를 알맞은 형태로 쓰시오.

1 그녀는 벽이 페인트칠되게 할 것이다. (paint)
→ She will have the wall ________.
2 그는 Nabi라고 불리는 작고 귀여운 고양이가 있다. (call)
→ He has a cute little cat ________ Nabi.
3 그 깨진 유리병은 네 것처럼 보인다. (break)
→ The ________ glass bottle looks like yours.

D
break 동 깨어지다

B 분사구문

분사구문은 「접속사+주어+동사」로 이루어진 부사절을 분사가 이끄는 구문으로 간결하게 나타낸 것으로, 문맥에 따라 다양한 의미를 나타낸다.

1 분사구문 만드는 법

~~When~~ he received the card, he felt happy. (부사절 / 주절)	① 「접속사+주어+동사」의 부사절에서 접속사를 없앤다.
→ ~~he~~ received the card, **he** felt happy.	② 부사절과 주절의 주어가 같으면, 부사절의 주어를 없앤다.
→ **Receiving** the card, he felt happy.	③ 남은 부사절의 동사를 현재분사 「v-ing」로 고친다.

~~While she~~ heard the news, she couldn't say anything.

Hearing the news, she couldn't say anything.

TIPS

1 분사구문의 부정형을 나타낼 때는 분사 앞에 부정어 not이나 never를 쓴다.
Not having much money, I didn't buy a cap. (돈이 많지 않아서, 나는 모자를 사지 않았다.)

2 분사구문이 Being으로 시작할 때, Being은 생략될 수도 있다.
(**Being**) **Satisfied** with the service, I gave big tip. (서비스에 만족해서, 나는 많은 팁을 주었다.)

2 분사구문의 의미

1) 때: …할 때(when, as), …하는 동안(while), …한 후에(after), …하자마자(as soon as)
Finishing his daily work, he had a cup of tea.
(← **After he finished** his daily work, he had a cup of tea.)

2) 이유: …하기 때문에(because, as, since)
Being a friendly person, Gary is loved by everybody.
(← **Because he is** a friendly person, Gary is loved by everybody.)

3) 조건: …하면(if)
Turning to the right, you will find the station.
(← **If you turn** to the right, you will find the station.)

4) 동시동작: …하면서(as)
I thought about my family, **looking** out the window.
(← I thought about my family **as I looked** out the window.)

5) 양보: …일지라도, …에도 불구하고(although, though)
Though hiding in a safe place, they still felt afraid.
(← **Though they hid** in a safe place, they still felt afraid.)
※ 양보를 나타내는 분사구문에서는 뜻을 분명히 나타내기 위해 접속사를 생략하지 않는 경우가 많다.

Check-Up

A 다음 괄호 안에서 알맞은 말을 고르시오.

1 (Cook / Cooking) dinner, he burnt himself.
2 (Be / Being) happy, the girl jumped up and down.
3 (To wave / Waving) her hands, Amanda said goodbye to us.
4 (Not having / Having not) enough time, they hurried to the bus stop.

B 다음 밑줄 친 부분을 바르게 고치시오.

1 Be hungry, he ate all the bread. → ______
2 Drank a cup of juice, I spilled some on my clothes. → ______
3 Read an article, Wendy underlined some important parts. → ______

C 다음 두 문장이 같은 뜻이 되도록 빈칸에 알맞은 말을 쓰시오.

1 While I took a shower, I sang out loud.
→ ______ a shower, I sang out loud.
2 Because she is stressed out, she is not feeling well.
→ ______ stressed out, she is not feeling well.
3 If you visit our website, you can download the video.
→ ______ our website, you can download the video.
4 When I lived abroad alone, I often missed my hometown.
→ ______ abroad alone, I often missed my hometown.

D 다음 밑줄 친 부분을 우리말로 옮기시오.

1 Walking to her house, she happened to meet an old friend.
→ ______, 그녀는 옛 친구를 우연히 만났다.
2 Having a lot of things to do, Henry had no time to relax.
→ ______, Henry는 휴식을 취할 시간이 없었다.

WORDS

A
burn oneself 불에 데다
wave 동 (손 · 팔을) 흔들다

B
spill 동 흘리다, 쏟다
underline 동 밑줄을 긋다

C
stress out 스트레스를 받게 하다
feel well 건강 상태가 좋다
abroad 부 해외에

D
happen to 우연히 …하다
relax 동 휴식을 취하다

Grammar Practice

A 다음 밑줄 친 부분을 바르게 고치시오.

1 Andrew had his hair <u>cutting</u>. → __________

2 They finally found the <u>burying</u> treasure. → __________

3 <u>Been</u> tired, she fell asleep on the sofa. → __________

4 <u>Answered</u> the phone, she reached for a pen. → __________

B 다음 괄호 안의 단어를 빈칸에 알맞은 형태로 쓰시오.

1 Eva put her __________ jeans in the box. (wear)

2 Look at the couple __________ on the bench. (sit)

3 The woman __________ her arms is my aunt. (raise)

4 I was __________ at hot and dry weather. (surprise)

5 I attended a wedding ceremony __________ in a church. (hold)

C 다음 빈칸에 들어갈 말을 보기 에서 골라 알맞은 형태로 쓰시오.

보기 thrill add hum

1 Albert heard a woman __________.

2 They checked the note __________ to the file.

3 Do you agree that the movie is __________?

D 다음 두 문장이 같은 뜻이 되도록 분사구문을 이용하여 문장을 완성하시오.

1 After she finished her bath, she put on body lotion.

→ ______________________________, she put on body lotion.

2 Because he wasn't busy, he decided to take a break.

→ ______________________________, he decided to take a break.

3 When I arrived in New York, I contacted one of my friends.

→ ______________________________, I contacted one of my friends.

WORDS

A
bury 동 묻다; (땅 속에) 숨기다
reach for (손을) 뻗다

B
wear 동 입다; *닳다, 해지다 (wore - worn)
raise 동 들어 올리다
wedding ceremony 결혼식
hold 동 잡다; *열다, 개최하다 (held - held)

C
add 동 추가하다, 덧붙이다
hum 동 콧노래를 부르다

D
put on (얼굴 · 피부 등에) …를 바르다
take a break 휴식을 취하다
contact 동 연락하다

내신 완성 Grammar Practice

1 다음 빈칸에 들어갈 말로 알맞은 것은?

I have a baseball ________ by my favorite player.

① autograph ② autographed
③ to autograph ④ autographing
⑤ have autographed

2 다음 문장의 밑줄 친 부분과 바꿔 쓸 수 있는 것은?

<u>Leaving the house</u>, please turn off all the lights.

① Since you leave the house
② While you leave the house
③ When you leave the house
④ Until you leave the house
⑤ Though you leave the house

3 다음 밑줄 친 부분 중 어법상 바르지 <u>못한</u> 것은?

① I saw Tony <u>diving</u> into the sea.
② He was <u>shocked</u> at his friend's accident.
③ The drummer's popularity is really <u>amazed</u>.
④ We had some pizza <u>delivered</u> to our house.
⑤ The man <u>sweeping</u> the sidewalk is my grandfather.

4 다음 문장을 분사구문을 포함한 문장으로 바꿔 쓰시오.

(1) If you open the refrigerator, you will see some orange juice.

→ ______________________________

(2) While she drove the car, she listened to music.

→ ______________________________

WORDS

1
autograph 동 사인하다

3
popularity 명 인기
sweep 동 (빗자루로) 쓸다, 청소하다
sidewalk 명 보도, 인도

4
refrigerator 명 냉장고

서술형에 나오는 WRITING

A 다음 우리말과 일치하도록 괄호 안의 말을 바르게 배열하시오.

1 모자를 쓰고 있는 남자는 누구인가요?
(the man, wearing, who, is)
→ ______________________________ a cap?

2 그녀는 먼지로 덮인 상자를 발견했다.
(a box, found, she, covered with)
→ ______________________________ dust.

3 그 질문을 이해하지 못해서, 나는 도움을 요청했다.
(asked for, the question, I, not, understanding)
→ ______________________________ help.

B 다음 우리말과 일치하도록 괄호 안의 단어를 이용하여 문장을 완성하시오.

1 Lisa는 수학여행에 대해 신나 보였다. (seem, excite)
→ Lisa ____________________ about the school trip.

2 Robert는 그의 자동차가 수리되게 했다. (have, car, repair)
→ Robert ____________________.

C 다음 밑줄 친 문장과 같은 뜻이 되도록 분사구문을 이용하여 문장을 완성하시오.

Friday, Dec. 21

My friend Jack and I planned to watch a musical. 1 <u>When I arrived at the meeting place, I couldn't find him.</u> He finally arrived, thirty minutes later. 2 <u>However, since we were too late, we couldn't get in the theater.</u>

1 ____________________, I couldn't find him.

2 However, ____________________, we couldn't get in the theater.

READING WITH GRAMMAR

1

In Ukraine, people put spider-shaped decorations on their Christmas trees. This tradition comes from a legend about a poor family. They had a Christmas tree, but they couldn't afford to decorate it. 더 예쁜 트리를 원했기 때문에, the children of the family began to cry on Christmas Eve. **Hearing** this sad sound, some spiders in the house made a plan. As the family slept, the spiders gathered at the Christmas tree. ① They put their white webs across the branches, **making** the tree beautiful. ② They built them to catch their prey overnight.

③ On Christmas morning, the family awoke and opened the curtains. ④ The morning sun hit the spider webs on the tree, **turning** them silver and gold! ⑤ This is why you can often see spider ornaments on Christmas trees.

1 위 글의 ①~⑤ 문장 중 글의 흐름과 관계없는 것은?

① ② ③ ④ ⑤

2 위 글의 밑줄 친 우리말을 다음 조건에 맞게 영작하시오.

조건 1 분사구문으로 작성할 것

조건 2 want, a prettier tree를 이용할 것

→ ______________________________

WORDS

decoration 명 장식품 tradition 명 ¹__________ legend 명 전설 afford 동 (…를 살[할]) 여유가 되다
decorate 동 장식하다 gather 동 ²__________ web 명 거미줄 branch 명 나뭇가지 prey 명 먹이
ornament 명 장식품

2

Today I attended an **exciting** boat race at the Todd River with my parents. However, it was much different from our expectations. The Todd River is often dried up, so people have ① interesting boat races on the sand instead of the water. When we got there, one of the boat races had just started. The boats had no bottom, so people ② standing inside the boats lifted them and ran! The team who reached the finish line first was the winner. Later, three big boats ③ named the *Navy*, the *Pirates*, and the *Vikings* battled each other. The teams fought **using** water guns and ④ tossing bags of flour **called** "flour bombs" at the other boats. We had a great time ⑤ watch the action!

1 Which is the best title for the passage?

① The Origins of the Todd River Race
② Unusual Boat Races on a Dry River
③ A Legendary Battle: Pirates vs. Vikings
④ An Interesting Boat Race on the Water
⑤ Some Warnings about the Todd River Race

2 Which is NOT grammatically correct?

① ② ③ ④ ⑤

WORDS expectation 명 예상 dry up 바싹 말리다 lift 동 [1] __________ finish line 결승선 navy 명 해군 pirate 명 해적 Viking 명 바이킹 battle 동 싸우다 명 전투 water gun 물총 toss 동 던지다 flour 명 밀가루 bomb 명 폭탄
문제 origin 명 기원 unusual 형 특이한, 색다른 legendary 형 전설적인 warning 명 경고(문), 주의

A 걱정 · 두려움 표현하기

A: You look depressed. What's going on?
(너 우울해 보여. 무슨 일이니?)

B: **I'm worried about** the dance contest.
(나는 춤 경연대회가 걱정돼.)

A: Don't worry. You'll do well.
(걱정하지 마. 넌 잘할 거야.)

'I'm worried about ...'은 '나는 …에 대해 걱정돼'의 의미로 걱정하는 바가 무엇인지 말할 때 쓰는 표현이다. 비슷한 표현으로 'I'm anxious[concerned] about ...'이 있다. 또한, 무서움이나 두려움을 표현할 때는 'I'm scared/afraid/frightened of ...'라는 표현을 쓸 수 있다.

EXPRESSION PLUS

- **I'm concerned about** my health. (나는 내 건강이 염려돼.)
- **I'm scared of** ghosts. (나는 귀신이 무서워.)
- **I'm afraid of** speaking in front of many people. (나는 많은 사람들 앞에서 말하는 것이 두려워.)

Check-Up

1 다음 대화의 빈칸에 들어갈 말로 알맞은 것은?

A: You don't look good. What's wrong?
B: I'm __________ about the audition tomorrow.
A: It's okay. Everything will be fine.

① mad ② sorry
③ worried ④ glad
⑤ curious

WORDS
1
audition 명 오디션
mad 형 화난
curious 형 궁금한

2 다음 우리말과 일치하도록 괄호 안의 단어를 바르게 배열하시오.

나는 혼자 여행하는 것이 두려워.
(afraid, alone, am, of, I, traveling)

→ ______________________________

B 기억 묻고 답하기

A: **Do you remember that** you borrowed some books from me last month**?**
(너는 네가 지난달 내게 책을 몇 권 빌린 것을 기억하니?)

B: Yes, I do. I'll give them back to you tomorrow.
(응, 기억해. 내가 내일 그것들을 너에게 돌려줄게.)

A: Thank you.
(고마워.)

'Do you remember (that) ...?'는 상대방에게 특정한 일에 대해 기억하는지 묻는 표현이다. 이와 비슷한 의미로 'Can you recall (that) ...?', 'I wonder if you remember ...'를 쓸 수 있다. 기억이 날 때는 'Yes, I remember ...', 기억이 나지 않을 때는 'No, I don't remember ...', 'I forgot ...' 등으로 대답할 수 있다.

⊕ EXPRESSION PLUS

A: **Can you recall** anyone calling you yesterday**?** (너는 어제 누군가 네게 전화한 것을 기억하니?)
B: **Yes, I remember** Eva called me. (응, Eva가 나에게 전화한 것이 기억나.)

A: **I wonder if you remember** my address. (나는 네가 내 주소를 기억하는지 궁금해.)
B: **No, I forgot** it. Can you tell me one more time? (아니, 잊어버렸어. 한 번 더 말해 줄래?)

TIPS 「Do you remember v-ing/to-v?」
remember의 목적어로 동명사가 오면 '너는 (과거에) …했던 것을 기억하니?'를, to부정사가 오면 '너는 (앞으로) …할 것을 기억하니?'를 의미한다.

Check-Up

1 다음 대화의 빈칸에 들어갈 말로 알맞지 않은 것은?

A: ______________________
B: Yes. The movie was about aliens.

① Do you remember to see that movie?
② Do you remember seeing that movie?
③ Can you recall the movie you saw last week?
④ Do you remember the movie you saw last week?
⑤ I wonder if you remember the movie you saw last week.

2 다음 우리말과 일치하도록 대화의 빈칸에 알맞은 말을 쓰시오.

A: You look worried. What's wrong?
B: ________ ________ where I put my wallet.
(나는 내 지갑을 어디에 뒀는지 잊어버렸어.)

WORDS

1
alien 명 외계인

2
wallet 명 지갑

FINAL TEST

1 다음 중 영어 단어와 우리말 뜻이 잘못 연결된 것은?

① spill - 쏟다
② toss - 두드리다
③ curious - 궁금한
④ legend - 전설
⑤ relax - 휴식을 취하다

2 다음 우리말과 일치하도록 빈칸에 알맞은 말을 쓰시오.

학생들은 티켓값을 지불할 여유가 된다.

→ Students can ________ to pay for the tickets.

3 다음 대화의 밑줄 친 문장과 바꿔 쓸 수 있는 것은?

A: You look nervous. Is there a problem?
B: The new semester begins soon. I'm afraid of meeting new friends.

① I forgot meeting new friends.
② I can't wait to meet new friends.
③ I really want to meet new friends.
④ I'm scared of meeting new friends.
⑤ I'm sorry that I can't meet new friends.

4 다음 빈칸에 들어갈 말이 바르게 짝지어진 것은?

• Can you ________ his name?
(너는 그의 이름을 기억하니?)
• I'm ________ about the deadline.
(나는 마감 기한에 대해 걱정돼.)

① forget - afraid
② forget - worried
③ recall - afraid
④ recall - worried
⑤ recall - shocked

5 다음 우리말과 일치하도록 괄호 안의 단어를 이용하여 문장을 완성하시오.

나는 그 발표가 걱정된다. (anxious)

→ I ________ ________ ________ the presentation.

[6-8] 다음 빈칸에 들어갈 말로 알맞은 것을 고르시오.

6

Joshua was trying to open the ________ door.

① lock
② locked
③ locking
④ to lock
⑤ to be locked

7

Do you know the couple ________ on the slope?

① ski
② skis
③ skied
④ skiing
⑤ to be skied

8

Some TV programs ________ in Korea are popular all over Asia.

① make
② made
③ making
④ were made
⑤ were making

9 다음 우리말과 일치하도록 괄호 안의 단어를 알맞은 형태로 쓰시오.

그녀는 그녀의 일이 지루해졌다. (bore)

→ She got ________ with her job.

10 다음 빈칸에 들어갈 말이 바르게 짝지어진 것은?

- I'll read the book __________ by Orwell.
- He felt someone __________ his shoulder.

① write - touched
② written - touched
③ written - touching
④ writing - touched
⑤ writing - touching

어려워요

11 다음 밑줄 친 부분의 쓰임이 나머지 넷과 다른 것은?

① The boy talking to her is Robert.
② Look at the flying bird over there!
③ I'm thinking about moving to Chicago.
④ Who is that girl sitting in the corner?
⑤ There were many people enjoying the sunny day.

12 다음 밑줄 친 부분 중 어법상 바르지 못한 것은?

① Finishing her work, she took a nap.
② Shopping in the market, I met Sam.
③ Being sick, they stayed in bed all day.
④ Waiting for her, I bought shoes at the mall.
⑤ Having not any money, he borrowed ten dollars from her.

어려워요

13 다음 대화를 읽고 분사를 이용하여 문장을 완성하시오.

Anna: Have you seen Serena?
Jamie: I saw her yesterday. She was studying at the library.

→ Jamie saw Serena __________ __________ __________ __________ yesterday.

14 다음 밑줄 친 단어를 알맞은 형태로 바꿔 쓰시오.

Keira's mother works at a hospital. She worked late last night. (1) Come home, she looked (2) tire. So Keira helped her with the household chores.

(1) __________ (2) __________

자주 나와요

15 다음 우리말을 영어로 옮길 때 빈칸에 들어갈 말로 알맞은 것은?

하루 종일 모니터를 쳐다봐서, 나는 눈이 아팠다.
→ __________, I had sore eyes.

① Stare at the monitor all day
② Stared at the monitor all day
③ Staring at the monitor all day
④ To stare at the monitor all day
⑤ To staring at the monitor all day

16 다음 두 문장을 한 문장으로 바꿀 때 빈칸에 알맞은 말을 쓰시오.

Dr. Smith received a present. The present was wrapped in beautiful paper.

→ Dr. Smith received a present ________ ________ ________ ________.

17 다음 중 어법상 바른 것은?

① I feel exciting when I shop.
② The night view was amazed.
③ He seemed surprising at my idea.
④ The road signs are pretty confused.
⑤ The trip to the jungle sounds really thrilling.

서술형

[18-19] 다음 우리말과 일치하도록 괄호 안의 단어를 바르게 배열하시오.

18 호수에서 헤엄치는 오리들은 귀엽다.
(in, the ducks, swimming, the lake)

→ ________________________ are cute.

19 그가 옳다고 믿었기 때문에, 그는 내 말을 전혀 듣지 않았다.
(was, right, believing, he)

→ ________________________, he didn't listen to me at all.

내신 완성 서술형

20 다음 문장을 분사구문을 포함한 문장으로 바꿔 쓰시오.

If you put some coins in the machine, you will get a drink.

→ ________________________
____

[21-22] 다음 글에서 어법상 틀린 곳을 모두 찾아 바르게 고치시오.

I ordered a plate decorating with flower patterns online. But when I received the plate, I found it break.

21 ________ → ________

22 ________ → ________

23 다음 그림을 보고, 조건에 맞게 영작하시오.

조건 1: have, her hair, perm을 이용할 것
조건 2: 주어를 포함하여 총 5단어로 작성할 것
조건 3: 과거시제로 작성할 것

→ Jisu ________________________.

WORD LIST

Grammar

□ chop	동 썰다, 다지다
□ film	명 영화
□ earthquake	명 지진
□ experiment	명 실험
□ flight	명 비행; 항공편
□ decision	명 결정
□ break	동 깨어지다
□ burn oneself	불에 데다
□ wave	동 (손 · 팔을) 흔들다
□ spill	동 흘리다, 쏟다
□ stress out	스트레스를 받게 하다
□ feel well	건강 상태가 좋다
□ abroad	부 해외에
□ happen to	우연히 …하다
□ relax	동 휴식을 취하다
□ reach for	(손을) 뻗다
□ wear	동 입다; 닳다, 해지다
□ raise	동 들어 올리다
□ wedding ceremony	결혼식
□ add	동 추가하다, 덧붙이다
□ hum	동 콧노래를 부르다
□ put on	(얼굴 · 피부 등에) …를 바르다
□ contact	동 연락하다
□ autograph	동 사인하다
□ popularity	명 인기
□ sweep	동 (빗자루로) 쓸다, 청소하다
□ refrigerator	명 냉장고

Reading

□ decoration	명 장식품
□ tradition	명 전통
□ legend	명 전설
□ afford	동 (…를 살[할]) 여유가 되다
□ decorate	동 장식하다
□ gather	동 모이다
□ web	명 거미줄
□ branch	명 나뭇가지
□ prey	명 먹이
□ expectation	명 예상
□ lift	동 들어 올리다
□ battle	동 싸우다 명 전투
□ toss	동 던지다
□ origin	명 기원
□ unusual	형 특이한, 색다른
□ warning	명 경고(문), 주의

Communication

□ anxious	형 불안해하는
□ audition	명 오디션
□ mad	형 화난
□ curious	형 궁금한
□ alien	명 외계인
□ wallet	명 지갑

Final Test

□ semester	명 학기
□ lock	동 잠그다
□ shoulder	명 어깨
□ household chore	집안일
□ wrap	동 싸다, 포장하다
□ perm	동 파마를 해 주다

CHAPTER 08

형용사와 부사

GET READY

I put **a little** syrup on my waffle.
(나는 내 와플에 약간의 시럽을 얹었다.)

I want to do something **interesting** today.
(나는 오늘 흥미로운 것을 하고 싶다.)

You should **turn on** the light because it's dark.
(어둡기 때문에 너는 불을 켜야 한다.)

명사를 수식하며 수나 양, 성질, 상태 등을 나타내는 말을 형용사라고 하고, 동사, 형용사, 부사 등을 수식하는 말을 부사라고 해요. 형용사와 부사를 써서 의미를 더 상세하게 표현할 수 있어요. 또한 부사는 동사와 짝을 이루어 하나의 동사처럼 쓰이기도 해요.

A 수량형용사

수량형용사는 뒤에 오는 명사의 수나 양을 나타낸다.

의미	셀 수 있는 명사의 복수형 앞	셀 수 없는 명사 앞
조금 있는, 약간의 (긍정적)	a few	a little
거의 없는 (부정적)	few	little
많은	many	much
	a lot of, lots of	

Many[A lot of / Lots of] *people* gathered to hear the speech.
I couldn't get **much[a lot of / lots of]** *information* from the book.
To make pancakes, I need **a few** *eggs* and **a little** *milk*.
This is a difficult topic, so **few** *students* understand it.
There is **little** *toothpaste* in the tube. We should buy a new one.

내신 POINT PLUS

most와 all의 수 일치
most(대부분의)와 all(모든)은 뒤에 나오는 명사의 수에 동사의 수를 일치시킨다.
Most people *believe* the rumor is true. (대부분의 사람들은 그 소문이 사실이라고 믿는다.)
All my money *was* stolen by the thief. (내 모든 돈이 도둑에 의해 도난당했다.)

B 형용사의 위치

1) 「-thing / -one / -body + 형용사」
-thing, -one, -body로 끝나는 대명사는 형용사가 뒤에서 수식한다.
There is nothing **wrong** with the car.
I have something **important** to tell you.

TIPS
수량형용사는 성질이나 상태를 나타내는 형용사의 앞에 위치한다.
many *big* boxes (많은 큰 상자들)
a few *old* men (몇 명의 노인들)

2) all의 위치
all이 명사를 수식할 때는 정관사(the), 지시형용사(this, that 등), 소유격(my, his 등), 다른 형용사의 앞에 위치한다.
All *the students* went on a field trip today.
I have already read **all** *these comic books*.

3) 「such + a(n) + 형용사 + 명사」/「so + 형용사 + a(n) + 명사」: '그만큼[매우] …한 ~'
형용사가 such와 함께 쓰이면 관사 뒤에, so와 함께 쓰이면 관사 앞에 위치한다.
I've never seen **such a beautiful sunset**.
→ I've never seen **so beautiful a sunset**.

Check-Up

WORDS

A 다음 괄호 안에서 알맞은 말을 고르시오.

1 Most kids (like / likes) sweet things.

2 There are (few / a little) characters in this novel.

3 Let's hurry. We don't have (many / much) time.

4 The tourists want to drink (something cold / cold something).

B 다음 문장에서 괄호 안의 단어가 들어갈 위치를 고르시오.

1 We ① want to hire ② someone ③. (outgoing)

2 I have never met ① so ② a ③ boy as Tom. (smart)

3 My grandfather ① made ② the ③ furniture. (all)

4 I can't believe that you did ① such ② a ③ thing. (foolish)

B
hire 동 고용하다
outgoing 형 외향적인, 사교적인
smart 형 똑똑한, 영리한
furniture 명 가구

C 다음 밑줄 친 부분을 바르게 고치시오.

1 Julia always has too <u>many</u> work to do. → ______

2 All my friends <u>calls</u> me by my nickname now. → ______

3 Did you buy <u>good anything</u> at the department store? → ______

4 I put <u>few</u> sugar in my coffee, so it didn't taste sweet. → ______

C
nickname 명 별명
department store 백화점

D 다음 우리말과 일치하도록 괄호 안의 단어를 바르게 배열하시오.

1 많은 사람들이 이 도시에 산다. (a, of, people, lot)
→ ______ live in this city.

2 캠핑은 매우 재미있는 활동이다. (such, activity, fun, a)
→ Camping is ______.

3 이 음악은 내게 새로운 것이 아니다. (new, nothing)
→ This music is ______ to me.

4 그녀의 모든 학생들이 그녀의 생일을 축하했다. (students, her, all)
→ ______ celebrated her birthday.

D
activity 명 활동

C 「동사+부사」

「동사+부사」 형태의 동사구는 하나의 동사 역할을 한다. 이때 동사구의 목적어에 따라 부사의 위치가 달라진다.

1 다양한 「동사+부사」 표현

명사나 대명사를 목적어로 취하는 「동사+부사」에는 다음과 같은 표현이 있다.

You may give back *my bicycle* anytime next week.
…를 돌려주다

Please hand in *your homework* by this Wednesday.
…를 제출하다

Did Amelia turn on *the fan* right after she grilled meat?
(전기 · 가스 · 수도 등을) 켜다

MORE EXPRESSIONS

- put out (불을) 끄다
- get on (버스 등에) 타다
- try on (옷 등을) 입어 보다
- throw away …를 버리다
- pay back (돈을) 갚다, 돌려주다
- look up (사전 등에서) 정보를 찾다
- turn up (라디오 등의) 소리를 크게 하다
- take off (옷 등을) 벗다
- put down …를 내려놓다
- fill out (양식 등에) 기입하다
- put off …를 미루다, 연기하다
- find out (사실 등을) 알아내다
- turn off (전기 · 가스 · 수도 등을) 끄다
- turn down (라디오 등의) 소리를 줄이다

2 동사구에서 목적어의 위치

1) 목적어가 명사인 경우: 부사 뒤 또는 동사와 부사 사이에 온다.

My little brother's crying **woke up** *my family*.
= My little brother's crying **woke** *my family* **up**.
She **put on** *her jacket* because it was cold.
= She **put** *her jacket* **on** because it was cold.

2) 목적어가 대명사인 경우: 동사와 부사 사이에 온다.

He dropped his package, so I **picked** *it* **up** for him.
He dropped his package, so I picked up it for him. (×)

TIPS

자동사로 쓰이는 「동사+부사」
「동사+부사」 형태지만 목적어를 취하지 않는 자동사로 쓰이는 표현들도 있다.

- get up 일어나다
- break down 고장 나다
- fall over 넘어지다
- hurry up 서두르다
- take off 이륙하다
- show up 나타나다
- go out 나가다
- pass away 사망하다[돌아가시다]

When I came close, the dog **ran away**. (내가 가까이 갔을 때, 그 개는 달아났다.)

Check-Up

A 다음 괄호 안에서 알맞은 말을 고르시오.

1 Can we (the meeting put / put the meeting) off?

2 Someone turned on the oven. Could you turn (it off / off it) again?

3 I didn't know those words, so I looked (them up / up them) in the dictionary.

WORDS

A
oven 명 오븐
dictionary 명 사전

B 다음 밑줄 친 부분을 바르게 고치시오.

1 Here's the order form. Please fill out it. → ____________

2 Sandy her scarf took off and put it in the closet. → ____________

3 It's dangerous to play with knives. Please put down them. → ____________

B
order form 주문서
closet 명 벽장

C 다음 우리말과 일치하도록 빈칸에 들어갈 말을 보기 에서 골라 쓰시오.

보기 find out　hurry up　throw away　put on

1 서둘러! 출발 전까지 10분밖에 안 남았어.
→ ____________! There are only ten minutes left before departure.

2 제가 이 플라스틱 병들을 어디에 버릴 수 있을까요?
→ Where can I ____________ these plastic bottles?

3 과학자들은 우주에 관한 새로운 정보를 알아낼 것이다.
→ Scientists will ____________ new information about space.

C
departure 명 떠남, 출발

D 다음 우리말과 일치하도록 괄호 안의 단어를 이용하여 문장을 완성하시오.

1 제가 그 스웨터를 다시 입어 봐도 될까요? (try)
→ Can I __________ __________ the sweater again?

2 그는 바깥의 소음 때문에 라디오 소리를 크게 했다. (turn)
→ He __________ __________ the radio because of the noise outside.

3 너는 내 노트를 나중에 돌려줘도 돼. (give)
→ You can __________ my notebook __________ to me later.

D
noise 명 소리, 소음

Grammar Practice

A 다음 밑줄 친 부분을 바르게 고치시오.

1 Have you ever heard so a funny story? → ____________

2 She eats light something between lunch and dinner. → ____________

3 Much teenagers came to enjoy the music festival. → ____________

4 There was a lot of trash in the park, but no one picked up it. → ____________

WORDS

A
light 형 밝은; *가벼운[간단한]

B 다음 괄호 안의 단어를 이용하여 빈칸에 알맞은 말을 쓰시오.

1 He scored ________ ________ ________ for his team. (lots, goal)

2 We have never had ________ ________ ________ meal before. (such, great)

3 I needed my bus fare. Luckily, I had ________ ________ ________ in my pocket. (few, coin)

B
fare 명 (교통) 요금
luckily 부 운 좋게, 다행히도
pocket 명 주머니

C 다음 빈칸에 들어갈 말을 보기에서 골라 쓰시오.

보기 put out　get on　turn it down　wake her up

1 The music is too loud. Could you ____________?

2 The firefighters tried to ____________ the forest fire.

3 We have to ____________ the airplane at gate 27.

C
firefighter 명 소방관
forest fire 산불

D 다음 우리말과 일치하도록 괄호 안의 단어를 바르게 배열하시오.

1 이번 여름에는 비가 거의 오지 않았다.
(rain, we, had, little)
→ ____________ this summer.

2 Sally는 그녀의 모든 돈을 배낭에 썼다.
(on, all, a backpack, money, her)
→ Sally spent ____________.

내신 완성 Grammar Practice

1 다음 빈칸에 들어갈 말로 알맞지 <u>않은</u> 것은?

There are ________ famous places nearby.

① few ② a few
③ many ④ a little
⑤ a lot of

2 다음 중 어법상 바르지 <u>못한</u> 것은?

① Most board games are fun for me.
② I will hand in my homework today.
③ These days, few people write letters by hand.
④ Ron almost fell over onto the bathroom floor.
⑤ Emily is having dinner with handsome someone.

3 다음 우리말과 일치하도록 괄호 안의 단어를 이용하여 빈칸에 알맞은 말을 쓰시오.

(1) 그 기계는 어제 고장 났다. 우리는 그것을 지금 사용할 수 없다. (break)

→ The machine ________ ________ yesterday. We can't use it now.

(2) Tim은 내일 일찍 일어날 것이다. 그는 아침에 회의가 있다. (get)

→ Tim will ________ ________ early tomorrow. He has a morning meeting.

4 다음 두 문장이 같은 뜻이 되도록 괄호 안의 단어를 이용하여 문장을 완성하시오.

(1) Harry painted so charming a picture.

→ Harry painted ________________________. (such)

(2) Do we have to buy much juice for the party?

→ Do we have to ________________________ for the party? (lots)

WORDS

1
nearby 부 인근에

2
almost 부 거의
bathroom 명 욕실, 화장실

4
charming 형 매력적인, 멋진

서술형에 나오는 WRITING

A **다음 우리말과 일치하도록 괄호 안의 말을 바르게 배열하시오.**

1 우리는 저 모든 아이들을 위한 충분한 장난감 차가 있다.
(all, have, for, we, enough toy cars, children, those)
→ ______________________________

2 제 수프에 약간의 후추를 넣어 주실래요?
(pepper, put, can, my soup, you, a little, in)
→ ______________________________

3 나는 그에 대해 어떤 나쁜 것도 말하지 않았다.
(him, say, I, bad, anything, didn't, about)
→ ______________________________

B **다음 우리말과 일치하도록 괄호 안의 단어를 이용하여 문장을 완성하시오.**

1 대부분의 운전자들이 이 자동차를 좋아한다. (driver, like)
→ ________ ________ ________ this car.

2 대기 오염 때문에 사람들이 거의 밖에 나가지 않았다. (people)
→ ________ ________ went outside because of the air pollution.

3 그는 연극이 시작되기 전에 그의 스마트폰을 껐다. (turn, smartphone)
→ He ________ ________ ________ ________ before the play started.

C **다음은 벼룩시장 광고이다. 괄호 안의 단어를 바르게 배열하여 문장을 완성하시오.**

Come to Our Flea Market

At the flea market, you can buy **1** ______________ (a, good, lot, things, of), from shoes to books. Most of the things are used, so you can buy them at **2** ______________ (price, a, low, such). There will be lots of bargains, and everybody is welcome!

1

Michelangelo is one of the greatest artists of all time. When he was young, however, he struggled to earn money. He traveled around Italy, looking for *patrons. Unfortunately, **most** people didn't want statues made by new artists. They preferred old statues by ancient Roman artists. So Michelangelo thought of clever something—he could make new statues that looked like old ones!

He made a statue called *Sleeping Cupid*. Then he **picked** it **up**, **threw** it **down**, and **rolled** it **around** in the dirt. A rich man bought *Sleeping Cupid*. He thought it was an ancient work of art. Later, however, Michelangelo accidentally told the truth. At first the man was very angry, but then he recognized Michelangelo's talent. He forgave Michelangelo and became his new patron.

*patron: 후원자

1 위 글에서 Michelangelo가 자신의 조각품을 땅에 던지고 굴린 이유는?

① 완성된 조각품이 만족스럽지 않아서
② 조각품을 더 단단하게 만들기 위해서
③ 조각품이 팔리지 않는 것에 화가 나서
④ 오래된 조각품처럼 보이게 하기 위해서
⑤ 사람들에게 자신의 열정을 보여 주기 위해서

서술형

2 위 글의 밑줄 친 문장을 바르게 고치시오.

→ So ______________________

WORDS

struggle 동 분투하다, 애쓰다　earn 동 (돈을) 벌다　unfortunately 부 불행하게도　statue 명 조각상　prefer 동 선호하다
ancient 형 고대의　clever 형 1 __________　dirt 명 먼지, 때; *흙　accidentally 부 우연히, 뜻하지 않게; *잘못하여
recognize 동 알아보다; 인정하다　talent 명 2 __________　forgive 동 용서하다

2

Brian was a middle school student suffering from cancer. He had to take ① lots of special medicine and visit **a lot of** doctors every week. Because of the ② many treatments, he found that he had less and less hair. Finally, he told his mother, "I don't want to go to school because I have so ③ little hair." He was afraid his friends would laugh at him. But his mother encouraged him to go to school.

A few days later, Brian went to school and saw **something surprising**. ④ His all classmates had shaved their heads! It was ⑤ such a meaningful surprise. One of them said to him, "Please don't quit school. Now you're not the only one without hair."

1 **How does Brian likely feel at the end?**

① satisfied ② angry
③ bored ④ scared
⑤ thankful

2 **Which is NOT grammatically correct?**

① ② ③ ④ ⑤

WORDS suffer from …로 고통받다 cancer 명 암 medicine 명 1__________ treatment 명 치료 laugh at …를 비웃다[놀리다] encourage 동 2__________ classmate 명 반 친구 shave 동 면도하다 meaningful 형 의미 있는 quit 동 그만두다

내신에 나오는 COMMUNICATION

A 상기시켜 주기

A: What will the weather be like today?
(오늘 날씨가 어떨까요?)

B: It's going to rain this afternoon.
Don't forget to take your umbrella.
(오늘 오후에 비가 올 거야. 우산 가져갈 것을 잊지 마.)

A: Okay, I won't.
(네, 잊지 않을게요.)

'Don't forget to-v ...'는 상대방에게 어떤 일을 하는 것을 잊지 않도록 상기시킬 때 쓰는 표현이다. 이와 유사한 표현으로는 'Remember to-v ...', 'Make sure to-v ...' 등이 있다. 이에 대해 잊지 않겠다고 대답할 때는 'I won't forget ...'이라고 말할 수 있다.

EXPRESSION PLUS

- **Remember to** set your alarm. (알람을 맞출 것을 기억해.)
- **Make sure to** close the windows. (꼭 창문을 닫도록 해.)

Check-Up

1 다음 대화의 괄호 안에서 알맞은 말을 고르시오.

A: Is there anything to prepare for our camping trip?
B: Hmm... Don't (forget / remember) to take warm clothes.
A: Okay, I (will / won't).

WORDS
1
prepare 동 준비하다
trip 명 여행

2 다음 대화의 빈칸에 들어갈 말을 보기 에서 모두 고르시오. (2개)

보기 ⓐ don't forget to ⓑ make sure to
ⓒ look forward to ⓓ never mind to

A: I'm leaving now. Can I get you something to eat?
B: No thanks. But ________________ come back before 8 p.m.

B 확신 여부 묻고 답하기

A: **Are you sure** you can do all that work**?**
(당신들이 그 모든 일을 할 수 있다고 확신하나요?)

B: **Yes, we're sure.**
(네, 저희는 확신합니다.)

C: **I'm certain that** we can.
(저는 저희가 할 수 있다고 확신합니다.)

어떤 사실이나 의견에 대해 확신하는지 물을 때는 'Are you sure (about) ...?'이나 'Are you sure (that)+주어+동사 ...?'라고 말할 수 있다. 확신할 때는 'Yes, I'm sure.', 확신하지 못할 때는 'No, I'm not sure.'이라고 대답할 수 있다.

EXPRESSION PLUS

1 확신하는지 묻기
- Would you like to leave now **for sure?** (너 지금 떠나고 싶은 것이 확실하니?)
- **Are you sure about** it**?** (너는 그것에 대해 확신하니?)
- **Is it certain that** he will teach math**?** (그가 수학을 가르칠 것이 확실하니?)

2 확신 여부 답하기
- **Of course. / Absolutely.** (물론이지.) / **Yes, certainly.** (응, 확실해.)
- **I have no doubt that** she will win. (나는 그녀가 우승할 거라는 것을 의심하지 않아.)
- **I'm not sure about** the plan. (난 그 계획에 대해서 확신할 수 없어.)

Check-Up

1 다음 대화의 빈칸에 들어갈 말로 알맞은 것은?

A: Did you know Emily got back from Europe?
B: ________________
A: Of course. I saw her yesterday.

① Are you afraid? ② Who is she?
③ Do you know her? ④ Are you sure?
⑤ Where did she go?

WORDS
1
get back 돌아오다

2 다음 대화의 밑줄 친 문장과 바꿔 쓸 수 있는 것은?

A: I'm ready to go now!
B: Are you certain that you have everything?
A: <u>Yes, I'm sure.</u>

① Absolutely. ② No, I haven't.
③ I think it's good. ④ No, I'm not sure.
⑤ That sounds great.

FINAL TEST

1 다음 밑줄 친 단어와 바꿔 쓸 수 있는 것은?

He solved all the puzzles. I think he is very <u>clever</u>!

① light ② smart ③ young
④ ancient ⑤ meaningful

2 다음 빈칸에 들어갈 말을 보기 에서 골라 쓰시오.

보기 hire quit forgive

(1) Why did you ________ the job?
(2) The company will ________ a project manager.

3 대화가 자연스럽게 이어지도록 (A)~(D)를 바르게 배열하시오.

(A) There's a popular place next to the bank.
(B) What about eating Italian food for dinner?
(C) Sounds great. Are there any good places nearby?
(D) Ah, I remember. Then don't forget to reserve the table.

________ → ________ → ________ → ________

4 다음 문장의 쓰임이 나머지 넷과 <u>다른</u> 것은?

① Why don't you join this club?
② Do you want to join this club for sure?
③ Are you sure you want to join this club?
④ Is it certain that you want to join this club?
⑤ Are you certain you want to join this club?

서술형

5 다음 우리말과 일치하도록 괄호 안의 단어를 바르게 배열하시오.

나는 네가 성공할 거라는 것을 의심하지 않는다.
(you, have, succeed, I, no, will, doubt, that)

→ ________________________

자주 나와요

6 다음 빈칸에 들어갈 말로 알맞은 것은?

I met Tony ________ weeks ago.

① much ② little ③ a little
④ a few ⑤ every

7 다음 빈칸에 들어갈 말로 알맞지 <u>않은</u> 것은?

There's ________ water left in the bottle.

① many ② little ③ a little
④ much ⑤ a lot of

[8-9] 다음 빈칸에 들어갈 말을 보기 에서 골라 알맞은 형태로 쓰시오.

보기 get on show up try on

8 I'm sorry, but you can't ________ the clothes before you buy them.

9 We ________ a train to go to Busan last weekend.

[10-11] 다음 빈칸에 공통으로 들어갈 말로 알맞은 것을 고르시오.

10

- Every year, ________ tourists visit this town.
- I've spent ________ time on my computer lately.

① many ② much ③ a lot of
④ a few ⑤ a little

11

- Jenny ________ up the television volume.
- The man ________ on the repaired printer.

① put ② got ③ picked
④ turned ⑤ threw

[12-13] 다음 우리말과 일치하도록 괄호 안의 단어를 이용하여 문장을 완성하시오.

12 우리 그 약속을 다음 달까지 연기해도 될까요? (put, the appointment)

→ Can we ________ ________ ________ ________ until next month?

13 그 헬리콥터는 정시에 이륙할 것이다. (take)

→ The helicopter will ________ ________ on time.

어려워요

14 다음 중 어법상 바르지 못한 것은?

① He tried to find out the reason.
② Can we take a break for a few minutes?
③ Jina doesn't have much experience in design.
④ Most restaurants here is crowded on weekends.
⑤ Selena put on this costume for the Christmas party.

15 다음 우리말을 영어로 바르게 옮긴 것은?

이 모든 가방들은 한국에서 만들어졌다.

① All these bags were made in Korea.
② These all bags were made in Korea.
③ These bags were made in all Korea.
④ All bags these were made in Korea.
⑤ Bags all these were made in Korea.

16 다음 빈칸에 들어갈 말이 바르게 짝지어진 것은?

- ________ warm milk can help you sleep well.
- The village was hit by ________ big a storm.

① A few – so ② A little – so
③ Many – so ④ Little – such
⑤ A little – such

서술형

17 다음 우리말과 일치하도록 괄호 안의 단어를 바르게 배열하시오.

아무런 새로운 일도 내게 일어나지 않았다.
(nothing, happened, new)

→ ______________ to me.

18 다음 중 어법상 바른 것은?

① This food has a lot cheese in it.
② Can you wake up me at seven?
③ Did you have many fun at the party?
④ I think Lisa is such a friendly person.
⑤ We had a round table, but we threw away it last night.

19 다음 빈칸에 들어갈 말을 보기 에서 골라 쓰시오.

보기 a few　few　a little　little

Eric did great on the test. He made ________ mistakes.

20 다음 질문에 대한 대답으로 가장 알맞은 것은?

A: When can you give my laptop back to me?
B: ______________

① I can give you back it tomorrow.
② I can give back it to you tomorrow.
③ I will it give back to you tomorrow.
④ I will give back it to you tomorrow.
⑤ I can give it back to you tomorrow.

내신 완성 서술형

[21-22] 다음 문장에서 어법상 틀린 것을 찾아 바르게 고치시오.

21 The all members should prepare for the speech by next Wednesday.

________ → ________

22 Much people participated in the audition.

________ → ________

23 다음 우리말과 일치하도록 괄호 안의 단어를 이용하여 문장을 완성하시오.

우리는 해변에서 정말 멋진 휴가를 보냈다.
(such, great, vacation)

→ We had ______________ at the beach.

24 다음 괄호 안의 단어와 공고문에 쓰인 형용사를 이용하여 문장을 완성하시오.

Work with Us!
We need a worker. He/She has to be diligent. Also we want him/her to be positive.

→ The company is looking for ________ ________ ________ ________. (someone)

WORD LIST

Grammar

□ hire	동 고용하다
□ furniture	명 가구
□ activity	명 활동
□ department store	백화점
□ closet	명 벽장
□ departure	명 떠남, 출발
□ noise	명 소리, 소음
□ light	형 밝은; *가벼운[간단한]
□ fare	명 (교통) 요금
□ luckily	부 운 좋게, 다행히도
□ pocket	명 주머니
□ firefighter	명 소방관
□ nearby	부 인근에
□ almost	부 거의
□ bathroom	명 욕실, 화장실
□ charming	형 매력적인, 멋진

Reading

□ struggle	동 분투하다, 애쓰다
□ earn	동 (돈을) 벌다
□ unfortunately	부 불행하게도
□ statue	명 조각상
□ prefer	동 선호하다
□ ancient	형 고대의
□ clever	형 영리한, 똑똑한
□ dirt	명 먼지, 때; 흙
□ accidentally	부 우연히, 뜻하지 않게; 잘못하여
□ recognize	동 알아보다; 인정하다
□ talent	명 재능, 재주
□ forgive	동 용서하다
□ suffer from	…로 고통 받다
□ cancer	명 암
□ medicine	명 약
□ treatment	명 치료
□ laugh at	…를 비웃다[놀리다]
□ encourage	동 격려하다, 용기를 북돋우다
□ classmate	명 반 친구
□ meaningful	형 의미 있는
□ quit	동 그만두다

Communication

□ prepare	동 준비하다
□ trip	명 여행
□ get back	돌아오다

Final Test

□ popular	형 인기 있는
□ reserve	동 예약하다
□ join	동 가입하다
□ succeed	동 성공하다
□ lately	부 최근에
□ repair	동 수리하다
□ appointment	명 약속
□ on time	정시에
□ experience	명 경험
□ crowded	형 붐비는
□ village	명 마을
□ storm	명 태풍
□ happen	동 발생하다
□ participate in	…에 참가하다
□ diligent	형 근면한, 성실한
□ positive	형 긍정적인

CHAPTER 09

전치사(구)

GET READY

Some children are playing **in** the park.
(몇몇 아이들이 공원에서 놀고 있다.)

The event will continue **until** May 8.
(그 행사는 5월 8일까지 계속될 것이다.)

The dog got out **through** a hole.
(그 개는 구멍을 통하여 나갔다.)

전치사는 명사나 대명사 앞에 쓰여 장소, 시간, 방향 등을 나타내요. 「전치사+명사(구)」로 이루어진 전치사구는 문장에서 형용사나 부사 역할을 해요.

A 전치사의 목적어와 전치사구의 역할

1 전치사의 목적어

전치사 뒤에 오는 단어 및 어구를 전치사의 목적어라고 한다. 전치사의 목적어로는 명사, 대명사, 동명사 등이 올 수 있으며, 전치사의 목적어로 대명사가 올 경우 목적격 형태로 쓴다.

I want to sit **next to** *you*. (목적어: 대명사)
A group of birds are flying **in** *the sky*. (목적어: 명사)
You can start the program **by** *pressing* this button. (목적어: 동명사)

내신 POINT PLUS

동사나 형용사가 전치사와 결합하여 숙어처럼 쓰이기도 한다.

I **agree with** your opinion. (나는 너의 의견에 동의한다.)
…에 동의하다

I will **look after** my nephew for a while. (나는 잠시 동안 내 조카를 돌볼 것이다.)
…를 돌보다

Sammy **is absent from** school today. (Sammy는 오늘 학교에 결석했다.)
…에 결석하다

She **is proud of** working for the public. (그녀는 대중을 위해 일하는 것을 자랑스러워한다.)
…를 자랑스러워하다

MORE EXPRESSIONS

- ask for …를 요청하다
- listen to …를 듣다
- be busy with …로 바쁘다
- be fond of …를 좋아하다
- be sure of …를 확신하다
- wait for …를 기다리다
- laugh at …를 비웃다
- be famous for …로 유명하다
- be poor at …하는 데 서투르다
- be full of[be filled with] …로 가득 차다
- belong to …에 속하다[…의 소유이다]
- be ready for …에 준비가 되다
- be different from …와 다르다
- be good at …하는 데 능숙하다

2 전치사구의 역할

전치사구는 「전치사+명사(구)」의 형태로, 문장에서 형용사나 부사 역할을 한다.

1) 형용사 역할: 명사나 대명사를 뒤에서 수식한다.

What's that **on your T-shirt**? (대명사 수식)

Let's watch the documentary **about tigers**. (명사 수식)

2) 부사 역할: 동사나 형용사를 수식한다.

Chris bought some tulips **at a flower shop**. (동사 수식)

Some students are worried **about the test**. (형용사 수식)

Check-Up

A 다음 문장에서 밑줄 친 부분이 수식하는 말에 동그라미(O) 표시하시오.

1 The black bag belongs to Mr. Brown.
2 I can't reach the cup on the top shelf.
3 My family usually eats out on Saturdays.
4 The food at that restaurant is quite delicious.

B 다음 괄호 안에서 알맞은 말을 고르시오.

1 The jar is full (of / with) honey.
2 Please ask (with / for) help when you need it.
3 The patient needs someone to look (on / after) him.
4 Have you thought about (leave / leaving) your neighborhood?

C 다음 밑줄 친 부분을 바르게 고치시오.

1 Can you wait for I for a second? → ________
2 Linda is busy of her homework now. → ________
3 We are looking forward to visit India soon. → ________
4 Is everything ready to the farewell party? → ________

D 다음 우리말과 일치하도록 괄호 안의 단어를 이용하여 문장을 완성하시오.

1 Anderson은 나를 비웃었다. (laugh)
→ Anderson ________ ________ me.
2 그 아이들은 초콜릿을 좋아한다. (fond)
→ The children ________ ________ ________ chocolate.
3 그 거리는 벚꽃으로 유명하다. (famous)
→ The street ________ ________ ________ its cherry blossoms.
4 리메이크작의 결말은 원작과 달랐다. (different)
→ The ending of the remake ________ ________ ________ the original.

WORDS

A
shelf 명 선반
eat out 외식하다
quite 부 꽤, 상당히

B
jar 명 병, 항아리
patient 명 환자
neighborhood 명 동네

C
for a second 잠시
farewell party 송별회

D
cherry blossom 벚꽃
ending 명 결말
original 명 원본, 원작

B 주요 전치사의 의미 차이

1 by: …까지 (완료 기한)　till[until]: …까지 (동작·상태의 계속)

Hand in your homework **by** this Thursday.
He waited **until** noon, but she didn't come.

2 from: …부터 (시작 시점)　since: … 이래로 (일정 시점으로부터 상태·상황의 계속)

The festival is held **from** May 5 to 7.
They have known each other **since** last year.

3 for: … 동안 (기간의 길이)　during: … 동안 (특정 기간)

Melissa and her team members did yoga **for** two hours.
I learned to ski **during** winter vacation.

TIPS

1 전치사 since(… 이래로)는 완료 시제와 함께 쓰인다.
2 for는 '얼마나 오래(how long)'를 나타내며 보통 뒤에 동작이나 상태가 지속되는 기간을 나타내는 표현이 온다.
during은 '언제(when)'를 나타내며 보통 뒤에 동작이나 상태가 일어난 시점이나 기간을 나타내는 표현이 온다.

4 along: …를 따라서　across: …를 가로질러 (횡단)　through: …를 통하여 (통과)

Let's take a walk **along** the beach.
The dog ran **across** the street.
Hot water flowed **through** the pipes.

5 by: …로 (교통수단)　with: …를 사용하여 (도구)

The students will go to the museum **by** bus.
He wrote his name **with** a blue pen.

내신 POINT PLUS

for와 in의 다양한 의미

1 The plane leaves **for** Sydney soon. (그 비행기는 곧 시드니를 향하여 출발할 것이다.)
…를 향하여 (방향 · 목적지)
The winning team jumped **for** joy. (그 우승팀은 기뻐서 뛰었다.)
…의 이유로 (이유 · 원인)

2 My wallet is **in** the car. (내 지갑은 차 안에 있다.)
… 안에 (장소)
I'll call you back **in** ten minutes. (제가 10분 후에 다시 전화할게요.)
… 후에, … 지나서 (경과)

Check-Up

A 다음 괄호 안에서 알맞은 말을 고르시오.

1 Sam stirred his tea (by / with) a teaspoon.

2 I met many new friends (since / during) my trip.

3 The express train will arrive (in / for) five minutes.

4 My uncle will stay at my house (until / by) next weekend.

WORDS

A
stir 동 젓다, 섞다
express train 급행 열차

B 다음 빈칸에 들어갈 말을 보기 에서 골라 쓰시오.

보기 during with along since

1 I cut the paper __________ scissors.

2 A lifeguard was walking __________ the shore.

3 A lot of people died of hunger __________ the war.

4 Jamie has worked at the hospital __________ 2016.

B
scissors 명 가위
lifeguard 명 안전 요원
shore 명 해안, 해변
die of …로 죽다

C 다음 밑줄 친 부분을 바르게 고치시오.

1 Can I get to the stadium <u>with</u> bus or subway? → __________

2 Please take this medicine <u>during</u> two weeks. → __________

3 The hair shop is open <u>since</u> Tuesday to Sunday. → __________

C
take medicine 약을 먹다

D 다음 우리말과 일치하도록 빈칸에 알맞은 전치사를 쓰시오.

1 내가 늦어서 미안해.
→ I am sorry __________ being late.

2 그 터널을 운전해서 통과하는 데 2분 걸린다.
→ It takes two minutes to drive __________ the tunnel.

3 우리는 역에 12시까지 가 있어야 한다.
→ We have to be at the station __________ twelve o'clock.

4 차가 올 때는 횡단보도를 건너지 마라.
→ Don't walk __________ the crosswalk when cars are coming.

D
crosswalk 명 횡단보도

Grammar Practice

A 다음 밑줄 친 부분을 바르게 고치시오.

1 Who is the man standing in front of she? → ________
2 We belong for the chess club at school. → ________
3 The concert hall was filled of excitement. → ________
4 My brother is not good at use chopsticks. → ________

WORDS

A
excitement 명 흥분
chopstick 명 젓가락

B 다음 보기 에서 알맞은 말을 골라 문장을 완성하시오. (한 번씩만 쓸 것)

보기 ask　proud　ready　busy

1 The old lady came over and ________ ________ help.
2 We ________ ________ ________ your courageous behavior.
3 Our soccer team ________ ________ ________ the game tomorrow.

B
courageous 형 용감한

C 다음 괄호 안의 말을 바르게 배열하여 문장을 완성하시오.

1 ________________ are not mine.
(the floor, those socks, on)
2 I ________________ of the movie.
(sure, not, the exact title, of, am)
3 The car ________________ expensive.
(looks, the parking lot, in)

C
exact 형 정확한
parking lot 주차장

D 다음 우리말과 일치하도록 괄호 안의 말을 이용하여 문장을 완성하시오.

1 나는 지난 수요일 이래로 James를 보지 못했다. (last Wednesday)
→ I haven't seen James ________ ________ ________.
2 대통령은 오늘 저녁 파리를 향하여 출발할 것이다. (Paris)
→ The president will depart ________ ________ this evening.
3 그녀는 비상구를 통하여 탈출했다. (the emergency exit)
→ She escaped ________ ________ ________ ________.

D
president 명 대통령
depart 동 떠나다[출발하다]
emergency exit 비상구
escape 동 탈출하다

내신 완성 Grammar Practice

1 다음 빈칸에 들어갈 말로 알맞은 것은?

Julie works ________ 9 a.m. to 6 p.m. every day.

① for ② to ③ till ④ from ⑤ by

2 다음 밑줄 친 부분의 역할이 나머지와 넷과 다른 것은?

① He put the gift in a small box.
② Thank you for inviting me today.
③ We will clean our house on Sunday.
④ Chloe apologized to us for being rude.
⑤ I have seen a poster about the festival.

3 다음 중 어법상 바르지 못한 것은?

① I am fond of cats and dogs.
② Jane listened of the announcement.
③ He is very poor at math and science.
④ The project will be finished in three weeks.
⑤ It has snowed a lot in Seoul since last night.

4 다음 우리말과 일치하도록 빈칸에 알맞은 말을 쓰시오.

(1) 그는 주말 내내 그의 아이들을 돌봐야 한다.
→ He has to ________ ________ his children all weekend.

(2) 그 방에 있는 낡은 가구는 내 소유였다.
→ The old furniture in the room ________ ________ me.

(3) 너는 요리 수업에 결석해서는 안 된다.
→ You should not ________ ________ ________ the cooking class.

WORDS

2
apologize 동 사과하다
rude 형 무례한

3
announcement 명 발표, 소식

서술형에 나오는 WRITING

A **다음 우리말과 일치하도록 괄호 안의 말을 바르게 배열하시오.**

1 Fiona는 칼로 양파를 썰었다.
(onions, a knife, with, chopped)
→ Fiona ______________________________.

2 선생님은 다른 학생들을 도와준 것을 이유로 Lisa를 칭찬했다.
(other students, Lisa, helping, praised, for)
→ The teacher ______________________________.

B **다음 우리말과 일치하도록 보기 의 전치사와 괄호 안의 말을 이용하여 문장을 완성하시오.**

보기 with during in for

1 나는 어제 여덟 시간 동안 잤다. (sleep, eight hours)
→ I ________ ________ ________ ________ yesterday.

2 결승전은 한 시간 후에 시작할 것이다. (begin, an hour)
→ The final match will ________ ________ ________ ________.

3 우리는 두 가지 이유 때문에 네 의견에 동의하지 않는다. (agree, your opinion)
→ We ________ ________ ________ ________ ________ for two reasons.

C **다음 그림을 보고, 괄호 안의 말을 이용하여 문장을 완성하시오.**

1

The boy is ______________________________ now.
(wait, a bus)

2

The city is ______________________________.
(famous, its night views)

1

Ask Anything about Crocodiles! — Crocodile Hunter

Q I read an article about crocodiles **on the Internet** last night. It said that crocodiles eat rocks. Is this true?

A It may sound strange that meat-eating *predators eat rocks, but it is true. Crocodiles have ten to fifteen pounds **of rocks in their stomach** on average. These rocks have an important function. Crocodiles usually don't chew their prey. Instead, they swallow it whole. The rocks **in their stomach** help them break down the food, especially animals **with hard shells and tough bones**. The rocks also add weight **to crocodiles' bodies**. This makes it possible for them to swim **in deep parts of the water**.

*predator: 포식 동물

1 위 글의 답변 내용을 요약할 때, 빈칸 (A)와 (B)에 알맞은 말을 본문에서 찾아 쓰시오.

Crocodiles swallow stones to (A) __________ __________ the food in their stomach and help them (B) __________ deep into the water.

(A) __________ __________ (B) __________

2 위 글의 밑줄 친 about crocodiles와 쓰임이 같은 것은?

① I put my bag on the desk.
② The wedding will be held at a church.
③ Liam works in the building on the corner.
④ How long can people live without water?
⑤ Olivia said she would come back in an hour.

WORDS
crocodile 명 악어 meat-eating 고기를 먹는 stomach 명 [1] __________ on average 평균적으로 function 명 기능
chew 동 씹다 prey 명 먹이 swallow 동 삼키다 whole 부 완전히; *전부, 통째로 break down 부수다; 분해하다
especially 부 특히 shell 명 껍데기, 껍질 tough 형 힘든; *단단한 bone 명 뼈 weight 명 [2] __________

2

A man spread a false rumor. "My neighbor is a thief," he said. Later, the neighbor was arrested **for a theft** because of the rumor. **In court**, the neighbor (for, spreading, the man, blamed, it). When the judge asked the man **about this**, he admitted it. "But they were just words. I didn't hurt anyone," he said. The judge told the man, "Write down everything you said **about your neighbor**. Cut the paper **into small pieces**, and throw them **into the air**. Then come back tomorrow." The man did as he was told.

The next day, the judge said, "Now find those pieces and put them back together." "That's impossible!" cried the man. "Exactly. There is also no way to fix a damaged reputation," said the judge. Finally the man realized his mistake and apologized **to his neighbor**.

1 What is the main idea of the passage?

① If you are patient, good things can happen.
② Don't judge someone by appearance alone.
③ Words once said cannot be taken back easily.
④ Don't try to do too many things at the same time.
⑤ The more you do something, the better you will become at it.

서술형

2 Unscramble the words in brackets.

→ ______________________________
(for, spreading, the man, blamed, it)

WORDS
spread 동 퍼트리다 rumor 명 소문 thief 명 [1]__________ arrest 동 체포하다 theft 명 절도 court 명 법정
blame 동 …를 탓하다 judge 명 판사 동 판단하다 admit 동 인정하다 cry 동 울다; *외치다 fix 동 고정시키다; *바로잡다
damaged 형 손해를 입은 reputation 명 평판 문제 patient 형 참을성 있는 appearance 명 외모

내신에 나오는 COMMUNICATION

A 기대 표현하기

A: The Halloween party is tomorrow.
(핼러윈 파티가 내일이야.)

B: Yeah. I'm **looking forward to** it.
(맞아. 난 그것을 기대하고 있어.)

A: Me too!
(나도!)

'look forward to+명사(구)'는 '…를 기대[고대]하다'의 의미로, 앞으로의 일에 대한 기대나 희망을 나타낼 때 쓰는 표현이다. 이와 유사한 의미의 표현으로는 'can't wait for+명사(구)', 'can't wait to-v' 등이 있다.

EXPRESSION PLUS

- I **can't wait for** his new album. (나는 그의 새 앨범이 너무 기다려져.)
- I **can't wait to go** on a picnic. (나는 빨리 소풍을 가고 싶어.)

TIPS 'look forward to ...'에서 to는 전치사이므로, 뒤에 명사(구), 대명사, 동명사(구)가 온다.
We **look forward to meeting** our new classmate. (우리는 새로운 반 친구를 만날 것을 기대하고 있다.)

Check-Up

1 다음 대화의 밑줄 친 문장과 바꿔 쓸 수 있는 것은?

A: I'll make you a cheese pizza for dinner.
B: Really? <u>I'm looking forward to eating it.</u>

① I love cheese pizza.
② I'm going to eat it.
③ I can't wait to eat it.
④ I don't want to eat it.
⑤ I want you to make it.

2 다음 우리말과 일치하도록 문장을 완성하시오.

나는 그녀로부터의 답장을 고대하고 있어.

→ I'm ________ ________ ________ a reply from her.

WORDS
2
reply 명 대답; *답장

B 도움 요청하고 답하기

A: **Can I ask you a favor,** Uncle Steve**?**
(제가 부탁 하나 해도 될까요, Steve 삼촌?)

B: **Sure.** How can I help you?
(물론이지. 내가 뭘 도와줄까?)

A: **Can you help me** do my history homework**?**
(제가 역사 숙제 하는 걸 도와주실 수 있나요?)

B: **No problem.**
(물론이지.)

상대방에게 부탁할 때는 'Can I ask you a favor?'라고 물을 수 있으며, 특정한 일에 대한 도움을 요청할 때는 'Can you help me ...?'라고 물을 수 있다. 요청에 응할 때는 'Sure.' 또는 'Of course.', 거절할 때는 'Sorry, I can't.'라고 말할 수 있다.

⊕ EXPRESSION PLUS

1 도움 요청하기
- Will you do me a favor? (너 내 부탁 좀 들어주겠니?)
- May I ask a favor of you? (제가 부탁 하나 해도 될까요?)
- Can I ask you to do something for me? (내가 부탁 좀 해도 될까?)

2 요청에 답하기
- Sure. / Of course. / No problem. / Absolutely. (물론이지.)
- I'm afraid I can't help you. (미안하지만 나는 널 도와줄 수 없어.)

Check-Up

1 다음 대화의 빈칸에 들어갈 말로 알맞지 않은 것은?

A: Can you help me carry my bags?
B: ____________

① Sure. ② Sorry, I can't.
③ No problem. ④ I'm afraid I can't.
⑤ I don't need your help.

WORDS
1
carry 동 …를 나르다

2 대화가 자연스럽게 이어지도록 (A)~(D)를 바르게 배열하시오.

(A) May I ask a favor of you?
(B) No problem. Here you go.
(C) Yes. What can I do for you?
(D) I can't find my cell phone. Can I use yours?

________ → ________ → ________ → ________

FINAL TEST

1 다음 영영 풀이에 해당하는 단어로 알맞은 것은?

completely correct in every detail

① stir ② exact
③ rumor ④ possible
⑤ courageous

2 다음 빈칸에 들어갈 말을 보기 에서 골라 쓰시오.

보기 shore reply swallow

(1) He sent a __________ to her letter.
(2) I can't __________ the vitamin pill because it's too big.

3 다음 대화의 빈칸에 들어갈 말로 알맞은 것은?

A: Do you have any plans for the vacation?
B: No, not really. I heard you'll be traveling abroad during the vacation!
A: Yes, ____________________.

① I can't wait for my trip
② I'm afraid I can't do that
③ I'm staying for vacation
④ let me know where you go
⑤ I'm looking forward to your visit

4 다음 중 의미가 같은 두 문장을 고르시오.

① How can I help you?
② Will you do me a favor?
③ Do you agree with my opinion?
④ Can I ask a couple of questions?
⑤ Can I ask you to do something for me?

5 다음 중 짝지어진 대화가 어색한 것은?

① A: Can I ask you a favor?
B: Sure. What can I do for you?
② A: The actor's new movie will be released tomorrow.
B: Yeah. I'm looking for it.
③ A: May I ask a favor of you?
B: Absolutely.
④ A: Lena is coming to the party.
B: Really? I can't wait to see her.
⑤ A: Can you help me wash the dishes?
B: Of course.

[6-8] 다음 빈칸에 들어갈 말로 알맞은 것을 고르시오.

6 The lights went out __________ a few minutes.

① by ② until ③ at
④ for ⑤ during

7 The war continued __________ 1953.

① along ② since ③ for
④ with ⑤ until

8 Elizabeth woke up several times __________ the night.

① on ② of ③ for
④ since ⑤ during

9 다음 우리말과 일치하도록 빈칸에 알맞은 말을 쓰시오.

우리는 그의 방문에 준비가 되어 있지 않다.

→ We ________ ________ ________ ________ his visit.

[10-12] 다음 빈칸에 들어갈 말이 바르게 짝지어진 것을 고르시오.

10

- They were sure ________ their victory.
- My two little brothers are different ________ each other.

① of – from ② of – with
③ to – with ④ to – from
⑤ with – of

! 자주 나와요

11

- London is famous ________ Tower Bridge.
- We should arrive at work ________ 11 a.m.

① of – at ② for – by
③ for – until ④ to – at
⑤ to – until

12

- His family never laughs ________ his dream.
- I am not good ________ speaking Japanese.

① of – on ② to – of
③ at – of ④ to – at
⑤ at – at

! 서술형

13 다음 우리말과 일치하도록 괄호 안의 단어를 바르게 배열하시오.

Katie는 길을 가로질러 걷고 있다.
(the road, walking, Katie, across, is)

→ ____________________________

[14-15] 다음 우리말을 영어로 바르게 옮긴 것을 고르시오.

14 나는 내일 배로 중국을 향해 떠날 것이다.

① I leave to China with ship tomorrow.
② I leave for China with ship tomorrow.
③ I will leave to China by ship tomorrow.
④ I will leave for China by ship tomorrow.
⑤ I will leave for China with ship tomorrow.

15 그들은 호텔에서 이틀 동안 머물렀다.

① They stayed at a hotel for two days.
② They stayed on a hotel for two days.
③ They stayed at a hotel until two days.
④ They stayed at a hotel to two days.
⑤ They stayed on a hotel from two days.

16 다음 밑줄 친 부분의 의미가 나머지 넷과 다른 것은?

① Dinner will be ready in a moment.
② Mr. Williams teaches English in Korea.
③ I left my new cap in a taxi yesterday.
④ My mother works in an advertising company.
⑤ Lyla put butter in a pan and melted it.

[17-18] 다음 우리말과 일치하도록 괄호 안의 단어를 이용하여 문장을 완성하시오.

17 우리 아빠는 일로 바쁘시다. (busy)

→ My father ________ ________ ________ his work.

18 길을 따라서 몇 그루의 나무가 심어져 있다. (the street)

→ Some trees are planted ________ ________ ________.

어려워요

19 다음 빈칸에 들어갈 말이 나머지 넷과 다른 것은?

① Brian is proud ________ his son.
② They decided to ask ________ support.
③ I've known Eric ________ over ten years.
④ Will you wait ________ me at the theater?
⑤ She cried ________ joy when she won the prize.

내신 완성 서술형

[20-21] 다음 글에서 밑줄 친 부분을 바르게 고치시오.

Ron is fond with basketball. One day he got hurt during a game. He couldn't walk during a week because of the pain.

20 is fond with → ________

21 during → ________

22 다음 우리말과 일치하도록 조건에 맞게 영작하시오.

그 차는 그의 소유가 아니다.

조건 1: the car, belong을 사용할 것
조건 2: 총 7단어로 작성할 것
→ ________________

23 다음 그림을 보고, 괄호 안의 말을 이용하여 문장을 완성하시오. (현재시제로 작성할 것)

→ Helen ________________.
(go to school, bicycle)

WORD LIST

Grammar

□ shelf	명 선반
□ quite	부 꽤, 상당히
□ patient	명 환자 형 참을성 있는
□ original	명 원본, 원작
□ stir	동 젓다, 섞다
□ scissors	명 가위
□ shore	명 해안, 해변
□ die of	…로 죽다
□ take medicine	약을 먹다
□ crosswalk	명 횡단보도
□ excitement	명 흥분
□ chopstick	명 젓가락
□ courageous	형 용감한
□ exact	형 정확한
□ parking lot	주차장
□ president	명 대통령
□ depart	동 떠나다[출발하다]
□ emergency exit	비상구
□ rude	형 무례한

Reading

□ stomach	명 위, 배
□ on average	평균적으로
□ chew	동 씹다
□ prey	명 먹이
□ swallow	동 삼키다
□ whole	부 완전히; 전부, 통째로
□ break down	부수다; 분해하다
□ especially	부 특히
□ shell	명 껍데기, 껍질
□ tough	형 힘든; 단단한
□ bone	명 뼈
□ weight	명 무게, 체중
□ spread	동 퍼트리다
□ rumor	명 소문
□ thief	명 도둑
□ arrest	동 체포하다
□ court	명 법정
□ blame	동 …를 탓하다
□ judge	명 판사 동 판단하다
□ admit	동 인정하다
□ cry	동 울다; 외치다
□ fix	동 고정시키다; 바로잡다
□ damaged	형 손해를 입은
□ appearance	명 외모

Communication

□ reply	명 대답; 답장
□ carry	동 …를 나르다

Final Test

□ abroad	부 해외에, 해외로
□ opinion	명 의견
□ release	동 풀어 주다; 공개하다
□ continue	동 계속되다
□ several	형 몇몇의
□ victory	명 승리
□ moment	명 잠시, 순간
□ melt	동 녹다, 녹이다
□ hurt	동 다치게 하다
□ pain	명 고통

CHAPTER 10

관계사

GET READY

The boy likes a girl **who** is his classmate.
(그 소년은 그의 반 친구인 소녀를 좋아한다.)

What they said made me happy.
(그들이 말한 것이 나를 행복하게 만들었다.)

This is the place **where** Dave was born.
(이곳은 Dave가 태어난 장소이다.)

관계사는 두 문장에서 공통으로 가리키는 대상이 있을 때 그 사이에서 앞·뒤 문장을 연결해 주는 역할을 해요. 관계사는 역할에 따라 관계대명사와 관계부사로 나눌 수 있어요.

GRAMMAR FOCUS

A 관계대명사 who, whom, whose, which

관계대명사는 「접속사 + 대명사」의 역할을 한다. 관계대명사가 이끄는 절은 앞에 나오는 명사인 선행사를 수식한다.

Do you know the girl? + She is singing now. (the girl = She)

→ Do you know the girl [**who** is singing now]?

관계대명사는 선행사의 종류와 관계대명사절 안에서의 역할에 따라 달라진다.

선행사	주격	목적격	소유격
사람	who	who(m)	whose
사물·동물	which	which	whose

1 선행사가 사람일 때

1) 주격 관계대명사 who: 선행사가 관계사절 안에서 주어 역할을 할 때 쓴다.

The boy is my brother. + He is playing soccer with Carl.

→ The boy [**who** is playing soccer with Carl] is my brother.

2) 목적격 관계대명사 who(m): 선행사가 관계사절 안에서 동사나 전치사의 목적어 역할을 할 때 쓴다. 구어체에서는 whom보다 who를 더 많이 쓴다.

Ariana and David have an old friend. + They've known her for nine years.

→ Ariana and David have an old friend [**whom** they've known for nine years].

3) 소유격 관계대명사 whose: 선행사가 관계사절 안에서 명사의 소유격 역할을 할 때 쓴다.

The police helped a boy. + His bike was stolen.

→ The police helped a boy [**whose** bike was stolen].

2 선행사가 사물·동물일 때

1) 주격·목적격 관계대명사 which: 선행사가 관계사절 안에서 주어 역할 또는 동사나 전치사의 목적어 역할을 할 때 쓴다.

We want to buy sneakers. + They are popular these days.

→ We want to buy sneakers [**which** are popular these days]. (주격)

She sold the picture. + She drew it a week ago.

→ She sold the picture [**which** she drew a week ago]. (목적격)

TIPS

관계대명사 which가 전치사의 목적어로 쓰일 때 전치사는 관계사절 맨 뒤나 관계사 앞에 위치할 수 있다.

2) 소유격 관계대명사 whose: 선행사가 관계사절 안에서 명사의 소유격 역할을 할 때 쓴다.

I saw a house. + Its windows were broken.

→ I saw a house [**whose** windows were broken].

Check-Up

A 다음 괄호 안에서 알맞은 말을 고르시오.

1 I have a friend (who / whose) wants to be a pilot.
2 Lena stayed in a hotel (whom / which) offered free breakfast.
3 He forgot about the novel (who / which) he read last month.
4 Tim is a researcher (who / which) studied biology in Germany.

WORDS

A
offer 동 (이용할 수 있도록) 내놓다, 제공하다
researcher 명 연구원
biology 명 생물학

B 다음 밑줄 친 관계대명사의 선행사에 동그라미(O) 표시하시오.

1 This is a restaurant which serves Mexican food.
2 They watched a movie whose title was *Spider-Man*.
3 I often wear the sweater which my grandmother made.
4 My cousin who traveled to New York sent me a postcard.

B
serve 동 (식당 등에서 음식을) 제공하다
cousin 명 사촌

C 다음 밑줄 친 부분을 바르게 고치시오.

1 We visited a building which walls were yellow. → ________
2 I work out at a gym whose is near my school. → ________
3 Do you know that boy which is playing with my son? → ________
4 Tracy lost the watch who her dad bought for her last year. → ________

D 다음 우리말과 일치하도록 빈칸에 알맞은 관계대명사를 쓰시오.

1 나는 다리에 금이 간 의자를 버렸다.
→ I threw away a chair ________ leg was cracked.
2 프랑스에 사는 나의 이모는 요리를 잘하신다.
→ My aunt ________ lives in France cooks well.
3 멋진 옷을 파는 가게에 가자.
→ Let's go to a shop ________ sells cool clothes.
4 저 여자가 내가 너에게 말했던 여배우이다.
→ That woman is the actress ________ I told you about.

D
crack 동 금이 가다

B 관계대명사 that, what

1 관계대명사 that

관계대명사 that은 선행사의 종류에 상관없이 주격, 목적격 관계대명사로 쓸 수 있다.

The children are Jack's friends. + They are standing over there.

→ The children [**that**[who] are standing over there] are Jack's friends. (주격)

I enjoyed the book. + My teacher recommended it.

→ I enjoyed the book [**that**[which] my teacher recommended]. (목적격)

TIPS

관계대명사 that을 주로 쓰는 경우

1 선행사가 '사람+동물[사물]'일 때
Look at the man and the dog **that** are running outside. (밖에서 달리고 있는 남자와 개를 봐.)

2 최상급 형용사, 서수, the only, the very, the same, the last, all, any, no 등이 선행사를 수식할 때
She's the only person **that** has won the prize twice. (그녀는 그 상을 두 번 받은 유일한 사람이다.)

3 선행사가 -thing으로 끝나는 대명사일 때
There is something **that** you should know. (네가 알아야 할 것이 있다.)

2 관계대명사 what

what은 선행사를 포함하는 관계대명사이며 the thing which[that]로 바꿔 쓸 수 있다.
what이 이끄는 관계사절은 문장에서 주어, 목적어, 보어 역할을 하며, '…하는 것'으로 해석한다.

[**What** we made for lunch] was mushroom pizza. (주어)

= [**The thing which**[**that**] we made for lunch] was mushroom pizza.

They couldn't hear [**what** she said] because of the noise. (목적어)

Exploring space is [**what** I want to do in the future]. (보어)

내신 POINT PLUS

관계대명사의 생략

1 「주격 관계대명사+be동사」의 생략
Who is the man (**that is**) driving the truck? (트럭을 운전하고 있는 저 남자는 누구니?)

2 목적격 관계대명사의 생략
목적격 관계대명사 who(m), which, that은 생략이 가능하다. 단, 전치사가 관계대명사 앞에 있는 경우에는 생략할 수 없다.
That is the house (**which**) my family used to live in. (저것은 우리 가족이 살았던 집이다.)
That is the house **in which** my family used to live. (o)
That is the house in ~~which~~ my family used to live. (x)

Check-Up

A 다음 괄호 안에서 알맞은 말을 고르시오.

1 I will give you some soap (that / what) I made myself.
2 Making sculptures is (that / what) we will do in this class.
3 Ethan wrote about people and things (that / who) he liked.
4 The dress (that / what) I saw yesterday was very expensive.
5 The doctor cared for children (that / whose) lives were in danger.

WORDS

A
sculpture 명 조각, 조각품
care for …를 보살피다[돌보다]
life 명 삶; *목숨, 생명
in danger 위험에 직면한, 위독한

B 다음 문장에서 생략 가능한 부분에 동그라미(O) 표시하시오.

1 She missed the bus that she needed to take.
2 I bathed the rabbits that were adopted by my mom.
3 Grace is wearing a coat which a famous person designed.

B
bathe 동 목욕시키다
adopt 동 입양하다

C 다음 밑줄 친 부분이 바르면 O를 쓰고, 틀리면 바르게 고치시오.

1 I visited a blog <u>who</u> is famous for film reviews. → ________
2 There must be something <u>that</u> we can do for him. → ________
3 You'd better write down the things <u>what</u> you learned in class. → ________
4 That song is <u>the thing that</u> makes this opera wonderful. → ________

C
review 명 논평, 비평

D 다음 문장의 빈칸에 that, what 중 알맞은 것을 골라 쓰시오.

1 I'll try hard to achieve ________ I dream of.
2 I patted the horse ________ was walking in the field.
3 She is interviewing an actor ________ recently won an Academy Award.
4 ________ Ben asked me to do was to come to his birthday party.

D
achieve 동 달성하다
pat 동 쓰다듬다, 토닥거리다

C 관계부사

1 관계부사의 역할

관계부사는 「접속사+부사」의 역할을 하며, 관계부사가 이끄는 절은 시간, 장소, 이유, 방법 등을 나타내는 선행사를 수식한다. 관계부사는 「전치사+관계대명사」로 바꿔 쓸 수 있다.

My family exercises at the gym. + Oliver works at the gym.

→ My family exercises at the gym **where** Oliver works.
(= **at which**)

내신 POINT PLUS

관계부사 = 「전치사 + 관계대명사」

when	on/in/at/during which	where	in/at/on/to which
why	for which	how	the way (in which)

2 관계부사 when, where, why, how

1) when: 선행사가 시간이나 때를 나타내는 경우 예 the time, the day, the year 등

I won't forget the day. + My team won the championship on that day.

→ I won't forget the day **when** my team won the championship.
(= **on which**)

2) where: 선행사가 장소를 나타내는 경우 예 the place, the town, the city 등

She visited the town. + She volunteered in the town once a month.

→ She visited the town **where** she volunteered once a month.
(= **in which**)

3) why: 선행사가 이유를 나타내는 경우 예 the reason

This is the reason. + Mike left for this reason.

→ This is the reason **why** Mike left.
(= **for which**)

4) how: 선행사가 방법이나 방식을 나타내는 경우에 쓴다. 선행사 the way와 관계부사 how는 함께 쓸 수 없으며, 둘 중 하나만 써야 한다.

Technology has changed the way. + Students study in the way.

→ Technology has changed **how** students study.

→ Technology has changed the way students study.

→ Technology has changed the way **in which** students study.

TIPS

관계부사 또는 선행사의 생략

선행사가 시간, 장소, 이유를 나타내는 일반적인 명사(the time, the place, the reason 등)일 경우 선행사나 관계부사 중 하나를 생략할 수도 있다.

I think about (**the time**) **when** we became friends.

= I think about **the time** (**when**) we became friends. (나는 우리가 친구가 되었던 때에 대해 생각한다.)

Check-Up

A 다음 괄호 안에서 알맞은 말을 고르시오.

1 Do you know the reason (why / when) Emma left early?
2 We went to the park (how / where) we always play baseball.
3 Jessica showed me (how / what) she guessed the password.
4 I haven't seen Amy since the year (when / where) we graduated.

WORDS

A
password 명 비밀번호
graduate 동 졸업하다

B 다음 밑줄 친 관계부사의 선행사에 동그라미(O) 표시하시오.

1 I drove past the city where I used to live.
2 Sue didn't tell me the reason why she was depressed.
3 Summer is a time when many people go on vacation.
4 They were left on an island where no people lived.

B
past 전 …를 지나서
depressed 형 우울한
island 명 섬

C 다음 밑줄 친 부분을 알맞은 관계부사로 고치시오.

1 March is where the new semester starts. → ________
2 Please explain the reason how my name isn't on the guest list. → ________
3 Is there a café when we can drink sweet milk tea? → ________

C
semester 명 학기
explain 동 설명하다

D 다음 우리말과 일치하도록 빈칸에 알맞은 관계부사를 쓰시오.

1 그는 그녀가 식물을 기르는 방식을 알고 싶어 한다.
→ He wants to know ________ she grows plants.
2 이곳이 내가 주로 책을 빌리는 도서관이다.
→ This is the library ________ I usually borrow books.
3 당신이 회의에 늦은 이유가 무엇입니까?
→ What is the reason ________ you are late for the meeting?
4 다음 주 목요일은 내가 이 숙제를 끝내야 하는 날이다.
→ Next Thursday is the day ________ I should finish this homework.

Grammar Practice

A 다음 밑줄 친 부분을 바르게 고치시오.

1 Sam helped the woman <u>whom</u> arms were hurt. → ________

2 Nurses are people <u>which</u> look after patients. → ________

3 The tourists will be taken to a place <u>when</u> they can spend the night. → ________

B 다음 빈칸에 들어갈 말을 보기에서 골라 쓰시오.

보기 how she practices dancing / why he seems nervous / when our vacation starts / whom you're talking about

1 I don't remember the boy ________________.

2 Tomorrow is the day ________________.

3 Do you know the reason ________________?

4 I will ask Amy ________________.

C 다음 두 문장이 같은 뜻이 되도록 빈칸에 알맞은 관계부사를 쓰시오.

1 This is the reason for which we quit the club.
→ This is the reason ________ we quit the club.

2 I'm looking for a shop at which I can buy electronics.
→ I'm looking for a shop ________ I can buy electronics.

3 Wednesday is the day on which he works.
→ Wednesday is the day ________ he works.

4 Jane told us the way she cooked the chicken soup.
→ Jane told us ________ she cooked the chicken soup.

D 다음 우리말과 일치하도록 괄호 안의 말과 관계대명사를 이용하여 문장을 완성하시오.

1 이 마을에 사는 어부들은 성실하다. (live in this town)
→ The fishermen ________________ are diligent.

2 내가 지난달에 산 휴대 전화가 고장 났다. (I bought last month)
→ The cell phone ________________ is broken.

3 아무도 내가 그들에게 말한 것을 믿지 않았다. (I told them)
→ Nobody believed ________________.

WORDS

A
nurse 명 간호사

B
nervous 형 불안해하는

C
quit 동 그만두다
electronics 명 전자 기기

D
diligent 형 근면한, 성실한

내신 완성 Grammar Practice

1 다음 빈칸에 들어갈 말로 알맞은 것은?

Did you check the time ________ we have to leave?

① how ② why ③ when ④ which ⑤ where

2 다음 중 어법상 바르지 못한 것은?

① My parents liked what I made for them.
② Alice saw a boy who looked like her brother.
③ I met an old lady whose hair was entirely white.
④ They praised the way how she took care of her baby.
⑤ The reason why I knocked on your door was to wake you up.

3 다음 밑줄 친 부분의 쓰임이 나머지 넷과 다른 것은?

① I ate the muffin which Soomi gave to me.
② He will buy a desk which fits well in his room.
③ I should take the bus which goes to the zoo.
④ The cat which has green eyes is very cute.
⑤ Henry read a book which was written for teenagers.

4 다음 두 문장을 보기 처럼 관계대명사를 이용하여 한 문장으로 바꿔 쓰시오.

보기 What is the name of the girl? She just called you.
→ What is the name of the girl who just called you?

(1) Tina drank lemonade. She bought it during her trip.
→ Tina drank lemonade ________________.

(2) This is the tent. We slept in it last night.
→ This is the tent in ________________.

WORDS

2
entirely 부 완전히
knock 동 (문 등을) 두드리다, 노크하다

3
fit 동 적합하다, 어울리다

A 다음 우리말과 일치하도록 괄호 안의 말을 바르게 배열하시오.

1 나는 네가 나에게 말했던 것에 대해 생각하고 있어.
(am, thinking about, me, told, you, I, what)
→ ______________________________

2 그 노래를 작곡한 소녀는 이 학교를 졸업했다.
(wrote, the song, this school, who, the girl, graduated from)
→ ______________________________

3 Jake는 지붕이 눈으로 덮인 집을 그렸다.
(roof, drew, snow, a house, whose, Jake, was covered with)
→ ______________________________

B 다음 우리말과 일치하도록 괄호 안의 말을 이용하여 문장을 완성하시오.

1 Stevenson 씨는 많은 학생들이 존경하는 선생님이다. (many students, respect)
→ Mr. Stevenson is a teacher ______________.

2 이 DVD는 과거에 사람들이 살았던 방식을 보여준다. (way, people, live)
→ This DVD shows ______________ in the past.

3 그 의사가 가지고 있는 노트북은 가장 최신 모델이다. (the doctor, have)
→ The laptop computer ______________ is the latest model.

C 다음 우리말과 일치하도록 괄호 안의 단어와 관계사를 이용하여 문장을 완성하시오.

1

This is a concert hall ________ ________ ________ fifty years ago. (build)
(이곳은 50년 전에 지어진 콘서트홀이다.)

2

Vincent was an artist ________ ________ the beauty of nature. (paint)
(Vincent는 자연의 아름다움을 그린 화가였다.)

READING WITH GRAMMAR

1

How can we stop starfish from killing coral? Scientists think they have found an answer—a robot **that** kills starfish. The robot is called the COTSbot. This is short for "*crown-of-thorns starfish robot." The crown-of-thorns starfish is a large starfish with sharp spines. It loves to eat coral. It has done a lot of damage to the Great Barrier Reef, the biggest *coral reef in the world. Scientists want to save the reef. This is **why** they invented COTSbot.

It swims around places (A) [which / where] crown-of-thorns starfish live. The spines of these starfish are (B) [that / what] it looks for. When it finds starfish, it uses poison to kill them. Scientists hope COTSbot will be protecting the Great Barrier Reef soon.

*crown-of-thorns starfish: 악마 불가사리
*coral reef: 산호초

1 위 글의 내용과 일치하지 않는 것은?

① 악마 불가사리는 뾰족한 가시를 가지고 있다.
② 악마 불가사리는 산호초를 잡아먹는다.
③ Great Barrier Reef는 세계에서 가장 큰 산호초 지대이다.
④ COTSbot은 산호초를 구하기 위해 만들어졌다.
⑤ COTSbot은 가시를 사용해 악마 불가사리를 죽인다.

2 위 글의 (A)와 (B)의 각 네모 안에서 어법에 맞는 표현을 골라 쓰시오.

(A) __________ (B) __________

WORDS starfish 명 불가사리 short for …의 생략[단축](형)인 sharp 형 날카로운, 뾰족한 spine 명 척추; *가시
damage 명 1__________ save 동 2__________ invent 동 발명하다 poison 명 독 protect 동 보호하다, 지키다

2

Have you ever ridden a bike for a free dinner? You can do it at a hotel in Denmark. Guests ① <u>who</u> stay there can ride special exercise bikes ② <u>which</u> make electricity for the hotel. The more you ride the bikes, the more electricity you make. Each bike has a screen ③ <u>whose</u> shows the amount of energy you create. The energy ④ <u>that</u> you make is stored in a battery. Later, the energy is moved to a room **which** the hotel uses for controlling the electricity.

Guests get a free dinner coupon every time they make about 10 *watts of electricity. This takes about 15 minutes of pedaling. This fun idea is ⑤ <u>how</u> the hotel helps the environment and its guests at the same time.

*watt: 와트 (전력의 단위)

1 Which is the best title for the passage?

① The Use of Electricity at a Hotel
② Special Events at a Hotel in Denmark
③ A Hotel's Environmentally Friendly Policy
④ The Bike Path around a Hotel in Denmark
⑤ The Advantages of Exercising with a Bike

2 Which is NOT grammatically correct?

① ② ③ ④ ⑤

WORDS electricity 명 전기 screen 명 화면 amount 명 1 ________ store 동 저장하다 control 동 통제하다, 관리하다 pedal 동 페달을 밟다 environment 명 2 ________ at the same time 동시에 문제 policy 명 정책, 방침 path 명 길 advantage 명 이점, 장점

내신에 나오는 COMMUNICATION

A 시간 약속 정하기

A: Sarah, let's go shopping together.
(Sarah, 우리 같이 쇼핑 가자.)

B: Sounds good. **Can you make it** at 6 p.m.**?**
(그거 좋겠다. 오후 6시에 만날 수 있니?)

A: Yes. See you then.
(응. 그때 봐.)

시간 약속을 정할 때는 'Can you make it + 시간/날짜?', 'Can we meet + 시간/날짜?', 'How about meeting + 시간/날짜?', 'Are you free[available] + 시간/날짜?' 등의 표현을 쓸 수 있다.

EXPRESSION PLUS

A: **Can we meet** at 2 o'clock**?** (우리 2시에 만날 수 있니?)
B: All right. (좋아.)

A: **How about meeting** this afternoon**?** (오늘 오후에 만나는 게 어때?)
B: Well, can we meet sometime later? (음, 우리 나중에 언젠가 만날 수 있니?)

A: **Are you available** this Friday**?** (너 이번 주 금요일에 시간 있니?)
B: Sorry, I already have other plans that day. (미안하지만, 나는 그날 이미 다른 계획들이 있어.)

Check-Up

1 다음 대화의 빈칸에 들어갈 말로 알맞은 것은?

A: Can you make it at 5 p.m.?
B: ______________________

① No. I'm free at 5 p.m.
② Yes. How did you make it?
③ Well, can we make it simpler?
④ Sorry, I had other plans yesterday.
⑤ Sorry, I can't. Can we meet sometime later?

WORDS

1
simple 형 간단한
sometime 부 언젠가

2 다음 우리말과 일치하도록 괄호 안의 단어를 이용하여 문장을 완성하시오.

너 오늘 저녁에 한가하니? (free)

→ __________ __________ __________ this evening?

B 의견 묻고 답하기

A: **What do you think of** the new car**?**
(너는 새 차에 대해 어떻게 생각하니?)

B: **I think** it's great.
(저는 그것이 아주 좋다고 생각해요.)

A: I think so, too.
(나도 그렇게 생각한단다.)

'What do you think of ...?'는 '…에 대해 어떻게 생각하니?'의 의미로 상대방의 의견을 물어볼 때 사용하는 표현이다. 이와 유사한 표현으로 'How do you like ...?', 'How do you feel about ...?' 등이 있다. 이에 대한 자신의 의견은 'I think[believe] ...'라고 말할 수 있다.

EXPRESSION PLUS

A: **How do you like** Indian food**?** (너는 인도 음식에 대해 어떻게 생각하니?)
B: I think it's delicious. (나는 그것이 아주 맛있다고 생각해.)

A: **How do you feel about** what he said**?** (너는 그가 말한 것에 대해 어떻게 생각하니?)
B: **I don't believe** it's true. (나는 그것이 사실이라고 믿지 않아.)

Check-Up

1 다음 대화의 빈칸에 들어갈 말로 알맞은 것을 모두 고르시오. (2개)

A: ______________________
B: I think the melody is fantastic.

① How do you like the music?
② Do you like to listen to music?
③ What kind of music do you like?
④ How do you feel about the music?
⑤ Why do you enjoy listening to music?

2 다음 괄호 안의 단어를 이용하여 대화를 완성하시오.

A: ________ ________ ________ ________
________ the foreign language class?
(what, think)
B: I think it's sometimes boring.

WORDS

1
melody 명 멜로디, 선율
fantastic 형 환상적인

2
foreign language 외국어

FINAL TEST

1 다음 중 영어 단어와 우리말 뜻이 잘못 연결된 것은?

① pilot - 조종사 ② poison - 약
③ explain - 설명하다 ④ store - 저장하다
⑤ graduate - 졸업하다

2 다음 우리말과 일치하도록 빈칸에 알맞은 말을 쓰시오.

전기를 낭비하지 않도록 노력하자.

→ Let's try not to waste ________.

3 대화가 자연스럽게 이어지도록 (A)~(D)를 바르게 배열하시오.

(A) I think it's amazing. May I see some other pictures you took?
(B) Great! I'm looking forward to seeing them.
(C) What do you think of this picture? I took it yesterday.
(D) I'm sorry, but they're at my home. I'll bring them tomorrow.

______ → ______ → ______ → ______

4 다음 질문에 대한 대답으로 알맞지 않은 것은?

Are you available this weekend?

① Why are you available?
② Sure. What time shall we meet?
③ No. Can we meet sometime later?
④ How about meeting tomorrow instead?
⑤ Sorry, I'm going camping with my family.

5 다음 중 짝지어진 대화가 어색한 것은?

① A: Can we meet next Friday?
B: Sorry, I have other plans that day.
② A: How about meeting tonight?
B: I can't make it today.
③ A: What do you think of this novel?
B: I want to write a novel someday.
④ A: How do you like Mr. Brown's class?
B: I think his class is very interesting.
⑤ A: Are you free this Saturday?
B: I'm sorry. I'm busy that day.

[6-7] 다음 빈칸에 들어갈 말로 알맞은 것을 고르시오.

6 The camel is an animal ________ lives in the desert.

① whom ② whose ③ which
④ when ⑤ what

7 I will call my uncle ________ I haven't seen for a while.

① how ② whose ③ when
④ which ⑤ whom

자주 나와요

8 다음 중 빈칸에 that이 들어갈 수 없는 것은?

① I thanked the man ________ saved me.
② Paris is the city ________ I want to visit.
③ I know a person ________ brother is a vet.
④ She hasn't found the money ________ she lost.
⑤ I like the singer ________ just released a new album.

[9-10] 다음 우리말을 영어로 바르게 옮긴 것을 고르시오.

9 나는 그에게 그가 경로를 찾은 방법을 물어봤다.

① I asked him why he found the path.
② I asked him how he found the path.
③ I asked the way how he found the path.
④ I asked him the way which he found the path.
⑤ I asked him the way how he found the path.

10 역사는 내가 대학에서 공부하고 싶은 것이다.

① History is which I want to study at university.
② History is that I want to study at university.
③ History is what I want to study at university.
④ That I want to study at university is history.
⑤ History is the thing I want to study it at university.

11 다음 빈칸에 알맞은 관계부사를 쓰시오.

I enjoyed the year ________ I lived in Japan.

12 다음 중 어법상 바른 것은?

① I know a bakery who sells nice pies.
② Surfing is that I will do during vacation.
③ Today is the day why she comes back to Korea.
④ This is the camera what I bought before.
⑤ I like the hat which you're wearing.

13 다음 두 문장을 한 문장으로 바르게 바꾼 것은?

I ate the cake. It was in the kitchen.

① I ate the cake that in the kitchen.
② I ate the cake who was in the kitchen.
③ I ate the cake what was in the kitchen.
④ I ate the cake where was in the kitchen.
⑤ I ate the cake which was in the kitchen.

14 다음 빈칸에 공통으로 들어갈 관계대명사를 쓰시오.

- This class is for children ________ like science.
- This is the beautiful park ________ I like the most.

15 다음 우리말과 일치하도록 괄호 안의 단어를 이용하여 문장을 완성하시오.

Billy는 기자들에게 그가 야구하는 것을 그만 둔 이유를 말했다. (the reason)

→ Billy told the reporters ________ ________ ________ he stopped playing baseball.

! 어려워요

16 다음 밑줄 친 부분 중 생략할 수 없는 것은?

① I miss the time when we were together.
② The country that he came from is Italy.
③ The waiter brought food which I didn't order.
④ We're waiting for the train that goes to Busan.
⑤ The players that are running on the field look excited.

17 다음 밑줄 친 부분의 쓰임이 나머지 넷과 다른 것은?

① That is a woman who I work with.
② I saw the man who lives next door.
③ We need someone who majored in art.
④ Julia met a writer who won the Nobel Prize.
⑤ Do you know anyone who is good at Spanish?

18 다음 두 문장을 한 문장으로 바꿀 때 빈칸에 알맞은 관계부사를 쓰시오.

I'm going to the museum. I saw Klimt's paintings there before.

→ I'm going to the museum __________ I saw Klimt's paintings before.

19 다음 빈칸에 들어갈 말로 알맞은 것은?

I have a friend __________ mom is a doctor.

① who ② when
③ whose ④ that
⑤ which

서술형

20 다음 우리말과 일치하도록 괄호 안의 단어를 바르게 배열하시오.

그가 말하는 방식은 나를 화나게 만든다.
(he, the way, me, makes, talks, upset)

→ ______________________________

내신 완성 서술형

21 다음 우리말과 일치하도록 조건에 맞게 영작하시오.

나는 내가 기른 감자들을 썰었다.

조건 1: cut, the potatoes, grow를 이용할 것
조건 2: 총 7단어로 작성할 것

→ ______________________________

22 다음 문장에서 어법상 틀린 곳을 찾아 바르게 고치시오.

That you did today was very brave.

__________ → __________

23 다음 대화에서 밑줄 친 부분을 바르게 고치시오.

Jim: I want to join the drawing club, but I'm not good at drawing.
Sue: Don't worry. Anyone whom is interested in drawing can join the drawing club.
Jim: Really? Then I will join.

whom → __________

WORD LIST

Grammar

□ offer	[동] (이용할 수 있도록) 내놓다, 제공하다
□ researcher	[명] 연구원
□ serve	[동] (식당 등에서 음식을) 제공하다
□ cousin	[명] 사촌
□ sculpture	[명] 조각, 조각품
□ care for	…를 보살피다[돌보다]
□ life	[명] 삶; 목숨, 생명
□ in danger	위험에 직면한, 위독한
□ bathe	[동] 목욕시키다
□ adopt	[동] 입양하다
□ review	[명] 논평, 비평
□ achieve	[동] 달성하다
□ pat	[동] 쓰다듬다, 토닥거리다
□ graduate	[동] 졸업하다
□ past	[전] …를 지나서
□ depressed	[형] 우울한
□ island	[명] 섬
□ semester	[명] 학기
□ explain	[동] 설명하다
□ nurse	[명] 간호사
□ quit	[동] 그만두다

Reading

□ sharp	[형] 날카로운, 뾰족한
□ damage	[명] 손상, 피해
□ save	[동] 구하다
□ invent	[동] 발명하다
□ poison	[명] 독
□ protect	[동] 보호하다, 지키다
□ electricity	[명] 전기
□ amount	[명] 양
□ store	[동] 저장하다
□ control	[동] 통제하다, 관리하다
□ environment	[명] 환경
□ at the same time	동시에
□ policy	[명] 정책, 방침
□ path	[명] 길
□ advantage	[명] 이점, 장점

Communication

□ simple	[형] 간단한
□ melody	[명] 멜로디, 선율
□ fantastic	[형] 환상적인
□ foreign language	외국어

Final Test

□ waste	[동] 낭비하다
□ available	[형] 이용할 수 있는; 시간이 있는
□ instead	[부] 대신에
□ novel	[명] 소설
□ someday	[부] 언젠가
□ desert	[명] 사막
□ university	[명] 대학
□ reporter	[명] 기자
□ order	[동] 주문하다
□ major in	…를 전공하다
□ brave	[형] 용감한

CHAPTER 11

접속사

GET READY

I tried hard **even though** I wanted to give up.
(비록 포기하고 싶었지만 나는 열심히 노력했다.)

We are wondering **if** you can come to the meeting.
(우리는 네가 회의에 올 수 있는지 궁금하다.)

Both my father **and** I wear glasses.
(나의 아버지와 나 둘 다 안경을 쓴다.)

접속사는 단어와 단어, 구와 구, 절과 절을 연결해 주는 말로, 시간·이유·양보·조건 등 여러 가지 의미를 나타내요. 접속사를 이용하여 문장에 풍부한 의미를 더할 수 있어요.

GRAMMAR FOCUS

A 부사절을 이끄는 접속사

1 시간

1) when: …할 때
I cried a lot **when** my grandfather passed away.

2) as: …하고 있을 때, …하면서
Ethan saw his sister **as** she was getting on the bus.

3) while: …하는 동안에
While I was sleeping, someone put a blanket on me.

4) before: … 전에 / **after:** … 후에
Let's warm up **before** we start exercising.
Joe found Nancy's cell phone on the table **after** she left.

5) until: …할 때까지
Please wait here **until** he comes.

2 이유

because[as / since]: … 때문에
She got angry at me **because** I forgot her name.
As I don't know the password, I can't log in to the computer.
Our flight was canceled **since** the weather was bad.

TIPS

1 as의 다양한 의미
1) …함에 따라
As he grew older, he became wiser.
(그는 나이가 들면서, 더 현명해졌다.)
2) … 대로
Do **as** I told you.
(내가 너에게 말한 대로 해라.)

2 because와 because of
because는 접속사이므로 뒤에 절이 오고, because of는 전치사이므로 뒤에 (대)명사, 동명사 등이 온다.

3 양보

though[although]: 비록 …이지만 / **even though:** 비록 …일지라도
Though[Although] he was hungry, he didn't eat anything.
Even though she couldn't swim well, she tried her best.

4 조건

1) if: (만약) …라면, …한다면
If you want to change the schedule, please let me know.

2) unless: (만약) …하지 않으면 (= if ... not)
We can talk now **unless** you're busy. (= We can talk now **if** you're **not** busy.)

TIPS

시간 · 조건의 부사절
시간이나 조건을 나타내는 접속사가 이끄는 부사절에서는 미래의 일이라도 현재시제로 나타낸다.
We'll go hiking **if** it *is* sunny tomorrow. (내일 날씨가 맑으면 우리는 하이킹을 갈 것이다.)
I'll tell him about the plan **when** he *comes*. (그가 오면 나는 그에게 계획에 대해 말할 것이다.)

Check-Up

A 다음 괄호 안에서 알맞은 말을 고르시오.

1 (If / While) I was doing yoga, I watched TV.

2 He sweated a lot (unless / after) he practiced dancing.

3 I asked her to join us (unless / although) I didn't know her well.

4 I couldn't concentrate (though / because) I was so sleepy.

WORDS

A
sweat 동 땀을 흘리다
concentrate 동 집중하다

B 다음 두 문장이 같은 뜻이 되도록 if나 unless를 이용하여 문장을 완성하시오.

1 If tickets aren't too expensive, we'll buy them.

→ ________ tickets ________ too expensive, we'll buy them.

2 Unless he apologizes, I'm not going to talk to him.

→ ________ he does ________ apologize, I'm not going to talk to him.

3 If you don't study for the exam, you'll get a low score.

→ ________ you ________ for the exam, you'll get a low score.

B
low 형 낮은

C 다음 우리말과 일치하도록 빈칸에 들어갈 말을 보기 에서 골라 쓰시오.

보기 when until as though

1 나는 하루 종일 걸었기 때문에 피곤하다.

→ I'm tired ________ I have walked all day.

2 그가 책을 펼쳤을 때, 그는 안에서 사진을 발견했다.

→ ________ he opened the book, he found a photo in it.

3 비록 방에 히터가 켜져 있었지만, 여전히 추웠다.

→ ________ the heater was on in the room, it was still cold.

4 나의 할머니는 내가 보이지 않을 때까지 문에 서 계셨다.

→ My grandmother stood at the door ________ I was out of sight.

C
out of sight 보이지 않는 곳에

GRAMMAR FOCUS

B 명사절을 이끄는 접속사

접속사 that, if, whether가 이끄는 명사절은 문장에서 주어, 목적어, 보어 역할을 한다.

1 that

1) 주어: '…하는 것은'으로 해석하며, that이 이끄는 명사절이 주어로 쓰일 때는 보통 「it(가주어) ... that절(진주어)」의 형태로 쓴다.

That he was fired is true. → **It** is true **that** he was fired.

가주어 진주어

2) 목적어: '…하는 것을'로 해석하며, that절을 목적어로 취하는 동사에는 think, believe, hope, say, know, tell 등이 있다. 이때 접속사 that은 생략할 수 있다.

I think (**that**) the book is helpful.

3) 보어: '…하는 것(이다)'

The problem is **that** they don't have enough money.

2 if/whether ... (or not): '…인지 (아닌지)'

We wonder **if** she can speak English.

I don't know **whether** I should sign up for the class (**or not**).

C 짝으로 이루어진 접속사

1) 「both A and B」: A와 B 둘 다

Both he **and** his brother are soccer fans.

2) 「either A or B」: A나 B 중 하나

I'll **either** send you a text message **or** call you.

3) 「neither A nor B」: A도 B도 아닌

She **neither** cried **nor** laughed.

4) 「not only A but (also) B」: A뿐만 아니라 B도 (= **B as well as A**)

The documentary is **not only** educational **but** (**also**) interesting.

= The documentary is interesting **as well as** educational.

5) 「not A but B」: A가 아니라 B인

The novel was written **not** in 2018 **but** in 2010.

TIPS

1 「both A and B」는 복수 취급하고, 나머지는 동사와 가까운 주어(B)에 동사의 수를 일치시킨다. 단, 「B as well as A」는 B에 수를 일치시킨다.

2 짝으로 이루어진 접속사로 연결되는 어구(A, B)는 문법적으로 성격이 같은 것이어야 한다.

+ 내신 POINT PLUS

접속사 역할을 하는 의문사

의문사가 접속사처럼 두 문장을 연결하는 경우에 의문사가 이끄는 절을 간접의문문이라고 한다. 간접의문문은 「의문사+주어+동사」의 어순으로 쓰고, 주로 동사 know, wonder, say, ask, tell 등의 목적어 역할을 한다.

I know **where** *the restaurant is*. (← I know. + Where is the restaurant?)

(나는 그 음식점이 어디에 있는지 안다.)

Check-Up

A 다음 괄호 안에서 알맞은 말을 고르시오.

1 He is not only kind (nor / but) also humorous.

2 Let me know (whether / that) you are busy or not.

3 (It / That) is surprising that the doll is popular with adults.

4 The sad man (either / neither) slept nor ate for several days.

5 (Both / Neither) *galbi* and *japchae* are traditional Korean dishes.

WORDS

A
humorous 형 재미있는, 유머러스한
adult 명 성인, 어른
traditional 형 전통의

B 다음 밑줄 친 부분을 바르게 고치시오.

1 Neither she nor you is wrong. → ________

2 Please tell me how can I get to the bank. → ________

3 They heard if Jake was promoted last week. → ________

4 My cup is not the white one but also the black one. → ________

5 You should either fix your camera and buy a new one. → ________

B
promote 동 승진시키다
fix 동 고정시키다; *수리하다

C 다음 우리말과 일치하도록 빈칸에 알맞은 접속사를 쓰시오.

1 그녀가 일등 상을 탈 것은 확실하다.
→ It is certain ________ she will win first prize.

2 나는 오늘 이 책을 다 끝낼 수 있을지 확실하지 않다.
→ I'm not sure ________ I can finish this book today.

3 이 음식은 맛있을 뿐만 아니라 영양가도 좋다.
→ This food is nutritious ________ ________ ________ delicious.

4 우리는 오늘 밤이나 내일 아침에 떠날 것이다.
→ We will leave ________ tonight ________ tomorrow morning.

5 Brown 씨는 영어 선생님이 아니라 수학 선생님이다.
→ Mr. Brown is ________ an English teacher ________ a math teacher.

C
certain 형 확실한, 틀림없는
nutritious 형 영양분이 풍부한

Grammar Practice

A 다음 밑줄 친 부분을 바르게 고치시오.

1 I think it she resembles her mother. → __________

2 Both he and I am going to attend the seminar. → __________

3 If you will see Sylvia, can you tell her to call me? → __________

4 All the leaves have fallen because the strong wind. → __________

B 다음 빈칸에 들어갈 말을 보기 에서 골라 쓰시오. (한 번씩만 쓸 것)

보기 before unless since even though whether

1 Let's get dressed __________ the guests arrive.

2 Tell me __________ you can study with us or not.

3 __________ I have enough time, I'll give you a ride.

4 They invited Matt to their party __________ they didn't like him.

5 __________ we walk faster, we will miss the beginning of the class.

C 다음 두 문장을 한 문장으로 바꿀 때 빈칸에 알맞은 말을 쓰시오.

1 Fred likes history. He likes science, too.

→ Fred likes __________ history __________ science.

2 We'll stay home. Or we'll take a walk.

→ We'll __________ stay home __________ __________ __________ __________.

3 He passed the exam. He also got a scholarship.

→ He __________ __________ passed the exam __________ __________ got a scholarship.

4 I want to know. When does the library close?

→ I want to know __________ __________ __________ __________.

WORDS

A
resemble 동 닮다
attend 동 참석하다

B
give A a ride A를 태워 주다
beginning 명 초반, 시작

C
scholarship 명 장학금

내신 완성 Grammar Practice

1 다음 빈칸에 공통으로 들어갈 말로 알맞은 것은?

- Sally dropped her wallet _________ she was getting up.
- He didn't show up on time again _________ we expected.

① if　　② as
③ until　　④ when
⑤ because

2 다음 밑줄 친 부분의 쓰임이 나머지 넷과 다른 것은?

① I hope that you enjoy your holidays.
② Carter thinks that everybody likes him.
③ She realized that she didn't have the key.
④ The bike that I bought a week ago is broken.
⑤ We know that the soccer team did their best.

3 다음 중 어법상 바르지 못한 것은?

① I wonder why she quit her job suddenly.
② As time passed, his condition got worse.
③ Neither my friend nor I want to see the movie.
④ Even though I was late, she welcomed me warmly.
⑤ Don't forget to turn off the TV when you will go out.

4 다음 우리말과 일치하도록 괄호 안의 단어를 이용하여 문장을 완성하시오.

(1) Victor는 비가 그칠 때까지 기다릴 것이다. (until, the rain, stop)

→ Victor will wait ______________________________.

(2) Jane뿐만 아니라 Jake도 꽃을 좋아한다. (well, like)

→ ______________________________ flowers.

WORDS

1
show up 나타나다
expect 동 예상하다

2
do one's best 최선을 다하다

3
get worse 악화되다
welcome 동 맞이하다, 환영하다
warmly 부 따뜻하게

서술형에 나오는 WRITING

A 다음 우리말과 일치하도록 괄호 단어를 바르게 배열하시오.

1 아무도 그가 떠났는지 아닌지 모른다.
(whether, knows, he, nobody, left)
→ ______________________________ or not.

2 우리는 Emma에게 그녀가 휴가로 어디에 가고 싶었는지 물었다.
(Emma, go, asked, wanted, we, to, where, she)
→ ______________________________ on vacation.

3 나는 그녀가 나에게 그 일정을 이야기할 때 주의 깊게 들었다.
(listened, as, I, she, told, carefully, me)
→ ______________________________ the schedule.

B 다음 두 문장을 괄호 안의 접속사를 이용하여 한 문장으로 바꿔 쓰시오.

1 Olivia's heart broke. She heard the news. (when)
→ Olivia's ______________________________.

2 I tried bungee jumping. I was a little afraid. (even though)
→ I ______________________________.

3 Tom always takes notes. He often forgets things. (since)
→ Tom ______________________________.

C 다음 그림을 보고, 보기 의 단어를 이용하여 빈칸에 알맞은 말을 쓰시오.

보기 both either neither

1

I bought __________ milk __________ orange juice.

2

The bag on the chair is __________ blue __________ brown.

1

What does space smell like? **Since** space is a vacuum, most people think **that** it doesn't smell like anything. However, many astronauts say this isn't true. Of course, they aren't able to smell space directly. But **when** astronauts go back inside the spacecraft after exploring space, they can smell space on their space helmets and suits.

One astronaut said **that** it smells like burnt metal. Others described the smell as similar to burnt meat. One space tourist even wrote that it smells like a burnt almond cookie! **Although** people may describe it in different ways, it's clear **that** ____________________. Scientists are still trying to figure out what causes this smell!

1 위 글의 빈칸에 들어갈 말로 가장 알맞은 것은?

① smelling space is impossible
② space does have a special smell
③ astronauts must wear spacesuits
④ astronauts like the smell of space
⑤ the smell is caused by burnt food

2 위 글의 밑줄 친 that과 쓰임이 다른 것은?

① I believed that he was wrong.
② The truth is that she is not talented.
③ This is the picture that I took yesterday.
④ We knew that he didn't have enough food.
⑤ It is important that we drink enough water.

WORDS
space 명 공간; *우주 vacuum 명 진공 astronaut 명 우주 비행사 directly 부 직접 spacecraft 명 우주선 explore 동 탐험하다 suit 명 정장; *(특정한 활동 때 입는) …옷[복] burnt 형 (불에) 탄 metal 명 [1] __________ describe 동 묘사하다 similar 형 [2] __________ figure out 알아내다 cause 동 …를 야기하다 문제 talented 형 재능이 있는

2

There are many ways to fix walls **when** they need repairs. ① German artist Jan Vormann's method is **both** imaginative **and** beautiful. ② Most repairmen use paint and *mortar to fix old walls, but Vormann fills gaps and holes with brightly colored Lego bricks. ③ Lego bricks were first made by a carpenter named Ole Kirk Christiansen. ④ After working on his first wall in Rome, Vormann began to get invited to places all around the world to use his technique. ⑤ Today, along with teams of volunteers, he still creates interesting pieces of Lego art. Vormann chose this technique **not only because** it is fun, <u>그것은 시선을 끌 수 있는 아주 좋은 방법이기도 하기 때문이다</u>. People passing by often stop and join in with Vormann, **as** they want to enjoy the fun, too.

*mortar: 회반죽

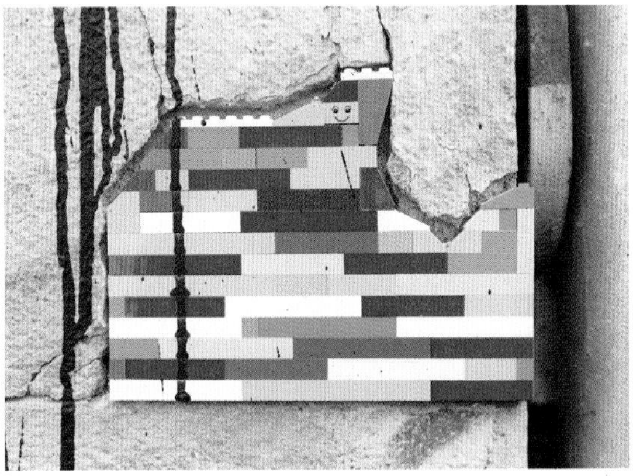

1 Which sentence is NOT needed in the passage?

① ② ③ ④ ⑤

2 Fill in the blanks to make the meaning same as the underlined part.

→ ________ ________ ________ it is a great way to get attention

WORDS repair 명 수리 method 명 방법 imaginative 형 창의적인, 상상력이 풍부한 gap 명 틈 brick 명 벽돌; *블록 carpenter 명 목수 technique 명 기법, 기술 along with …와 함께 volunteer 명 [1]________ pass by 지나가다
문제 attention 명 주의, 관심

내신에 나오는 COMMUNICATION

A 장래 희망 묻고 답하기

A: **What do you want to be in the future?**
(너는 미래에 무엇이 되고 싶니?)

B: **I want to be** an engineer. **What do you hope to be in the future?**
(나는 엔지니어가 되고 싶어. 너는 미래에 무엇이 되길 바라니?)

A: **I want to be** a doctor.
(나는 의사가 되고 싶어.)

'What do you want to be in the future?'는 상대방의 장래 희망을 물을 때 쓰는 표현이다. 이와 유사한 표현으로는 'What are you going to be in the future?'나 'What do you hope to be in the future?' 등이 있다. 대답할 때는 'I want to be ...'나 'I'm going to be ...' 등으로 말할 수 있다.

⊕ EXPRESSION PLUS

A: **What are you going to be in the future?** (너는 미래에 무엇이 될 거니?)
B: **I'm going to be** a ballerina. (나는 발레리나가 될 거야.)

Check-Up

1 다음 대화의 빈칸에 들어갈 말로 알맞은 것은?

A: What do you want to be in the future?
B: ____________________

① I'm a teacher.
② I want to be a cook.
③ I'd like to play soccer now.
④ I want you to be a scientist.
⑤ I'm going to read a history book.

2 다음 괄호 안의 단어를 바르게 배열하여 대화를 완성하시오.

A: ________________________________ in the future?
(to, you, what, be, are, going)
B: I hope to be an architect.

WORDS

2
architect 명 건축가

B 제안하기

A: Mom, we're hungry.
(엄마, 저희 배고파요.)

B: **Why don't we** have some pizza**?**
(우리 피자를 먹는 게 어때?)

A: **Sounds great!**
(좋아요!)

'Why don't we[you] ...?'는 상대방에게 제안할 때 쓰는 표현이다. 제안할 때 쓰는 다른 표현으로는 'Shall we ...?', 'How[What] about v-ing?', 'Let's ...' 등이 있다. 제안에 승낙할 때는 'Sounds great.', 'That's a good idea.', 'I'd like to.' 등으로, 거절할 때는 'Sorry, but I can't.', 'I'd like to, but I can't.', 'Maybe next time.' 등으로 대답한다.

⊕ EXPRESSION PLUS

A: **How about** going to the movies tonight**?** (오늘 밤 영화 보러 가는 게 어때?)
B: **That's a good idea.** (좋은 생각이야.) / **I'm sorry, but I can't.** (미안하지만, 나는 안 돼.)

A: **Shall we** go hiking this afternoon**?** (우리 오늘 오후에 하이킹 갈래?)
B: **Maybe next time.** I'm too tired right now. (나중에. 나는 지금 너무 피곤해.)

Check-Up

1 다음 중 의미하는 바가 나머지 넷과 다른 것은?

① Shall we have steak for dinner?
② Why do we have steak for dinner?
③ How about having steak for dinner?
④ What about having steak for dinner?
⑤ Why don't we have steak for dinner?

2 다음 괄호 안의 말을 바르게 배열하여 대화를 완성하시오.

A: If you really like Julie, ______________________
______________ to her?
(you, write a letter, don't, why)
B: That's a good idea.

WORDS

1
steak 명 스테이크

FINAL TEST

1 다음 밑줄 친 단어와 바꿔 쓸 수 있는 것은?

The story is very humorous.

① sad
② scary
③ funny
④ traditional
⑤ imaginative

2 다음 빈칸에 들어갈 말을 보기 에서 골라 쓰시오.

보기 sweat cause describe

(1) Driving fast can __________ an accident.
(2) I __________ a lot when I eat spicy food.

3 다음 질문에 대한 대답으로 알맞지 않은 것은?

Shall we go for a walk after dinner?

① Sounds great.
② Sorry, but I can't.
③ That's a good idea.
④ I'd like to, but I can't.
⑤ Never mind. I'm all right.

4 대화가 자연스럽게 이어지도록 (A)~(D)를 바르게 배열하시오.

(A) Yes. I'd like to write fantasy novels.
(B) I want to be a best-selling author.
(C) Cool! Do you want to write novels?
(D) What are you going to be in the future?

_______ → _______ → _______ → _______

5 다음 괄호 안의 단어를 이용하여 빈칸에 알맞은 말을 쓰시오.

A: __________ __________ __________ __________ __________ __________ in the future? (what, want)
B: I want to be a firefighter.

[6-8] 다음 빈칸에 들어갈 말로 알맞은 것을 고르시오.

6

Emily and her friends saw wild animals __________ they went to the zoo.

① until ② when ③ that
④ unless ⑤ whether

7

I can't meet you tomorrow __________ I finish all my work today.

① that ② after ③ since
④ unless ⑤ whether

8

My hands were trembling __________ I was very nervous.

① until ② unless ③ because
④ although ⑤ even though

9 다음 우리말과 일치하도록 빈칸에 알맞은 말을 쓰시오.

당신은 버스나 택시 중 하나를 타면 됩니다.

→ You can take __________ __________ __________ __________ a taxi.

[10-11] 다음 우리말과 일치하도록 할 때, 빈칸에 들어갈 말로 알맞은 것을 고르시오.

10 안전벨트를 매지 않으면, 너는 벌금을 내야 할 것이다.

→ ______________, you will have to pay a fine.

① If you wear a seat belt
② If you will wear a seat belt
③ Unless you wear a seat belt
④ Unless you won't wear a seat belt
⑤ Unless you don't wear a seat belt

11 그녀도 나도 일본 음식을 좋아하지 않는다.

→ Neither she nor I ________ Japanese food.

① like ② likes
③ liking ④ don't like
⑤ doesn't like

12 다음 밑줄 친 부분이 의미상 어색한 것은?

① We had lunch before the show started.
② While I was away, Dan watched my bag.
③ He doesn't gain weight because he eats a lot.
④ Turn off the TV if you're not watching it.
⑤ He had a stomachache after he ate too much ice cream.

서술형

13 다음 우리말과 일치하도록 괄호 안의 단어를 바르게 배열하시오.

Ann은 똑똑할 뿐만 아니라 친절하기도 하다.
(smart, not, is, also, but, Ann, only, kind)

→ ______________________________

14 다음 밑줄 친 부분 중 어법상 바르지 못한 것은?

A: Do you know when ① does the concert start?
B: It will start ② in five or ten minutes.
A: I ③ can't believe ④ that I will ⑤ be able to see my favorite singer soon.

서술형

15 다음 우리말과 일치하도록 괄호 안의 단어를 이용하여 문장을 완성하시오.

그녀가 선물을 열었을 때 그녀는 기뻐 보였다.
(when, open, the gift)

→ She looked pleased ______________ ______________.

16 다음 두 문장을 한 문장으로 바꿀 때 빈칸에 들어갈 말로 알맞은 것은?

It was raining heavily. But we went out for dinner.
→ __________ it was raining heavily, we went out for dinner.

① If ② Until
③ Unless ④ Because
⑤ Although

어려워요

17 다음 빈칸 (A), (B)에 알맞은 접속사를 쓰시오.

- The fact is ___(A)___ the tower was built in 2017.
- The class will last ___(B)___ the bell rings.

(A) ________ (B) ________

18 다음 빈칸에 공통으로 들어갈 말로 알맞은 것은?

- Sophia fell asleep ________ the speech was boring.
- David called me ________ I was washing the dishes.

① as ② if
③ while ④ since
⑤ whether

자주 나와요

19 다음 밑줄 친 부분의 의미가 나머지 넷과 다른 것은?

① I'll lend her my laptop if she needs it.
② Turn on the air conditioner if it's hot.
③ I don't know if I should take his advice.
④ We can get another one free if we buy this cup.
⑤ You should visit Insa-dong if you go to Seoul.

내신 완성 서술형

20 다음 글에서 틀린 부분을 찾아 바르게 고치시오.

Last week, my cousin wanted to go to the baseball stadium. However, the game was canceled because rain, so he had to stay home.

________ → ________

21 다음 우리말과 일치하도록 조건에 맞게 영작하시오.

비록 슬펐지만, 그는 미소 지었다.

조건 1: Although로 시작할 것
조건 2: sad, smile을 이용할 것
조건 3: 총 6단어로 작성할 것
→ ________________________

[22-23] 다음 그림을 보고, 괄호 안의 말을 이용하여 문장을 완성하시오. (현재진행형으로 작성할 것)

22 ________ Owen and Matilda ______________. (carry a bag)

23 ________ Owen nor Matilda ______________. (wear glasses)

WORD LIST

Grammar

☐ sweat	동 땀을 흘리다
☐ concentrate	동 집중하다
☐ low	형 낮은
☐ out of sight	보이지 않는 곳에
☐ humorous	형 재미있는, 유머러스한
☐ adult	명 성인, 어른
☐ traditional	형 전통의
☐ promote	동 승진시키다
☐ certain	형 확실한, 틀림없는
☐ nutritious	형 영양분이 풍부한
☐ resemble	동 닮다
☐ attend	동 참석하다
☐ give A a ride	A를 태워 주다
☐ beginning	명 초반, 시작
☐ scholarship	명 장학금
☐ show up	나타나다
☐ expect	동 예상하다
☐ do one's best	최선을 다하다
☐ get worse	악화되다
☐ welcome	동 맞이하다, 환영하다
☐ warmly	부 따뜻하게

Reading

☐ space	명 공간; 우주
☐ astronaut	명 우주 비행사
☐ directly	부 직접
☐ spacecraft	명 우주선
☐ explore	동 탐험하다
☐ burnt	형 (불에) 탄
☐ metal	명 금속
☐ describe	동 묘사하다
☐ similar	형 비슷한
☐ figure out	알아내다
☐ cause	동 …를 야기하다
☐ talented	형 재능이 있는
☐ repair	명 수리
☐ imaginative	형 창의적인, 상상력이 풍부한
☐ gap	명 틈
☐ carpenter	명 목수
☐ technique	명 기법, 기술
☐ along with	…와 함께
☐ volunteer	명 자원봉사자
☐ pass by	지나가다
☐ attention	명 주의, 관심

Communication

☐ architect	명 건축가
☐ steak	명 스테이크

Final Test

☐ author	명 작가
☐ wild	형 야생의
☐ pay	동 지불하다
☐ fine	명 벌금
☐ gain weight	체중이 늘다
☐ minute	명 (시간 단위의) 분
☐ heavily	부 심하게
☐ last	동 계속되다
☐ fall asleep	잠들다
☐ laptop	명 노트북 컴퓨터
☐ advice	명 조언, 충고
☐ free	부 무료로
☐ stadium	명 경기장
☐ smile	동 웃다, 미소 짓다

CHAPTER 12

대명사가 만드는 중요 구문

GET READY

I lost my *cell phone*, so I bought a new **one**.
(나는 휴대폰을 잃어버려서, 새것을 샀다.)

Some students like English, and **others** like math.
(어떤 학생들은 영어를 좋아하고, 다른 학생들은 수학을 좋아한다.)

I won first prize, so I was proud of **myself**.
(나는 1등을 해서, 나 자신이 자랑스러웠다.)

대명사는 앞에 나온 명사를 대신하여 쓰는 말이에요. 대명사 중에서 막연한 사람이나 사물을 가리키는 말을 부정대명사라고 하고 '… 자신, … 자체'라는 의미를 나타내는 말을 재귀대명사라고 해요.

GRAMMAR FOCUS

A 부정대명사

부정대명사는 막연한 사람이나 사물을 가리키는 대명사로, 일부는 명사를 수식하는 형용사처럼 쓰이기도 한다.

1 one

앞에 나온 명사와 같은 종류의 사물이나 사람 중에 불특정한 것을 가리킬 때 쓰며, 가리키는 대상이 복수형일 때는 ones를 쓴다.

A: Is there a supermarket near here?
B: There's **one** across from the bakery. (one = a supermarket)

These shoes are big for me. Do you have smaller **ones**? (ones = shoes)

TIPS
앞에 나온 명사를 다시 가리킬 때는 대명사 it을 쓴다.
I can't find **my bag**. Have you seen **it**?
(나는 내 가방을 못 찾겠어. 너는 그것을 본 적 있니?)

2 another

'또 하나 다른 것(의), 또 하나(의)'라는 의미로, 앞에 나온 명사와 같은 종류의 사물이나 사람을 추가적으로 나타낼 때 쓴다.

I've already eaten a piece of apple pie and ordered **another**.

3 all

'모두, 모든 것'이라는 의미로, 사람을 가리킬 때는 복수 취급을, 사물이나 상황을 나타낼 때는 단수 취급을 한다. 「all (of)+(대)명사」 형태로 쓰인 경우 (대)명사의 수에 동사를 일치시킨다.

All *were* tired after the long trip.
All (of) the rooms in the hotel *were* booked.
All *is* going well these days.
All (of) the money *was* paid back.

4 both

'둘 다(의), 양쪽(의)'이라는 의미로, 복수 취급하며 「both (of)+복수명사」 형태로 쓸 수 있다.

Ron and Teresa want to be astronauts. **Both** *are* interested in space.
Both (of) the scientists *were* pleased with the research results.

5 each, every

each는 '각자(의), 각각(의)'이라는 의미로, 「each+단수명사」 또는 「each of+복수명사」 형태로 쓸 수 있으며 단수 취급한다. every는 '모든'이라는 의미로, 「every+단수명사」의 형태로 쓰며 단수 취급한다.

Each person *gets* three cards.
Each of the actors *has* become famous for a different movie.
Every student *has* to return the library books within ten days.

TIPS
「every+기간」은 '…마다'의 의미이다.
They hold an event **every two years**.
(그들은 2년마다 행사를 개최한다.)

Check-Up

A 다음 괄호 안에서 알맞은 말을 고르시오.

1 (All / Each) soccer team has eleven players.
2 All the animals in this forest (is / are) endangered.
3 He has two sisters, and (both / each) of them work at banks.
4 My jeans were old, so my mom bought me new (them / ones).

WORDS

A
endangered 형 멸종 위기의, 위험한

B 다음 빈칸에 들어갈 말을 보기 에서 골라 쓰시오. (한 번씩만 쓸 것)

보기 all both every another

1 The World Cup is held ________ four years.
2 We dropped three vases, and ________ of them broke.
3 There are two restaurants on the corner. ________ are nice.
4 I drink one coffee in the morning and ________ coffee in the afternoon.

B
vase 명 꽃병

C 다음 밑줄 친 부분을 바르게 고치시오.

1 Each speaker have five minutes for their presentation. → ________
2 Can I ride your bicycle? I'll give one back tomorrow. → ________
3 Every items in this store is on sale until next week. → ________

C
presentation 명 발표
item 명 물품
on sale 판매되는; *할인 중인

D 다음 우리말과 일치하도록 빈칸에 알맞은 부정대명사를 쓰시오.

1 각각의 나라에는 그곳만의 문화와 전통이 있다.
→ ________ country has its own culture and traditions.
2 이 문제는 저것보다 더 풀기 쉽니?
→ Is this problem easier to solve than that ________?
3 모든 선수들이 그 경기 규칙들을 따른다.
→ ________ player follows the rules of the game.
4 이 샌드위치는 정말 맛있어요. 또 하나 먹어도 되나요?
→ This sandwich is really good. Can I have ________?

D
culture 명 문화
tradition 명 전통

B 부정대명사 구문

구문	의미
one ... the other ~	(둘 중의) 하나는 …, 나머지 하나는 ~
one ... another ~ the other(s) ~	하나는 …, 다른 하나는 ~, 나머지 (하나)는 ~
some ... others ~	어떤 것[사람]들은 …, 다른 어떤 것[사람]들은 ~
some ... the others ~	어떤 것[사람]들은 …, 나머지 전부는 ~
each other / one another	서로

I have two pets. **One** is a parrot, and **the other** is a monkey.
There are three cars. **One** is blue, **another** is red, and **the other** is black.
Some tourists rested at the hotel, and **others** went shopping.
Some of the cookies are here, but where are **the others**?
Jim and Chloe are talking to **each other**.
The basketball players are passing the ball to **one another**.

TIPS
보통 each other는 둘일 때, one another는 셋 이상일 때 쓰지만 구분 없이 쓸 수 있다.

C 재귀대명사

재귀대명사는 인칭대명사의 소유격이나 목적격에 -self(단수)/-selves(복수)를 붙인 형태로, '… 자신'이라는 뜻이다.

TIPS
재귀대명사의 종류
myself, yourself, himself, herself, itself, ourselves, yourselves, themselves

1 재귀 용법

목적어가 주어 자신일 때 사용하며, 동사나 전치사의 목적어 역할을 한다. 이때 재귀대명사는 생략할 수 없다.
Some people express **themselves** through their clothes. (동사의 목적어)
Amy looked at **herself** in the mirror. (전치사의 목적어)

2 강조 용법

'자신이, 직접, 자체'의 의미로 주어, 목적어, 보어를 강조하며, 주로 강조하고자 하는 단어 뒤나 문장 맨 뒤에 위치한다. 이때 재귀대명사는 생략 가능하다.
I changed the bulb **myself**. / I **myself** changed the bulb. (주어 강조)
You can't change the design **itself**. (목적어 강조)

내신 POINT PLUS

재귀대명사의 관용적 표현
- by oneself 혼자서, 혼자 힘으로
- in itself 그 자체가
- enjoy oneself 즐거운 시간을 보내다
- make oneself at home 편안하게 지내다
- beside oneself 제정신이 아닌
- help oneself (to) …를 마음껏 먹다
- between ourselves 우리끼리 얘기지만
- burn[hurt] oneself 불에 데다[다치다]

Check-Up

A 다음 괄호 안에서 알맞은 말을 고르시오.

1 The teacher told (us / ourselves) to be careful in the laboratory.
2 The woman was beside (her / herself) when she lost her child.
3 (One / Some) possible topic for the speech is school life, and the other is hobbies.
4 You need three ingredients. One is flour, another is milk, and (the other / others) is an egg.
5 The old couple looked at (one / each) other happily.

WORDS

A
laboratory 명 실험실
ingredient 명 재료

B 다음 밑줄 친 부분을 생략할 수 있으면 O, 없으면 X 표시하시오.

1 I made this model ship myself.
2 Jeff is selfish. He only cares about himself.
3 Hailey fell down the stairs and hurt herself last week.
4 I didn't like the book, but I loved the main character herself.

B
selfish 형 이기적인
stair 명 계단

C 다음 밑줄 친 부분을 바르게 고치시오.

1 Many children are enjoying them at the pool. → ________
2 This village is very small, so many people know one anothers. → ________
3 Ella has two cousins. One is a nurse, and others is a police officer. → ________

C
village 명 마을

D 다음 우리말과 일치하도록 빈칸에 알맞은 대명사를 쓰시오.

1 이 망고 주스를 마음껏 마셔. 내가 너를 위해 그걸 만들었어.
→ Help ________ to this mango juice. I made it for you.
2 어떤 사람들은 공포 영화를 좋아하지만, 다른 어떤 사람들은 좋아하지 않는다.
→ ________ people like horror movies, but ________ don't.
3 나는 엽서 두 장이 있다. 하나는 너를 위한 것이고, 나머지 하나는 우리 엄마를 위한 것이다.
→ I have two postcards. ________ is for you, and ________ ________ is for my mom.

D
postcard 명 엽서

Grammar Practice

A 다음 밑줄 친 부분을 바르게 고치시오.

1 I burnt me while I was ironing my shirts. → __________
2 She lost her student card. I think she left one in the bus. → __________
3 Can I exchange these gray socks for white one? → __________
4 All the schools was closed because of the heavy storm. → __________

B 다음 빈칸에 들어갈 말을 보기에서 골라 쓰시오.

보기 the other one each some

1 I'm looking for a tie. Can you recommend a popular __________?
2 An international film festival is held in Busan __________ year.
3 Lisa doesn't like two kinds of food. One is seafood, and __________ is curry.
4 There are 20 people on the bus. __________ are sitting, and the others are standing.

C 다음 우리말과 일치하도록 빈칸에 알맞은 말을 쓰시오.

1 모두가 집에 갔다. Chris는 혼자서 남겨졌다.
→ Everyone went home. Chris was left __________ __________.
2 Ann은 그 상을 받았을 때 자신이 자랑스러웠다.
→ Ann was proud of __________ when she received the award.
3 어떤 사람들은 선물로 물건을 원하고, 다른 어떤 사람들은 돈을 원한다.
→ __________ people want items for gifts, and __________ want money.
4 식사는 세 가지 코스를 포함한다. 하나는 샐러드, 다른 하나는 수프, 나머지 하나는 스테이크이다.
→ The meal includes three courses. __________ is salad, __________ is soup, and __________ __________ is steak.

WORDS

A
iron 동 다림질하다
exchange 동 교환하다
storm 명 폭풍

B
international 형 국제적인

C
award 명 상
include 동 포함하다

내신 완성 Grammar Practice

WORDS

1 다음 빈칸에 들어갈 말로 알맞은 것은?

She has a piano in her bedroom. She has ________ piano in the living room.

① each ② both
③ every ④ another
⑤ some

2 다음 중 어법상 바르지 못한 것은?

① Each person have a different personality.
② She really likes to take pictures of herself.
③ I participate in the meeting every three years.
④ These two sweaters look pretty. I will buy both.
⑤ All of the dishes in the restaurant were sold out.

2
personality 명 성격
participate in …에 참가하다
sold out 다 팔린, 매진된

3 다음 밑줄 친 부분 중 생략할 수 있는 것은?

① Julia calls herself a good student.
② Tim taught himself how to play the violin.
③ I introduced myself to my new neighbors.
④ He took a plane by himself for the first time.
⑤ They picked all the apples from the tree themselves.

4 다음 우리말과 일치하도록 괄호 안의 단어를 이용하여 문장을 완성하시오.

(1) 모든 전문가들은 실험을 하기 위해 서로를 도왔다. (help, another)
→ All the experts ________________ to do the experiment.

(2) 환영합니다! 저는 여러분들이 편안하게 지내기를 바랍니다. (make, home)
→ Welcome! I hope you will ________________.

4
expert 명 전문가
experiment 명 실험

서술형에 나오는 WRITING

A 다음 우리말과 일치하도록 괄호 안의 말을 바르게 배열하시오.

1 모든 구성원들은 새해 첫날에 연하장을 쓴다.
(the members, write, all, greeting cards, of)
→ ______________________ on New Year's Day.

2 나의 이모들은 둘 다 뉴욕으로 이사 가려고 계획하고 있다.
(my aunts, planning, move, both, are, of, to)
→ ______________________ to New York.

3 나는 오늘 신발 한 켤레를 샀고, 내일 또 다른 한 켤레를 살 것이다.
(will, another, I, pair, buy)
→ I bought a pair of shoes today, and ______________________ tomorrow.

B 다음 우리말과 일치하도록 괄호 안의 말을 이용하여 문장을 완성하시오.

1 각각의 승객들은 이 양식을 작성해야 한다. (the passengers, have to)
→ ______________________ fill out this form.

2 그녀는 해변에 누워 있는 자신을 상상했다. (imagine)
→ ______________________ lying on the beach.

3 우리는 바구니에 있는 과일을 마음껏 먹었다. (help, to)
→ We ______________________ the fruit in the basket.

C 다음 그림을 보고, 빈칸에 알맞은 대명사를 쓰시오.

1

Which ball do you want? __________ is a baseball, and __________ is a soccer ball.

2

There are three boys. __________ is wearing an orange shirt, __________ is wearing a striped shirt, and __________ is wearing a black shirt.

1

One day, two frogs fell into a hole. They tried to jump out, but the hole was too deep. **All the other** frogs gathered around the hole and looked down at the unlucky pair. "How awful this is!" they said. "That hole is really deep. You'll never get out of there!" Hearing this, ① one of the frogs gave up and stopped trying to jump out of the hole. But __________ kept jumping higher and higher. Finally, ② he was able to escape from that terrible hole.

Some frogs who were watching asked ③ him why he didn't give up, but he didn't answer. In fact, ④ he was deaf and thought **the other** frogs were cheering for ⑤ him.

1 위 글의 밑줄 친 ①~⑤ 중 가리키는 바가 다른 하나는?

① ② ③ ④ ⑤

2 위 글의 빈칸에 들어갈 말로 가장 알맞은 것은?

① other
② others
③ the other
④ the others
⑤ another

WORDS hole 명 구멍; *구덩이 deep 형 [1] __________ look down at …를 내려다보다 unlucky 형 운이 나쁜 pair 명 한 쌍 awful 형 끔찍한 get out (of) (…에서) 나오다 give up [2] __________ escape 동 탈출하다, 벗어나다 terrible 형 끔찍한 deaf 형 귀가 먹은, 청각 장애가 있는 cheer for 응원하다

2

There is nowhere to hide in open water. However, **some** sharks have overcome this problem. The *lantern shark, one of the smallest sharks in the ocean, can hide themselves in a special way. The shark has organs that absorb light from the sun and reproduce it. These allow the lantern shark to glow, like its name suggests.

But how does this hide the shark? Imagine that *predators or prey are swimming below the shark on a sunny day. Normally, they can see the silhouette of the shark under the sunlight. However, when the lantern shark glows, it simply looks like the sunlight **itself** in the water. This keeps both predators and prey from finding the lantern shark by making it "invisible."

*lantern shark: 랜턴상어
*predator: 포식 동물

1 Read the summary below and find the best pair for blanks (A) and (B).

The lantern shark protects itself by sending out ____(A)____ with its ____(B)____.

	(A)		(B)
①	sound	-	body
②	sound	-	organs
③	light	-	organs
④	light	-	silhouette
⑤	air	-	silhouette

2 Correct the underlined word.

→ ______________

WORDS
nowhere 부 아무 데도 (··· 없다) overcome 동 극복하다 organ 명 장기, 기관 absorb 동 1 __________ glow 동 빛나다 suggest 동 제안하다; *시사하다 prey 명 먹이 normally 부 보통 silhouette 명 윤곽, 실루엣 simply 부 그냥, 그저 invisible 형 2 __________ 문제 send out (빛·소리 등을) 내다[발하다]

내신에 나오는 COMMUNICATION

A 이해 점검하기

A: Go straight two blocks and turn right.
Do you know what I mean?
(두 블록 직진해서 오른쪽으로 도세요. 제 말 이해하시겠어요?)

B: **Yes, I understand.**
(네, 이해해요.)

'Do you know what I mean?'은 자신이 한 말을 상대방이 이해했는지 확인하고 싶을 때 쓰는 표현이다. 상대방의 말을 이해한 경우에는 'Yes, I understand.', 이해하지 못한 경우에는 'No, I don't understand.'라고 대답할 수 있다.

EXPRESSION PLUS

1 이해 점검하기
- Do you understand? (이해하니?)
- Is everything clear? (다 이해하니?)
- Are you with me? (내 말 이해하니?)

2 대답하기
- Not really. (그렇지 않아.) / Not exactly. (잘 모르겠어.)
- Sorry, but I don't understand. (미안하지만, 이해가 안 돼.)

Check-Up

1 다음 대화의 빈칸에 들어갈 말로 알맞은 것을 모두 고르시오. (2개)

A: Transfer to Line 2 at City Hall Station. Do you know what I mean?
B: ______________________

① Not really.
② I'm sorry to hear that.
③ Sorry, but I don't understand.
④ I know you should transfer to Line 2.
⑤ Do you need a dictionary to find the meaning?

WORDS

1
transfer 동 옮기다; *갈아타다
dictionary 명 사전

2 다음 괄호 안의 단어를 이용하여 대화를 완성하시오.

A: That's how you solve the problem. __________ __________ __________? (understand)
B: Yes, I understand.

B 조언 구하고 답하기

A: I have a terrible toothache. **Do you think I should** see a dentist**?**
(나 치통이 너무 심해. 내가 치과에 가야 한다고 생각하니?)

B: **Yes, I think you should.**
(응, 내 생각에 너는 그래야 해.)

'Do you think I should ...?'는 상대방에게 조언을 구할 때 쓰는 표현으로 'What should I do?' 등으로도 말할 수 있다. 상대방에게 조언할 때는 '(I think) You should ...'나 'You'd better[You had better] ...'라고 말할 수 있다. 이때 'You'd better ...'는 강한 충고의 표현이므로, 윗사람에게는 쓰지 않도록 주의한다.

⊕ EXPRESSION PLUS

A: I can't sleep well. **What should I do?** (나는 잠을 잘 못 자. 내가 무엇을 해야 할까?)

B: **You should** drink some hot milk before bed. (너는 자기 전에 따뜻한 우유를 좀 마셔야 해.)
Why don't you take a warm bath before bed**?** (자기 전에 따뜻한 목욕을 하는 게 어때?)
You'd better stop using your cell phone before bed. (너는 자기 전에 휴대 전화 사용을 하지 않는 게 좋겠어.)

Check-Up

1 다음 대화의 빈칸에 들어갈 말로 알맞은 것은?

A: I have a cold. What should I do?
B: ____________________

① I caught a cold, too.
② Well, I don't think so.
③ I think you should do that.
④ No, I don't think you should.
⑤ Why don't you see a doctor?

WORDS

1
have[catch] a cold 감기에 걸리다

2 다음 우리말과 일치하도록 괄호 안의 말을 바르게 배열하시오.

내 생각에 너는 그에게 사과해야 해.
(should, think, apologize to him, you, I)

→ ______________________________

FINAL TEST

1 다음 중 영어 단어와 우리말 뜻이 잘못 연결된 것은?

① selfish – 이기적인　② glow – 빛나다
③ personality – 성격　④ culture – 문화
⑤ overcome – 포기하다

2 다음 우리말과 일치하도록 빈칸에 알맞은 말을 쓰시오.

Helen은 한 쌍의 부츠를 샀다.

→ Helen bought a ________ of boots.

3 대화가 자연스럽게 이어지도록 (A)~(D)를 바르게 배열하시오.

(A) OK. I'll try that.
(B) You look worried. What's wrong?
(C) I think you should go to the lost and found.
(D) I left my key on the subway. What should I do?

______ → ______ → ______ → ______

4 다음 대화의 빈칸에 들어갈 말로 알맞은 것은?

A: ______________________
B: No. Could you explain again?

① How can you say that?
② Are you happy about that?
③ Do you know what I mean?
④ Could you repeat that again?
⑤ What do you think I should do?

5 다음 문장이 들어갈 위치로 가장 알맞은 곳은?

Is everything clear?

A: How can I make tomato spaghetti? (①)
B: (②) First, boil some noodles for about nine minutes.
A: OK. What's next? (③)
B: After that, chop some tomatoes and mix them with some vegetables, sauce, and a little salt. (④)
A: Yes, I understand. (⑤)

[6-7] 다음 빈칸에 들어갈 말로 알맞은 것을 고르시오.

6

A new president is elected ________ five years in my country.

① each　② every　③ another
④ both　⑤ the other

7

________ of these paintings were painted by Monet.

① All　② One　③ Each
④ Every　⑤ Other

8 다음 밑줄 친 부분의 쓰임이 나머지 넷과 다른 것은?

① I solved this puzzle myself.
② We should believe in ourselves.
③ Sue is too old to take care of herself.
④ You need to be honest with yourself.
⑤ Jason hurt himself moving heavy boxes.

[9-10] 다음 우리말과 일치하도록 빈칸에 알맞은 말을 쓰시오.

9 그들 자신이 결정을 해야 한다.

→ They ________ have to make a decision.

10 그는 화가 나서 제정신이 아니었다.

→ He was ________ ________ with anger.

11 다음 밑줄 친 부분과 바꿔 쓸 수 있는 것은?

I'm still hungry. I can eat one more piece of pizza.

① it
② both
③ some
④ every
⑤ another

12 다음 빈칸에 들어갈 말이 바르게 짝지어진 것은?

All of my friends ________ to go camping. However, each of them ________ to camp in a different place.

① like - want
② like - wants
③ like - wanting
④ likes - want
⑤ likes - wanting

13 다음 중 어법상 바르지 못한 것은?

① Each ticket costs 100 dollars.
② All the kids take the school bus.
③ Both of the girls wear glasses.
④ Every student were in the classroom.
⑤ Some like summer, but others like winter.

[14-15] 다음 우리말을 영어로 바르게 옮긴 것을 고르시오.

14 우리 둘 다에게 충분한 공간은 없다.

① There's enough space for all of us.
② There's enough space for each of us.
③ There's not enough space for one of us.
④ There's not enough space for both of us.
⑤ There's not enough space for each other.

15 그의 계획 그 자체는 나쁘지 않았다.

① His plan it was not bad.
② His plan in it was not bad.
③ His plan in itself was not bad.
④ His plan was not bad by itself.
⑤ His plan was not bad for itself.

! 자주 나와요

16 다음 빈칸에 공통으로 들어갈 말로 알맞은 것은?

- I don't have a white shirt, so I'll buy ________.
- I read two books. ________ was a comic book, and the other was a magazine.

① it[It]
② one[One]
③ some[Some]
④ other[Other]
⑤ another[Another]

어려워요

17 다음 밑줄 친 부분 중 어법상 바르지 못한 것은?

There ① are three girls in the picture. They're holding hands with ② one another. One ③ is wearing jeans, ④ another is wearing a skirt, and ⑤ other is wearing a school uniform.

18 다음 빈칸에 it이 들어갈 수 없는 것은?

① This watch is nice. I love _____.
② I like that hat. I want to buy _____.
③ I forgot my pen. Can I borrow _____?
④ I can't find the switch. Where is _____?
⑤ He wrapped a present and put _____ in a box.

19 다음 두 문장이 같은 뜻이 되도록 빈칸에 알맞은 말을 쓰시오.

Did you travel to Vietnam alone last year?

→ Did you travel to Vietnam __________ __________ last year?

내신 완성 서술형

[20-21] 다음 문장에서 어법상 틀린 곳을 모두 찾아 바르게 고치시오.

Every actor were backstage.
All of them was practicing before the show.

20 __________ → __________

21 __________ → __________

22 다음 우리말과 일치하도록 조건에 맞게 영작하시오.

그 세 남자들은 서로 격려했다.

조건 1: encourage, another를 이용할 것
조건 2: 총 6단어로 작성할 것

→ ______________________________

____

23 다음은 Grace의 반 학생들이 좋아하는 스포츠에 관한 그래프이다. 그래프와 일치하도록 알맞은 대명사를 이용하여 문장을 완성하시오.

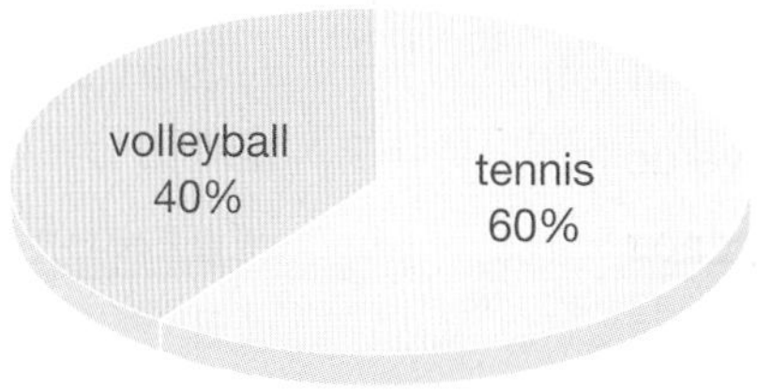

→ In Grace's class, __________ of the students like tennis and __________ __________ like volleyball.

WORD LIST

Grammar

□ endangered	형 멸종 위기의, 위험한
□ vase	명 꽃병
□ presentation	명 발표
□ item	명 물품
□ on sale	판매되는; *할인 중인
□ culture	명 문화
□ tradition	명 전통
□ laboratory	명 실험실
□ selfish	형 이기적인
□ stair	명 계단
□ iron	동 다림질하다
□ exchange	동 교환하다
□ international	형 국제적인
□ award	명 상
□ personality	명 성격
□ participate in	…에 참가하다
□ sold out	다 팔린, 매진된
□ experiment	명 실험

Reading

□ hole	명 구멍; 구덩이
□ deep	형 깊은
□ look down at	…를 내려다보다
□ pair	명 한 쌍
□ awful	형 끔찍한
□ get out (of)	(…에서) 나오다
□ give up	포기하다
□ escape	동 탈출하다, 벗어나다
□ terrible	형 끔찍한
□ deaf	형 귀가 먹은, 청각 장애가 있는
□ cheer for	응원하다
□ nowhere	부 아무 데도 (… 없다)
□ overcome	동 극복하다
□ absorb	동 흡수하다
□ glow	동 빛나다
□ suggest	동 제안하다; 시사하다
□ normally	부 보통
□ simply	부 그냥, 그저
□ invisible	형 보이지 않는

Communication

□ transfer	동 옮기다; 갈아타다
□ dictionary	명 사전
□ have[catch] a cold	감기에 걸리다

Final Test

□ lost and found	분실물 취급소
□ explain	동 설명하다
□ repeat	동 반복하다
□ boil	동 끓이다
□ chop	동 썰다
□ president	명 대통령
□ elect	동 선출하다
□ take care of	…를 돌보다
□ still	부 아직(도)
□ cost	동 (값·비용이) …이다
□ enough	형 충분한
□ magazine	명 잡지
□ wrap	동 싸다, 포장하다
□ encourage	동 격려하다

CHAPTER 13

비교 구문

GET READY

Jacob is **as smart as** Amy.
(Jacob은 Amy만큼 똑똑하다.)

Jacob is **smarter than** Amy.
(Jacob은 Amy보다 더 똑똑하다.)

Jacob is **the smartest** student in his class.
(Jacob은 그의 반에서 가장 똑똑한 학생이다.)

둘 이상의 사람이나 사물을 비교할 때는 형용사나 부사의 원급, 비교급, 최상급을 사용해요. 원급은 형용사나 부사의 원래 형태이며, 비교급은 '더 …한[하게]'의 의미를, 최상급은 '가장 …한[하게]'의 의미를 나타내요.

GRAMMAR FOCUS

A 비교 구문의 형태

1 원급 비교

원급 비교 구문 「**as + 형용사 / 부사의 원급 + as**」는 '…만큼 ~한[하게]'의 의미이다. 부정형은 「not as[so] + 형용사 / 부사의 원급 + as」이며, '…만큼 ~하지 않은[않게]'이라고 해석한다.

He is **as gentle as** his father.

Jane plays the piano **as well as** Sammy.

Today is **not as[so] cold as** yesterday.

2 비교급 비교

「**형용사 / 부사의 비교급 + than**」: '…보다 더 ~한[하게]'

The round table is **cheaper than** the old lamp.

This T-shirt is **more comfortable than** that one.

Wilson likes fish **more than** meat.

> **TIPS**
>
> 비교급의 강조
>
> 비교급 앞에 '훨씬'의 의미를 나타내는 much, far, still, even, a lot 등의 부사를 붙여 비교급을 강조할 수 있다. 단, 부사 very는 비교급을 수식할 수 없다.
>
> He exercises **much** *harder than* I do.
>
> (그는 나보다 훨씬 더 열심히 운동한다.)

3 최상급 비교

「**the + 형용사 / 부사의 최상급**」: '가장 …한[하게]'

Health is **the most important** thing.

최상급 비교 구문 뒤에 전치사와 함께 장소나 범위, 또는 비교 대상이 되는 명사가 올 수 있다.

1) 「**the + 최상급 + in + 장소 / 범위**」: '…에서 가장 ~한[하게]'

The panda is **the most popular** animal *in the zoo*.

2) 「**the + 최상급 + of + 복수명사**」: '…중에서 가장 ~한[하게]'

Bill is **the tallest** *of his brothers*.

내신 POINT PLUS

비교급과 최상급 만드는 법

	형용사/부사의 형태	비교급/최상급 만드는 법	예
규칙 변화	대부분의 단어	원급 + -er / -est	rich - rich**er** - rich**est**
	-e로 끝나는 단어	원급 + -r / -st	nice - nice**r** - nice**st**
	「자음 + y」로 끝나는 단어	y를 i로 고치고 + -er / -est	easy - eas**ier** - eas**iest**
	「단모음 + 단자음」으로 끝나는 단어	자음을 한 번 더 쓰고 + -er / -est	big - big**ger** - big**gest**
	일부 2음절 단어, 3음절 이상의 단어	more / most + 원급	famous - **more** famous - **most** famous
불규칙 변화	good / well - **better** - **best**		bad / ill - **worse** - **worst**
	many / much - **more** - **most**		little - **less** - **least**
	late - **later** - **latest** (시간이) 늦은		far - **farther** - **farthest** (거리) 먼
	late - **latter** - **last** (순서가) 나중인		far - **further** - **furthest** (정도) 나아간, (거리) 먼

Check-Up

A 다음 단어의 비교급과 최상급을 쓰시오.

1 hot – ________ – ________

2 good – ________ – ________

3 wise – ________ – ________

4 beautiful – ________ – ________

WORDS

B 다음 괄호 안에서 알맞은 말을 고르시오.

1 Light is (very / much) faster than sound.

2 Naomi is the (more / most) famous singer in Japan.

3 Bob can jump as (high / higher) as his older brother.

4 I think baseball is more interesting (as / than) basketball.

C 다음 밑줄 친 부분을 바르게 고치시오.

1 His hair is not as <u>darkest</u> as Ted's. → ________

2 This dress is <u>pretty</u> than my skirt. → ________

3 Fixing the car cost <u>little</u> than I expected. → ________

4 Elizabeth is <u>the more diligent</u> worker in her department. → ________

C
cost 동 (값·비용이) 들다
diligent 형 부지런한
department 명 부서

D 다음 우리말과 일치하도록 괄호 안의 단어를 이용하여 문장을 완성하시오.

1 Bruno는 Alice보다 훨씬 더 늦게 도착했다. (far, late)
→ Bruno arrived ________ ________ ________ Alice.

2 이 동네에서 가장 큰 가게는 무엇인가요? (large)
→ What is ________ ________ store in this town?

3 그 아기의 피부는 눈만큼 새하얗다. (white)
→ The baby's skin is ________ ________ ________ snow.

4 영어 시험이 나의 모든 시험들 중에서 가장 어려웠다. (difficult)
→ The English test was ________ ________ ________ of all my tests.

D
skin 명 피부

B 주요 비교 표현

1 원급을 이용한 표현

1) 「**as+원급+as possible**」: '가능한 한 …한[하게]'
= 「**as+원급+as+주어+can**」: '…가 할 수 있는 한 ~한[하게]'
She shouted **as loudly as possible**.
= She shouted **as loudly as she could**.

2) 「**배수사+as+원급+as**」: '…보다 몇 배로 ~한[하게]'
This book is **four times as thick as** that one.
The flight to Bali takes **twice as long as** the flight to Hong Kong.

TIPS

배수사를 이용한 표현
배수사는 twice[two times], three times와 같이 '… 배'를 나타낸다. 「배수사+as+원급+as」는 「배수사+비교급+than」으로도 나타낼 수 있다. 단, 배수사 twice는 보통 「twice+as+원급+as」로 나타낸다.
My bag is **three times as heavy as** yours. (내 가방은 네 것보다 세 배 더 무겁다.)
= My bag is **three times heavier than** yours.

2 비교급을 이용한 표현

1) 「**비교급+and+비교급**」: '점점 더 …한[하게]'
More and more people are traveling abroad.
The days get **shorter and shorter** as winter begins.

2) 「**the+비교급, the+비교급**」: '…하면 할수록, 더 ~하다'
The higher we climb, **the thinner** the air gets.
The longer he waited for her, **the angrier** he became.

3) 「**Which[Who] ... 비교급, A or B?**」: 'A와 B 중에서 어느 것이[누가] 더 …하니?'
Which do you like **better,** pizza **or** fried chicken**?**
Who is **more handsome,** Brad **or** Charles**?**

3 최상급을 이용한 표현

1) 「**one of the+최상급+복수명사**」: '가장 …한 것들 중 하나'
Busan is **one of the biggest cities** in Korea.
She is **one of the greatest poets** of all time.

2) 「**the+최상급+명사+(that)+주어+have ever v-ed**」: '…가 지금까지 ~한 것[사람] 중 가장 …한 (명사)'
That is **the scariest movie** *I've ever seen*.
You have **the most beautiful voice** *we have ever heard*.

Check-Up

A 다음 괄호 안에서 알맞은 말을 고르시오.

1 She is (kinder / the kindest) person I've ever met.

2 I will send you the file as (soon / sooner) as possible.

3 The tower is (four / four times) as high as this building.

4 He's one of the most respected (pianist / pianists) in the world.

B 다음 괄호 안의 단어를 빈칸에 알맞은 형태로 쓰시오.

1 They ate breakfast as ________ as they could. (quickly)

2 The office is five times ________ ________ my room. (big)

3 The ________ I got to know him, the ________ I liked him. (much)

C 다음 밑줄 친 부분을 바르게 고치시오.

1 The situation is getting bad and bad. → ________

2 Which is more valuable to you, money and friends? → ________

3 The cold it becomes, the easier you can catch a cold. → ________

D 다음 우리말과 일치하도록 괄호 안의 단어를 이용하여 문장을 완성하시오.

1 우리 아빠는 가능한 한 자주 자전거로 출근하신다. (often)
→ My father rides his bike to work ________ ________ ________ ________.

2 Jeff는 내가 지금까지 만난 사람 중 가장 독특한 사람이다. (unique)
→ Jeff is ________ ________ ________ person I ________ ________ met.

3 돌고래는 지구상에서 가장 똑똑한 동물들 중 하나이다. (smart)
→ Dolphins are ________ ________ ________ ________ animals on Earth.

WORDS

A
respect 동 존경하다

C
situation 명 상황
valuable 형 소중한

D
unique 형 독특한
dolphin 명 돌고래
earth 명 지구; 세상

Grammar Practice

A 다음 밑줄 친 부분을 바르게 고치시오.

1 Apples are as not sour as lemons. → ____________
2 Is Earth farthest from the Sun than Mars? → ____________
3 That was the long movie we've ever seen. → ____________
4 The closer our vacation gets, the happy we are. → ____________

WORDS

A
sour 형 (맛이) 신

B 다음 빈칸에 들어갈 말을 보기 에서 골라 알맞은 형태로 쓰시오.

보기 warm famous brief fluently

1 Marco speaks Spanish ________ than Korean.
2 The weather is becoming ________ and ________.
3 Please be as ________ as possible when you write a report.
4 Many people agree that he is the ________ artist in history.

B
brief 형 간결한, 간단한
fluently 부 유창하게

C 다음 보기 처럼 괄호 안의 단어를 이용하여 주어진 문장을 비교 문장으로 바꾸시오.

보기 It was 15°C yesterday. Today, it is 20°C. (warm)
→ Today is warmer than yesterday.

1 I weigh 50kg. My brother weighs 63kg. (heavy)
→ My brother is ________ ________ me.
2 Emily swims 50 meters in 30 seconds. Joy also swims 50 meters in 30 seconds. (fast)
→ Joy swims ________ ________ ________ Emily.
3 Owen is 170cm tall. Jim is 174cm tall. Thomas is 180cm tall. (tall)
→ Thomas is ________ ________ boy of the three.
4 The silver ring is $40. The gold ring is $120. (times, expensive)
→ The gold ring is ________ ________ ________ ________ than the silver ring.

C
weigh 동 무게가 …이다

내신 완성 Grammar Practice

1 다음 빈칸에 들어갈 말로 알맞은 것은?

Jessie earns ________ her sister.

① two as much
② two as much as
③ twice as more as
④ twice as much as
⑤ twice as much than

2 다음 빈칸에 들어갈 말이 바르게 짝지어진 것은?

- The scientists will do ________ research.
- Brian eats the ________ of the three people.

① far – little
② farther – less
③ farther – least
④ further – less
⑤ further – least

3 다음 중 어법상 바르지 못한 것을 모두 고르시오. (2개)

William's Shop is ① the cheapest store in our town. Most of their products are ② very cheaper than those ③ of other stores. But the store is not the ④ most popular because their products are ⑤ the baddest in town.

4 다음 우리말과 일치하도록 괄호 안의 단어를 이용하여 문장을 완성하시오.

(1) 나에게는 포크가 젓가락보다 더 편리하다. (convenient)

→ A fork ________ ________ ________ ________ chopsticks for me.

(2) 이야기를 하면서, 그녀는 점점 더 신이 났다. (more, excited)

→ As she talked, she got ________ ________ ________ ________.

WORDS

1
earn 동 (돈을) 벌다

2
research 명 연구

3
product 명 상품, 제품

4
convenient 형 편리한
chopstick 명 젓가락 (한 짝)

서술형에 나오는 WRITING

A 다음 우리말과 일치하도록 괄호 안의 말을 바르게 배열하시오.

1 이곳은 그가 지금까지 방문한 곳 중 가장 큰 박물관이다.
(visited, is, museum, he, this, ever, the largest, has)
→ ______________________________

2 네가 더 열심히 공부하면 할수록, 네 성적은 더 나아질 것이다.
(study, the, be, your grades, harder, the, will, better, you)
→ ______________________________

B 다음 우리말과 일치하도록 괄호 안의 단어를 이용하여 문장을 완성하시오.

1 낙타와 코끼리 중 어느 것이 더 작니? (small)
→ ________ ________ ________, a camel ________ an elephant?

2 그것은 세상에서 가장 깊은 호수들 중 하나이다. (deep, lake)
→ It is one of ________ ________ ________ in the world.

3 저 드레스는 네 것보다 훨씬 더 매력적이다. (much, attractive)
→ That dress is ________ ________ ________ ________ yours.

C 다음 호텔 정보를 보고, 괄호 안의 단어를 이용하여 문장을 완성하시오.

Hills Hotel
- built in 2009
- rooms: 70
- $140 per night

Star Hotel
- built in 2009
- rooms: 50
- $180 per night

Beachside Hotel
- built in 2018
- rooms: 100
- $230 per night

1 The Hills Hotel is ________ ________ ________ the Star Hotel. (old)
2 The Beachside Hotel has ________ ________ rooms of the three hotels. (many)
3 The Star Hotel is ________ ________ ________ the Hills Hotel. (expensive)

READING WITH GRAMMAR

1

Look at this number: 10,000,000,000,000,000,000,000,000,000,000,000,000,000,000,000,000,000,000,000,000,000,000,000,000,000,000,000,000,000,000,000,000,000,000. Is it **the largest number you've ever seen**? What is it? A trillion? No, it's not. Having 100 zeros, it's **much bigger than** a trillion.

Mathematician Dr. Edward Kasner wrote it down in 1938. Then he asked his nephew to think of a name for it. The nine-year-old boy decided on "googol." So, how big is a googol? Imagine how many pieces of sand could fit in the universe. A googol is (greater, times, 10 billion, than) that. It also inspired the name of **one of the most successful technology companies** in the world. That's right—Google is a misspelling of googol! That company chose the name to show that their search engine can find lots and lots of information.

1 위 글의 제목으로 가장 알맞은 것은?

① The Size of the Universe
② Googol: The Number with 100 Zeros
③ The Greatest Mathematician in History
④ A Nine-Year-Old Boy Who Was a Math Genius
⑤ How Google Has Become a Successful Company

서술형

2 위 글의 괄호 안의 단어를 바르게 배열하시오.

→ A googol is ______________________________ that.
(greater, times, 10 billion, than)

WORDS

trillion 명 1조 mathematician 명 수학자 nephew 명 (남자) 조카 sand 명 모래 universe 명 우주 billion 명 10억 inspire 동 고무하다; *영감을 주다 successful 형 [1] __________ technology 명 기술 company 명 회사 misspelling 명 틀린 철자 문제 genius 명 천재

2

You buy a beautiful shirt, but you don't have pants to match it. So you buy new pants and decide that you need matching shoes. Over and over, you go out and buy new stuff to match what you already own. This is called "the Diderot Effect."

In the 18th century, a man named Denis Diderot received a beautiful dressing gown. Compared to this gown, the rest of his home seemed **less attractive**. He thought he needed **more** works of art on his walls and **nicer** furniture in his rooms. He started to buy **the best** and **newest** things in order to match the special gown. The ___(A)___ he bought, the ___(B)___ he wanted new things. Ever since Diderot mentioned this story in an essay, people have used the expression "the Diderot Effect" to describe similar situations.

1 Fill in the blank with a word from the passage.

The Diderot Effect means that you keep buying new things to ________ what you already have.

2 Which is the best pair for blanks (A) and (B)?

	(A)	(B)		(A)	(B)
①	much	– more	②	much	– better
③	more	– more	④	more	– better
⑤	better	– many			

WORDS match 동 어울리다, 맞추다 over and over 반복해서 stuff 명 물건 dressing gown (잠옷 위에 입는) 가운, 실내복 compared to …와 비교하여 attractive 형 매력적인, 멋진 furniture 명 [1] ________ mention 동 말하다, 언급하다 expression 명 [2] ________ describe 동 묘사하다 similar 형 비슷한, 유사한 문제 keep v-ing …를 계속하다

내신에 나오는 COMMUNICATION

A 비교하기

A: **Who is faster**, Ethan **or** Tony**?**
(Ethan과 Tony 중 누가 더 빠르니?)

B: Ethan is **faster than** Tony.
(Ethan이 Tony보다 더 빨라.)

A: Really?
(정말이니?)

B: Yes. Ethan even runs **faster than** Carl!
(응. Ethan은 심지어 Carl보다 더 빨리 달려!)

두 대상을 비교하여 설명할 때 '비교급+than'으로 표현할 수 있다. 비교의 정도가 같거나 비슷할 때는 'as+원급+as'로 표현할 수 있다.

EXPRESSION PLUS

A: **Which country** do you think **is bigger**, Canada **or** Russia**?**
(너는 캐나다와 러시아 중 어느 나라가 더 크다고 생각하니?)

B: I think Russia is **bigger than** Canada. (나는 러시아가 캐나다보다 더 크다고 생각해.)

A: I think Ava is **more popular than** Jessica. (나는 Ava가 Jessica보다 더 인기 있다고 생각해.)

B: No, Jessica is **as popular as** Ava. (아니야, Jessica는 Ava만큼 인기 있어.)

Check-Up

1 다음 대화의 빈칸에 들어갈 말로 알맞지 않은 것은?

A: Is this film longer than what we watched last time?
B: ______________________

① I don't know, but maybe not.
② I have never watched a film before.
③ No, this film is much shorter than that one.
④ This film is 20 minutes longer than that one.
⑤ This film is as long as what we watched last time.

WORDS
1
film 명 영화

2 다음 괄호 안의 단어를 이용하여 대화를 완성하시오.

A: Which subject do you think is __________ __________, math __________ science? (interesting)
B: I think science is more interesting.

B 경고하기

A: The water looks very deep over there.
(저쪽은 물이 매우 깊어 보여.)

B: It does. **Make sure not to** swim there.
(맞아. 저기에서 수영하지 않도록 해.)

A: Okay. I'll keep that in mind.
(알겠어. 명심하도록 할게.)

상대방에게 어떤 행동을 하거나 하지 말도록 경고할 때는 'Make sure to-v' 또는 'Make sure not to-v' 등으로 말할 수 있다. 이와 유사한 표현으로는 'Make sure (that) you+동사원형', 'Be sure to-v' 등이 있으며, 아랫사람에게 강한 경고의 의미로 'You had better+동사원형'이라고 말할 수도 있다.

EXPRESSION PLUS

- **Make sure you** wear your seat belt. (안전벨트를 매도록 해라.)
- **Be sure not to** come home late. (집에 늦게 오지 않도록 해라.)
- **Be careful not to** burn yourself while cooking. (요리할 때 불에 데지 않도록 조심해라.)
- **Be sure that you** don't waste water. (물을 낭비하지 않도록 해라.)
- **You had better not** drive tonight. (오늘 밤엔 운전하지 않도록 해라.)

Check-Up

1 다음 그림을 보고 할 수 있는 경고 표현으로 알맞지 않은 것은?

① Make sure to be quiet.
② Be sure that you are quiet.
③ Make sure you make any noise.
④ Be careful not to make any noise.
⑤ You had better not make any noise.

WORDS

1
make a noise
떠들다, 소란을 피우다

2 다음 우리말과 일치하도록 괄호 안의 말을 바르게 배열하시오.

같은 실수를 다시 하지 않도록 해라.
(not, be, sure, again, make the same mistake, to)

→ ______________________________

FINAL TEST

1 다음 중 영어 단어와 우리말 뜻이 잘못 연결된 것은?

① skin - 피부
② similar - 비슷한
③ brief - 간결한
④ universe - 우주
⑤ valuable - 평범한

2 다음 빈칸에 들어갈 말을 보기 에서 골라 쓰시오.

보기 diligent　sour　convenient

→ This photo print is ________ to use.

3 다음 대화의 빈칸에 들어갈 말로 알맞은 것은?

A: These two are our best-selling jackets.
B: I like both of them. ________
A: The white one is cheaper than the black one.

① Which one is cheaper?
② What are you looking for?
③ Do you think it will suit me?
④ How can I buy the black one?
⑤ Why is the white one cheaper?

4 대화가 자연스럽게 이어지도록 (A)~(D)를 바르게 배열하시오.

(A) Be sure to bring stomach medicine.
(B) I heard you're traveling overseas for the holidays.
(C) Okay. I'll buy some in advance.
(D) Yes. It will be my first trip abroad. Can you give me any advice?

________ → ________ → ________ → ________

5 다음 대화의 밑줄 친 부분과 바꿔 쓸 수 없는 것은?

A: I'm going to the court to watch a tennis match.
B: Sounds interesting! But make sure to stay seated during the match.
A: Oh, I'll keep that in mind.

① be sure to stay seated
② make sure you stay seated
③ be sure that you stay seated
④ be careful not to stay seated
⑤ make sure that you stay seated

! 자주 나와요

[6-8] 다음 빈칸에 들어갈 말로 알맞은 것을 고르시오.

6 This is ________ restaurant in the neighborhood.

① nice
② nicer
③ the nicest
④ more nice
⑤ the most nice

7 The situation was ________ than I thought.

① serious
② more serious
③ even serious
④ the more serious
⑤ the most serious

8 The earlier we get there, ________ our seats will be.

① good
② better
③ best
④ the better
⑤ the best

[9-10] 다음 빈칸에 들어갈 말로 알맞지 않은 것을 고르시오.

9 The magic show was ________ more popular than the musical.

① far ② even ③ much
④ very ⑤ a lot

10 My new tent is not so ________ as my old one.

① big ② small ③ worse
④ heavy ⑤ expensive

! 자주 나와요

11 다음 빈칸에 공통으로 들어갈 말로 알맞은 것은?

- I think that inner beauty is ________ important than appearance.
- Who is ________ intelligent, Amy or Sally?

① even ② better ③ little
④ more ⑤ most

! 어려워요

[12-13] 다음 우리말과 일치하도록 괄호 안의 단어를 이용하여 문장을 완성하시오.

12 그녀의 방이 내 것보다 훨씬 더 크다. (far, large)

→ Her room ________ ________ ________ ________ ________.

13 그곳은 서울에서 가장 유명한 역사적인 장소들 중 하나이다. (famous)

→ That is ________ ________ ________ ________ ________ historical places in Seoul.

14 다음 중 어법상 바르지 못한 것은?

① It grew darker and darker outside.
② The tree is three times as tall as I am.
③ I think you are more talented than Bella.
④ The Nile River is the longest river in the world.
⑤ This is hotter summer that I've ever experienced.

! 어려워요

15 다음 중 어법상 바른 것은?

① The colder it gets, harder it is to sleep.
② He has twice as much shoes as Nick.
③ Her English skills are a lot good than mine.
④ The theater is little crowded than yesterday.
⑤ More and more people are getting interested in camping.

16 다음 빈칸에 들어갈 말이 바르게 짝지어진 것은?

- Driving is ________ difficult thing he has ever tried.
- She is not ________ funny as her sister.

① still - so ② more - so
③ more - as ④ the most - as
⑤ the most - more

17 다음 우리말을 영어로 바르게 옮긴 것을 모두 고르시오. (2개)

이 전구는 저것보다 10배 더 밝다.

① This bulb is ten times bright than that one.
② This bulb is ten times as bright as that one.
③ This bulb is ten times brighter than that one.
④ This bulb is ten times brightest than that one.
⑤ This bulb is as ten times brighter than that one.

18 다음 괄호 안의 단어를 이용하여 대화를 완성하시오.

A: It's freezing outside. Right now the temperature is -10˚C.
B: What will the weather be like tomorrow?
A: It will be -8˚C. So, tomorrow will be ________ ________ today. (warm)

내신 완성 서술형

[19-20] 다음 글에서 밑줄 친 부분을 바르게 고치시오.

This vase is the <u>more</u> expensive product in our store. We try to be as careful <u>than</u> we can when we move it.

19 more → ________

20 than → ________

[21-23] 다음 표를 보고, 괄호 안의 단어를 이용하여 문장을 완성하시오.

	Patrick	Andy	Tim
Age	18	15	17
Weight	68kg	60kg	60kg
Height	178cm	165cm	170cm

21 Andy is ________ ________ Patrick. (young)

22 Tim is ________ ________ ________ Andy. (heavy)

23 Patrick is ________ ________ ________ the three. (tall)

WORD LIST

Grammar

□ cost	동 (값 · 비용이) 들다
□ diligent	형 부지런한
□ department	명 부서
□ skin	명 피부
□ respect	동 존경하다
□ situation	명 상황
□ valuable	형 소중한
□ unique	형 독특한
□ dolphin	명 돌고래
□ earth	명 지구; 세상
□ sour	형 (맛이) 신
□ brief	형 간결한, 간단한
□ fluently	부 유창하게
□ weigh	동 무게가 …이다
□ research	명 연구
□ product	명 상품, 제품
□ convenient	형 편리한

Reading

□ nephew	명 (남자) 조카
□ sand	명 모래
□ universe	명 우주
□ inspire	동 고무하다; 영감을 주다
□ successful	형 성공적인
□ technology	명 기술
□ company	명 회사
□ genius	명 천재
□ match	동 어울리다, 맞추다
□ over and over	반복해서
□ stuff	명 물건
□ compared to	…와 비교하여
□ attractive	형 매력적인, 멋진
□ furniture	명 가구
□ mention	동 말하다, 언급하다
□ expression	명 표현
□ describe	동 묘사하다
□ similar	형 비슷한, 유사한

Communication

□ film	명 영화
□ make a noise	떠들다, 소란을 피우다

Final Test

□ overseas	부 해외로
□ neighborhood	명 근처, 인근
□ serious	형 심각한
□ inner	형 내부의, 내면의
□ intelligent	형 똑똑한
□ experience	동 경험하다
□ crowded	형 붐비는
□ bulb	명 전구
□ freezing	형 너무나 추운
□ temperature	명 온도
□ vase	명 꽃병
□ weight	명 무게, 체중
□ height	명 높이, 키

CHAPTER 14

가정법

GET READY

If I **were** taller, I **could reach** the shelf.
(내가 키가 더 크다면, 선반에 손이 닿을 수 있을 텐데.)

If you **had booked** the tickets, we **could have seen** the movie.
(네가 표를 예매했었다면, 우리는 영화를 볼 수 있었을 텐데.)

I wish I **could travel** to the past.
(내가 과거로 여행할 수 있다면 좋을 텐데.)

이루어질 수 없는 일을 가정하거나 상상할 때 가정법을 사용해요. 현재 사실과 반대되는 상황이나 실현 가능성이 희박한 일을 가정할 때는 가정법 과거를, 과거 사실과 반대되는 상황을 가정할 때는 가정법 과거완료를 써요.

GRAMMAR FOCUS

A 가정법의 의미와 형태

1 가정법의 의미

가정법은 실제로 일어나지 않은 일이나 실현 가능성이 희박한 일에 대한 가정이나 소망을 표현할 때 쓴다. 가정법에서는 문장의 형식상의 시제와 의미상의 시제가 일치하지 않으므로 해석에 유의한다.

2 가정법 과거

가정법 과거는 현재 사실과 반대되는 상황이나 현재 또는 미래에 실현 가능성이 희박한 일을 가정할 때 쓴다. 현재시제로 해석한다는 점에 유의한다.

1) 형태: 「If+주어+동사의 과거형, 주어+would[should/could/might]+동사원형」

2) 의미: 만약 …라면, ~할 텐데

If they **were** in Rome, they **could look** around the Colosseum.
(← As they're not in Rome, they can't look around the Colosseum.)

If I **played** soccer well, I **could join** the soccer team.
(← As I don't play soccer well, I can't join the soccer team.)

> **TIPS**
> 가정법 과거 문장의 if절에서 be동사를 쓸 경우, 보통 주어의 인칭과 수에 관계없이 were를 쓰지만 was를 쓰기도 한다.

3 가정법 과거완료

가정법 과거완료는 과거 사실과 반대되는 상황을 가정할 때 쓴다. 과거시제로 해석한다는 점에 유의한다.

1) 형태: 「If+주어+had v-ed, 주어+would[should/could/might]+have v-ed」

2) 의미: 만약 …했다면, ~했을 텐데

If Abby **had taken** a train, she **wouldn't have been** late for the class.
(← As Abby didn't take a train, she was late for the class.)

If it **had** not **rained**, we **could have gone** on a picnic.
(← As it rained, we couldn't go on a picnic.)

> **+ 내신 POINT PLUS**
>
> 단순 조건문과 가정법 과거
>
> 1 단순 조건문(직설법): if는 단순 조건문을 만드는 접속사로도 쓰여 실제로 발생 가능한 일을 가정한다.
> **If** she **knows** his address, she **will tell** you. (그녀가 그의 주소를 알면, 네게 말해 줄 거야.)
> → 그녀가 그의 주소를 알 가능성이 어느 정도 있음
>
> 2 가정법 과거: 현재 사실과 반대되거나 실현 가능성이 희박할 경우에 쓴다.
> **If** she **knew** his address, she **would tell** you. (만약 그녀가 그의 주소를 안다면, 네게 말해 줄 텐데.)
> → 그녀가 그의 주소를 알 가능성이 거의 없음

Check-Up

A 다음 괄호 안에서 알맞은 말을 고르시오.

1 If I (have / had) two fans, I could give you one.

2 If you (turn / turned) right, you will find the theater.

3 If I (ran / had run), I wouldn't have missed the bus.

4 What (will / would) you do if you were the president?

B 다음 밑줄 친 부분을 바르게 고치시오.

1 If I were you, I <u>can drive</u> safely. → ________

2 If he had had more money, he <u>would buy</u> two jackets. → ________

3 If it <u>rained</u> tomorrow, the festival will be canceled. → ________

4 If they <u>don't have</u> a test tomorrow, they could play computer games. → ________

C 다음 우리말과 일치하도록 괄호 안의 단어를 빈칸에 알맞은 형태로 쓰시오.

1 내가 그곳에 있다면, 초과 근무를 해야 할 텐데. (be)

→ If I ________ there, I would have to do overtime.

2 네가 더 일찍 왔었다면, 그녀를 볼 수 있었을 텐데. (come)

→ If you ________ ________ earlier, you could have seen her.

3 우리가 자리를 예약했었다면, 한 시간 동안 기다리지 않았을 텐데. (wait)

→ If we had reserved a table, we wouldn't ________ ________ for an hour.

D 다음 두 문장이 같은 뜻이 되도록 빈칸에 알맞은 말을 쓰시오.

1 As I have a lot of things to do, I can't join you.

→ If I ________ ________ a lot of things to do, I ________ ________ you.

2 As I threw away the receipt, I couldn't exchange the shirt.

→ If I ________ ________ ________ the receipt, I ________ ________ ________ the shirt.

WORDS

A
fan 명 선풍기

B
cancel 동 취소하다

C
do overtime 초과 근무를 하다
reserve 동 예약하다

D
throw away 버리다
receipt 명 영수증

B I wish 가정법

1 I wish 가정법 과거

현재나 미래에 이루기 힘들거나 실현 가능성이 거의 없는 소망을 나타내는 표현이다.

1) 형태: 「I wish+주어+동사의 과거형」

2) 의미: …라면 좋을 텐데

I wish I **were** a famous model.
(← I'm sorry that I am not a famous model.)

I wish I **spent** more time with you.
(← I'm sorry that I don't spend more time with you.)

I wish I **could speak** well in front of an audience.
(← I'm sorry that I can't speak well in front of an audience.)

2 I wish 가정법 과거완료

과거 사실에 반대되는 소망이나 과거의 일에 대한 아쉬움을 나타내는 표현이다.

1) 형태: 「I wish+주어+had v-ed」

2) 의미: …했더라면 좋았을 텐데

I wish I **had invented** the item.
(← I'm sorry that I didn't invent the item.)

I wish I **had studied** hard for the exam.
(← I'm sorry that I didn't study hard for the exam.)

I can't open the door. **I wish** I **hadn't lost** the key.
(← I'm sorry that I lost the key.)

TIPS

wish와 hope

wish는 실현되지 않은 일이나 실현 불가능한 일에 대한 소망을, hope는 실현 가능한 일에 대한 소망을 나타낸다.

I **wish** you were my sister.
(네가 내 여동생이라면 좋을 텐데.)

I **hope** you will come back now.
(나는 네가 지금 돌아오면 좋겠어.)

+ 내신 POINT PLUS

wish의 여러 가지 의미

wish는 뒤에 오는 목적어의 형태에 따라 다양한 의미를 나타낸다.

I **wish to speak** with the manager. (저는 관리자와 이야기하고 싶습니다.)
「wish+to-v」: …를 원하다

I **wish you a Merry Christmas.** (즐거운 크리스마스 되길 기원합니다.)
「wish+목적어+목적격 보어(명사)」: …에게 ~를 기원하다

I **wish (that) I were** in Africa. (내가 아프리카에 있다면 좋을 텐데.)
「wish+(that)+가정법」: …가 ~라면 좋을 텐데

Check-Up

A 다음 괄호 안에서 알맞은 말을 고르시오.

1 I (wish / hope) I will win the final match.

2 It is only Monday. I wish today (is / were) Saturday.

3 I wish I (can / could) play many musical instruments.

4 I bought two postcards in Spain. I wish I (bought / had bought) more.

WORDS

A
musical instrument 악기

B 다음 밑줄 친 부분을 바르게 고치시오.

1 I wish I can record a song in this studio. → ________

2 It's really cold these days. I wish it is spring. → ________

3 I wish you come to my birthday party yesterday. → ________

4 I wish I brought my camera when I traveled to Japan. → ________

B
record 동 기록하다; *녹음하다

C 다음 우리말과 일치하도록 괄호 안의 단어를 빈칸에 알맞은 형태로 쓰시오.

1 내가 지난밤에 늦게까지 깨어 있지 않았더라면 좋았을 텐데. (stay)
→ I wish I ________ ________ up late last night.

2 우리 집에 수영장이 있다면 좋을 텐데. (have)
→ I wish I ________ a swimming pool at my house.

3 버스가 덜 붐비면 좋을 텐데. (be)
→ I wish the bus ________ less crowded.

D 다음 두 문장이 같은 뜻이 되도록 빈칸에 알맞은 말을 쓰시오.

1 I'm sorry that I didn't wear rain boots.
→ I wish I ________ ________ rain boots.

2 I'm sorry that I spent all my money shopping.
→ I wish I ________ ________ all my money shopping.

3 I'm sorry that I don't have a beautiful voice like Fred.
→ I wish I ________ a beautiful voice like Fred.

D
voice 명 목소리

Grammar Practice

A 다음 밑줄 친 부분을 바르게 고치시오.

1 I wish Bruce didn't quit his job last year. → ________

2 If there is enough oxygen on Mars, we could live there. → ________

3 I wish many seats had been left in the library now. → ________

4 If they didn't watch the horror movie last night, they could have slept well. → ________

B 다음 괄호 안의 단어를 빈칸에 알맞은 형태로 쓰시오.

1 If I ________ braver, I would become a firefighter. (be)

2 I wish I ________ ________ Spanish before I went to Spain. (learn)

3 If Jinsu hadn't played for our team, we wouldn't ________ ________. (win)

4 I am poor at painting landscapes. I wish I ________ ________ landscapes well. (can, paint)

C 다음 두 문장이 같은 뜻이 되도록 빈칸에 알맞은 말을 쓰시오.

1 I'm sorry that my school is not close to my house.
→ I wish my school ________ ________ to my house.

2 As Jack doesn't know Anna's phone number, he can't call her.
→ If Jack ________ Anna's phone number, he ________ ________ her.

3 As I had an appointment, I didn't stay home.
→ If I ________ ________ an appointment, I would ________ ________ home.

4 I wish you had seen the musical with us last weekend.
→ I'm sorry you ________ ________ the musical with us last weekend.

WORDS

A
oxygen 명 산소

B
be poor at …를 못하다
landscape 명 풍경(화)

C
appointment 명 약속

내신 완성 Grammar Practice

1 다음 빈칸에 들어갈 말로 알맞은 것은?

I wish you __________ Professor Park's lecture last week.

① attend
② attended
③ have attended
④ had attended
⑤ could attend

WORDS

1
professor 명 교수

2 다음 문장을 가정법으로 바르게 고친 것은?

As Ben hurt his leg, he couldn't go skiing.

① If Ben hurt his leg, he could go skiing.
② If Ben didn't hurt his leg, he could go skiing.
③ If Ben didn't hurt his leg, he couldn't go skiing.
④ If Ben hadn't hurt his leg, he could gone skiing.
⑤ If Ben hadn't hurt his leg, he could have gone skiing.

3 다음 중 어법상 바르지 못한 것은?

① I wish my family were on vacation now.
② I wish I had put on sunblock before I left my home.
③ What would happen if there are no trees in the world?
④ If Jolie had enough time, she could read these books today.
⑤ If I hadn't dropped my cell phone, it wouldn't have broken.

3
put on …를 바르다

4 다음 우리말과 일치하도록 괄호 안의 단어를 이용하여 문장을 완성하시오.

(1) 내가 그때 너의 충고를 받아들였더라면 좋았을 텐데. (take, advice)
→ I wish I ______________________ at that time.

(2) 그녀가 우유에 알레르기가 없다면, 그것들을 먹을 수 있을 텐데. (have, eat)
→ If she __________ an allergy to milk, she __________ them.

4
take advice 충고를 받아들이다
allergy 명 알레르기

서술형에 나오는 WRITING

A 다음 우리말과 일치하도록 괄호 안의 말을 바르게 배열하시오.

1 내가 더 오래 머무를 수 있으면 좋을 텐데.
(could, I, stay, wish, I, longer)
→ ______________________________

2 Bill이 운전하지 않았다면, 그 사고는 일어나지 않았을 텐데.
(driven, if, not, wouldn't, had, the accident, have, Bill, happened)
→ ______________________________

3 내가 그 의자를 다른 색으로 샀더라면 좋았을 텐데.
(the chair, I, bought, I, had, in another color, wish)
→ ______________________________

B 다음 문장을 가정법 문장으로 바꿔 쓰시오.

1 I'm sorry that I forgot about my sister's birthday.
→ I wish ______________________________.

2 As I didn't know your address, I didn't pick you up.
→ If I ______________________________.

3 As you don't have enough apples, you can't make an apple pie.
→ If you ______________________________.

C 다음 괄호 안의 말을 이용하여 문자 메시지를 완성하시오.

Joe

Hey, Charles! It has been a year since you went back to Chicago. I miss the time we took an art class together. There will be a Klimt exhibition at City Museum. If you were here, we **1** ______________ (go there) together. I wish I **2** ______________ (can, have conversations) about his paintings with you. I'm looking forward to seeing you someday.

1

When two young women were dining at a fancy restaurant, ① a lady came to their table and spoke to one of them. "I'm sorry to bother you, but you look just like my daughter. ② She died last year. **I wish** I **could see** her one last time. May I ask you a favor? Could you wave to me and say, 'Good-bye, ③ Mom,' when I leave?" The woman felt sorry for ④ her, so she agreed to do as the lady had asked. But before the lady left, the young woman stood up and offered to pay for the lady's dinner. When her friend asked why, she replied. "At this moment, ⑤ she thinks I am her daughter. If her daughter ________ alive, she would do the same thing."

1 위 글의 밑줄 친 ①~⑤ 중 가리키는 바가 다른 하나는?

① ② ③ ④ ⑤

2 위 글의 빈칸에 be동사를 알맞은 형태로 쓰시오.

→ ________

WORDS
dine 동 식사를 하다 fancy 형 값비싼, 고급의 bother 동 [1] ________ favor 명 부탁 wave 동 손을 흔들다
feel sorry for …를 안쓰럽게 여기다 offer 동 제의[제안]하다 pay 동 지불하다 reply 동 [2] ________ moment 명 순간
alive 형 살아 있는

2

Have you ever thought, "(wish, I, my, wings, car, had) so I could fly over the traffic"? An American company has developed a car that could make your dream come true. It has two seats, four wheels, and foldable wings. To extend the wings, you just need to push a button. The car will then transform into a plane in just thirty seconds! It can fly distances of around 800 kilometers and at speeds of up to 185 km/h. Because of its flying function, it requires a runway to take off, and drivers need a pilot's license. It sounds just like other planes, but in bad weather, it can still land successfully and drive on the road.

The company that made the car believes it will be on sale soon. Now, imagine what it **would be** like **if** you **had** this amazing car. How wonderful it would be!

1 Which is NOT true about the flying car?

① It has wings that can be folded or extended.
② It can be used both as a car and as a plane.
③ It can reach speeds of 185 km/h in the air.
④ It can take off without a runway.
⑤ To drive it, owners must have a pilot's license.

! 서술형

2 Unscramble the words in brackets.

→ ______________________________
(wish, I, my, wings, car, had)

WORDS
traffic 명 차량들, 교통(량)　develop 동 [1] __________　come true 실현되다　wheel 명 바퀴　foldable 형 접을 수 있는　extend 동 펼치다　transform 동 변하다　distance 명 거리　function 명 [2] __________　require 동 필요하다　runway 명 활주로　take off 이륙하다　license 명 면허증　land 동 착륙하다　문제 reach 동 (특정 속도에) 이르다[달하다]

A 기원하기

A: I have a singing contest tomorrow.
(나는 내일 노래 대회가 있어.)

B: **I wish you the best of luck.**
(너에게 행운이 있길 빌게.)

A: Thank you so much.
(정말 고마워.)

상대방에게 행운을 빌어 줄 때는 'I wish you the best of luck.'이라고 말할 수 있다. 이와 유사한 표현으로는 'I wish you all the best.', 'I wish you good luck.' 등이 있으며, 'I hope ...'(…하기를 바랄게)라는 표현을 이용하여 상대방에게 좋은 일을 기원해 줄 수 있다.

EXPRESSION PLUS

- I wish you well. / Good luck to you. (행운을 빌게.)
- I'll keep my fingers crossed for you. (널 위해 행운을 빌어 줄게.)
- I hope everything goes well. (모든 일이 잘되기를 바랄게.)

Check-Up

1 다음 중 쓰임이 나머지 넷과 다른 것은?

① Good luck.
② I wish you well.
③ I think you are very lucky.
④ I hope everything goes well.
⑤ I'll keep my fingers crossed for you.

WORDS

2 다음 대화의 빈칸에 들어갈 말로 알맞은 것은?

A: I'm nervous about my presentation.
B: Don't worry. ____________

① How are you feeling?
② Would you say that again?
③ I wish you the best of luck.
④ How can I listen to your presentation?
⑤ You're not good at giving presentations.

2
nervous 형 불안해하는
presentation 명 발표

B 반복 요청하기

A: What's your phone number?
(네 전화번호가 뭐니?)
B: It's 212-483-8749.
(212-483-8749야.)
A: **Can you say that again?**
(다시 말해 줄 수 있니?)

상대방의 말을 잘 듣지 못했거나 이해하지 못한 경우에는 'Can[Would/Could] you say that again?'이라는 표현으로 반복해 주기를 요청할 수 있다. 이와 유사한 표현으로는 'Can you repeat that, please?' 등이 있다.

EXPRESSION PLUS

- I'm sorry? (뭐라고 했니?)
- Pardon me? (뭐라고?)
- I beg your pardon? (뭐라고 하셨죠?)
- What did you say? (뭐라고 말했니?)
- Would you mind repeating that? (한 번 더 말씀해 주시겠어요?)

Check-Up

1 다음 대화의 빈칸에 들어갈 말로 알맞지 않은 것은?

A: I wonder where the public restroom is.
B: ____________________

① I'm sorry?
② What did you say?
③ Can you repeat after me?
④ Can you say that again?
⑤ Would you mind repeating that?

2 다음 우리말과 일치하도록 괄호 안의 단어를 이용하여 문장을 완성하시오.

뭐라고 하셨죠? (beg, pardon)

→ ________ ________ ________ ________?

WORDS

1
wonder 동 궁금하다
public 형 대중의, 공공의
restroom 명 화장실

FINAL TEST

1 다음 밑줄 친 단어와 유사한 의미의 단어는?

They stayed at a fancy hotel near the ocean.

① big ② quiet ③ alive
④ foldable ⑤ expensive

2 다음 우리말과 일치하도록 빈칸에 알맞은 말을 쓰시오.

서울에서 부산까지 거리는 얼마인가요?

→ What's the ________ from Seoul to Busan?

3 다음 대화의 빈칸에 들어갈 말로 알맞지 않은 것은?

A: I'm going to have a history test tomorrow.
B: ______________________

① I hope you do well.
② Good luck to you.
③ I wish you good luck.
④ I think you can do well.
⑤ I wish you had done well on the test.

4 다음 괄호 안의 단어를 이용하여 대화를 완성하시오.

A: My team will play a soccer match next week.
B: I'll ________ ________ ________ ________ for you. (keep, fingers)

5 다음 대화의 밑줄 친 문장과 바꿔 쓸 수 없는 것은?

A: To make the tea sweet, add sugar and stir for five minutes on low heat.
B: Can you repeat that, please?

① I'm sorry?
② What did you say?
③ I beg your pardon?
④ Why did you tell me that?
⑤ Would you mind repeating that?

[6-7] 다음 빈칸에 들어갈 말로 알맞은 것을 고르시오.

6 I wish I ________ time to rest now.

① have ② had
③ have had ④ had had
⑤ could have had

7 If you ________ an umbrella, you wouldn't have gotten wet.

① bring ② brought
③ have brought ④ had brought
⑤ were brought

! 자주 나와요

8 다음 빈칸에 공통으로 들어갈 말로 알맞은 것은?

- I wish we ________ at the beach.
- If I ________ you, I wouldn't buy such an expensive car.

① be ② am
③ are ④ were
⑤ have been

9 다음 빈칸에 들어갈 말이 바르게 짝지어진 것은?

I'm lost. If I ________ English, I could ________ someone the way.

① spoke - ask
② spoke - asked
③ had spoken - ask
④ had spoken - asked
⑤ have spoken - ask

13 다음 두 문장이 같은 뜻이 되도록 할 때, 빈칸에 들어갈 말로 알맞은 것은?

I'm sorry that you didn't go to the national park with me.
→ I wish you ________ to the national park with me.

① go ② went
③ didn't go ④ had gone
⑤ have gone

자주 나와요

[10-11] 다음 괄호 안의 단어를 이용하여 문장을 완성하시오.

10 If Lauren hadn't been sick, she could ________ ________ in the Boston marathon a week ago. (participate)

11 I wish you ________ ________ to the party last night. (come)

12 다음 대화의 빈칸에 들어갈 말로 알맞은 것은?

A: What would you do if you won the lottery?
B: If I won the lottery, ________.

① I can buy a car
② I will buy a house
③ I move to another country
④ I would have given it to my parents
⑤ I would donate the money to charity

서술형

[14-15] 다음 문장을 가정법 문장으로 바꿔 쓰시오.

14 As I wasn't careful, I hurt myself.

→ ________________________, I wouldn't have hurt myself.

15 I'm sorry that I am not as tall as Tom.

→ I wish ________________________.

16 다음 주어진 문장과 의미가 같은 것은?

If I weren't busy, I could drop by your house.

① As I'm busy, I will drop by your house.
② As I'm busy, I can't drop by your house.
③ If I'm not busy, I will drop by your house.
④ As I was busy, I dropped by your house.
⑤ I could drop by your house as I was not busy.

! 어려워요

17 다음 중 어법상 바르지 못한 것은?

① I wish you are with me at that time.
② I wish I could ride a bike by myself.
③ If I were you, I wouldn't believe him.
④ If we leave now, we will arrive on time.
⑤ I wish I had remembered her name.

18 다음 우리말을 영어로 바르게 옮긴 것은?

내가 어제 가방을 잃어버리지 않았더라면 좋았을 텐데.

① I wish I lose my bag yesterday.
② I wish I didn't lose my bag yesterday.
③ I wish I had lost my bag yesterday.
④ I wish I hadn't lost my bag yesterday.
⑤ I wish I couldn't lose my bag yesterday.

19 다음 밑줄 친 부분 중 어법상 바르지 못한 것은?

I ① played games until late at night yesterday. So I ② overslept this morning and ③ was late for school. If I ④ get up early, I wouldn't ⑤ have been late.

내신 완성 서술형

20 다음 문장을 If로 시작하는 가정법으로 바꿔 쓰시오.

As I didn't go to Arizona, I couldn't visit the Grand Canyon.

→ ______________________________

____

21 다음 우리말과 일치하도록 조건에 맞게 영작하시오.

내가 그 문제를 너와 함께 상의했더라면 좋았을텐데.

조건 1: discuss the matter with를 이용할 것
조건 2: 총 9단어로 작성할 것
→ ______________________________

____

[22-23] 다음 그림을 보고, 주어진 표현을 이용하여 대화를 완성하시오.

(fly in the sky)

(talk with animals)

Q: What would you do if you had superhuman powers?

22 Joan: If I had a superhuman power, ______________________________.

23 Eric: If I had a superhuman power, ______________________________.

WORD LIST

Grammar

□ cancel	동 취소하다
□ reserve	동 예약하다
□ throw away	버리다
□ receipt	명 영수증
□ musical instrument	악기
□ record	동 기록하다; 녹음하다
□ voice	명 목소리
□ oxygen	명 산소
□ landscape	명 풍경(화)
□ appointment	명 약속
□ professor	명 교수
□ put on	…를 바르다
□ take advice	충고를 받아들이다
□ allergy	명 알레르기

Reading

□ dine	동 식사를 하다
□ fancy	형 값비싼, 고급의
□ bother	동 귀찮게 하다
□ favor	명 부탁
□ wave	동 손을 흔들다
□ feel sorry for	…를 안쓰럽게 여기다
□ offer	동 제의[제안]하다
□ pay	동 지불하다
□ reply	동 대답하다
□ moment	명 순간
□ alive	형 살아 있는
□ traffic	명 차량들, 교통(량)
□ develop	동 개발하다
□ come true	실현되다
□ wheel	명 바퀴
□ foldable	형 접을 수 있는
□ extend	동 펼치다
□ transform	동 변하다
□ distance	명 거리
□ function	명 기능
□ require	동 필요하다
□ runway	명 활주로
□ take off	이륙하다
□ license	명 면허증
□ land	동 착륙하다
□ reach	동 (특정 속도에) 이르다[달하다]

Communication

□ presentation	명 발표
□ wonder	동 궁금하다
□ public	형 대중의, 공공의
□ restroom	명 화장실

Final Test

□ match	명 경기, 시합
□ sweet	형 달콤한
□ stir	동 젓다
□ participate	동 참가하다
□ donate	동 기부하다
□ charity	명 자선 단체
□ drop by	(…에) 들르다
□ at that time	그때
□ oversleep	동 늦잠 자다
□ discuss	동 상의[논의]하다
□ matter	명 문제, 일

MEMO

MEMO

MEMO

MEMO

MEMO

MEMO

MEMO

지은이

NE능률 영어교육연구소

NE능률 영어교육연구소는 혁신적이며 효율적인 영어 교재를 개발하고
영어 학습의 질을 한 단계 높이고자 노력하는 NE능률의 연구조직입니다.

능률중학영어 〈중2〉

펴 낸 이 주민홍
펴 낸 곳 서울특별시 마포구 월드컵북로 396(상암동) 누리꿈스퀘어 비즈니스타워 10층
㈜NE능률 (우편번호 03925)
펴 낸 날 2019년 1월 5일 개정판 제1쇄 발행
2023년 11월 15일 제13쇄
전 화 02 2014 7114
팩 스 02 3142 0356
홈페이지 www.neungyule.com
등록번호 제1-68호
I S B N 979-11-253-2450-8 53740
정 가 13,000원

NE 능률

고객센터

교재 내용 문의 : contact.nebooks.co.kr (별도의 가입 절차 없이 작성 가능)
제품 구매, 교환, 불량, 반품 문의 : 02-2014-7114
☎ 전화문의는 본사 업무시간 중에만 가능합니다.

NE능률 교재 MAP

문법 구문

아래 교재 MAP을 참고하여 본인의 현재 혹은 목표 수준에 따라 교재를 선택하세요.
NE능률 교재들과 함께 영어실력을 쑥쑥~ 올려보세요!
MP3 등 교재 부가 학습 서비스 및 자세한 교재 정보는 www.nebooks.co.kr 에서 확인하세요.

초1-2

초3
- 그래머버디 1
- 초등영어 문법이 된다 Starter 1

초3-4
- 그래머버디 2
- 초등영어 문법이 된다 Starter 2
- 초등 Grammar Inside 1
- 초등 Grammar Inside 2

초4-5
- 그래머버디 3
- Grammar Bean 1
- Grammar Bean 2
- 초등영어 문법이 된다 1
- 초등 Grammar Inside 3
- 초등 Grammar Inside 4

초5-6
- Grammar Bean 3
- Grammar Bean 4
- 초등영어 문법이 된다 2
- 초등 Grammar Inside 5
- 초등 Grammar Inside 6

초6-예비중
- 능률중학영어 예비중
- Grammar Inside Starter
- 원리를 더한 영문법 STARTER

중1
- 능률중학영어 중1
- Grammar Zone 입문편
- Grammar Zone 워크북 입문편
- 1316 Grammar 1
- 문제로 마스터하는 중학영문법 1
- Grammar Inside 1
- 열중 16강 문법 1
- 쓰기로 마스터하는 중학서술형 1학년
- 중학 천문장 1

중1-2
- 능률중학영어 중2
- 1316 Grammar 2
- 문제로 마스터하는 중학영문법 2
- Grammar Inside 2
- 열중 16강 문법 2
- 원리를 더한 영문법 1
- 중학영문법 총정리 모의고사 1
- 중학 천문장 2

중2-3
- Grammar Zone 기초편
- Grammar Zone 워크북 기초편
- 1316 Grammar 3
- 원리를 더한 영문법 2
- 중학영문법 총정리 모의고사 2
- 쓰기로 마스터하는 중학서술형 2학년
- 중학 천문장 3

중3
- 능률중학영어 중3
- 문제로 마스터하는 중학영문법 3
- Grammar Inside 3
- 열중 16강 문법 3
- 중학영문법 총정리 모의고사 3
- 쓰기로 마스터하는 중학서술형 3학년

예비고–고1
- 문제로 마스터하는 고등영문법
- 올클 수능 어법 start
- 천문장 입문

고1
- Grammar Zone 기본편 1
- Grammar Zone 워크북 기본편 1
- Grammar Zone 기본편 2
- Grammar Zone 워크북 기본편 2
- 필히 통하는 고등 영문법 기본편
- 필히 통하는 고등 서술형 기본편
- 천문장 기본

고1-2
- 필히 통하는 고등 영문법 실력편
- 필히 통하는 고등 서술형 실전편
- TEPS BY STEP G+R Basic

고2-3
- Grammar Zone 종합편
- Grammar Zone 워크북 종합편
- 올클 수능 어법 완성
- 천문장 완성

고3

수능 이상/ 토플 80-89 · 텝스 600-699점
- TEPS BY STEP G+R 1

수능 이상/ 토플 90-99 · 텝스 700-799점
- TEPS BY STEP G+R 2

수능 이상/ 토플 100 · 텝스 800점 이상
- TEPS BY STEP G+R 3

중학 내신 완벽 대비 종합서

능률 중학 영어

중2

정답 및 해설

NE 능률

중학 내신 완벽 대비 종합서

능률 중학 영어

중2

정답 및 해설

CHAPTER 01 문장의 형식

GRAMMAR FOCUS

p. 8

A 감각동사와 수여동사

1 그 환자들은 오늘 좋아 보인다.
그의 아이디어는 굉장하게 들린다.
그 커피는 좋은 냄새가 난다.
그 우유는 신맛이 난다.
Fred의 가족은 피곤했다.

2 나는 내 여동생에게 아이스크림을 좀 사 줬다.
그 점원은 우리에게 새 옷들을 보여 주었다.

Check-Up

p. 9

A 1 sounded like 2 good 3 for 4 nervous
B 1 wonderful 2 to 3 great 4 to Anne
C 1 for me 2 to them 3 to us
D 1 soup tastes spicy 2 lent me some money
3 showed her the map

GRAMMAR FOCUS

p. 10

B 목적격 보어를 가지는 동사

2 1) 그들은 그들의 고양이를 Mimi라고 이름 지었다.
TV 쇼는 그 소년을 스타로 만들었다.
2) 나는 문을 열린 채로 두었다.
Eric은 그 영화가 지루하다는 것을 알게 되었다.
3) 너는 내가 너를 돕기를 원하니?
엄마는 우리가 컴퓨터 게임을 하도록 허락해 주셨다.

3 1) 내가 네 교과서를 빌리게 해 줘.
그녀의 아빠는 그녀가 일찍 자게 했다.
2) 우리는 땅이 흔들리는 것을 느꼈다.
Jessica는 누군가 울고 있는 것을 들었다.

Check-Up

p. 11

A 1 waving 2 to be 3 listen 4 angry
B 1 to tell 2 run[running] 3 pick 4 clean
C 1 easy 2 tremble[trembling] 3 to make
4 to wear
D 1 bark[barking] 2 expected, to win
3 call him a genius

Grammar Practice

p. 12

A 1 scream[screaming] 2 expensive
3 to sing 4 hide 5 beautiful
B 1 to go 2 hungry 3 warm 4 touch
C 1 coupons to the customers
2 delicious noodles for us
3 her student card to her boyfriend
4 the story of her childhood to me

문제해설

A 1 지각동사 hear는 목적격 보어로 동사원형이나 현재분사를 쓴다.
2 감각동사(look) 뒤에는 부사가 아닌 형용사가 와야 한다.
3 동사 expect는 목적격 보어로 to부정사를 쓴다.
4 사역동사 have는 목적격 보어로 동사원형을 쓴다.
5 동사 think의 목적격 보어로 부사가 아닌 형용사를 써야 한다.

B 1 동사 advise는 목적격 보어로 to부정사를 쓴다.
2 감각동사 feel 뒤에는 형용사를 쓴다.
3 동사 keep은 목적격 보어로 형용사를 쓴다.
4 사역동사 let은 목적격 보어로 동사원형을 쓴다.

C 수여동사 send, show, tell이 있는 문장은 전치사 to를, cook이 있는 문장은 전치사 for를 사용하여 3형식 문장으로 바꿀 수 있다.

내신 완성 Grammar Practice

p. 13

1 ①, ④ 2 ③ 3 ③ 4 (1) laugh (2) to you

문제해설

1 ①, ④ 동사 help는 목적격 보어로 동사원형이나 to부정사를 쓴다.

2 「감각동사+like+명사」는 '…처럼 ~하다'의 의미이다.
동사 allow는 목적격 보어로 to부정사를 쓴다.

3 ③ 동사 get은 사역의 의미지만 목적격 보어로 to부정사를 쓴다.
따라서 sign을 to sign으로 고쳐야 한다.

4 (1) 사역동사 make는 목적격 보어로 동사원형을 쓴다.
(2) 수여동사 give가 있는 3형식 문장은 간접목적어 앞에 전치사 to를 쓴다.

서술형에 나오는 WRITING

p. 14

A 1 This Indian curry tastes good.
2 Would you bring me a towel?
3 He persuaded his mom to raise his allowance.
B 1 They call him a hero.
2 The idea sounds creative.
3 Min taught me Chinese.[Min taught Chinese to me.]
C 1 make your parents happy
2 They smell fresh and sweet

문제해설

B 1 동사 call은 목적격 보어로 명사를 쓴다.
3 수여동사 teach가 쓰인 4형식 문장은 「teach+간접목적어+직접목적어」, 3형식 문장은 「teach+직접목적어+to+간접목적어」로 나타낸다.

C Emily의 꽃집
당신은 부모님을 행복하게 해드리고 싶나요? 저희는 아름다운 꽃을 많이 가지고 있습니다. 그것들은 신선하고 달콤한 향이 납니다. 당신의 부모님께서 그것들을 정말 좋아하실 거예요!
▶ 1 「make+목적어+형용사」의 어순으로 쓴다.
2 「smell+형용사」의 어순으로 쓴다.

READING WITH GRAMMAR

pp. 15~16

Reading 1 | 1 ④ 2 (A) strange (B) to lend
Words | [1] 효과적인 [2] 상상하다

해석 | 당신은 하루 동안 이웃의 자전거를 빌리고 싶다. 하지만 당신은 그녀가 안 된다고 말할까 봐 두렵다. 당신은 무엇을 해야 할까? 그것을 한 달 동안 빌려달라고 요청해라! 이것은 이상하게 들릴지 모르지만, 그것은 실제로 사람들을 설득하는 효과적인 방법이다. 그것은 '면전에서 문 닫기 기법'이라고 불린다.

다음에 나오는 상황을 상상해 보아라: 당신이 이웃의 문을 두드리고 그녀에게 한 달 동안 그녀의 자전거를 빌려달라고 요청한다. 물론, 그녀는 안 된다고 말하지만, 그녀는 당신에게 미안하다고 느낀다. 당신은 실망스럽지만, 대신에 그것을 단 하루 동안만 빌려달라고 부탁한다. 당신의 이웃은 안심해서, 흔쾌히 동의하고 그녀의 자전거를 당신에게 준다. 면전에서 문 닫기 기법으로, 당신은 그녀가 하루 동안 당신에게 자전거를 빌려주도록 설득할 수 있다.

구문해설

1행 You **want to borrow** your neighbor's bicycle *for* a day.
▶ want는 to부정사를 목적어로 취한다.
▶ for: … 동안

2행 **This** may sound strange, but it's actually an effective way *to persuade* people.
▶ This는 앞 문장의 내용을 가리킨다.
▶ to persuade는 명사구 an effective way를 수식하는 형용사적 용법의 to부정사이다.

문제해설

1 ④ 이웃이 자전거를 한 달 동안 빌려주는 것을 거절해서 그 대신 하루만 자전거를 빌려달라고 다시 요청하는 상황 다음에 이웃이 당신에게 자전거를 빌려주는 것에 흔쾌히 동의한다는 내용의 주어진 문장이 오는 것이 자연스럽다.

2 (A) 감각동사 sound 뒤에는 형용사가 주격 보어로 와야 한다.
(B) 동사 ask는 5형식 문장에서 목적격 보어로 to부정사를 취한다.

Reading 2 | 1 ④ 2 ②
Words | [1] 생산하다 [2] 해로운

해석 | 이곳 베이징은 겨울이야. 이 도시 사람들은 마스크를 쓰고 있어. 왜 그런지 아니? 이것은 더러운 공기 때문이야. 사람들이 그들의 집을 따뜻하게 하려고 석탄을 태우기 때문에 겨울에 공기 오염이 더 심해져. 이것은 해로운 가스를 만들어내고, 이 가스들이 미세먼지를 형성하지.

어떤 사람들은 이것이 대단한 일이 아니라고 생각할지 모르지만, 그것은 우리의 일상생활에 영향을 미쳐. 우선, 공기 중의 미세먼지는 눈에 잘 보이는 정도를 줄여. 이런 이유로, 많은 공항이 지난주에 폐쇄되었어. 또한, 사람들이 숨을 쉴 때, 미세먼지가 폐로 들어가서 그들을 아프게 만들 수 있어. 나는 오늘 저녁에 조깅을 가고 싶었는데, 부모님께서는 내가 밖으로 나가는 것을 허락하지 않으셨어. 부모님께서 정부가 사람들에게 건강을 위해서 실내에 머무를 것을 권고했다고 말하셨어. 하늘은 언제 다시 맑아질까?

구문해설

4행 **This** produces harmful gases, ...
▶ This는 앞 문장의 because 이하의 내용을 가리킨다.

6행 Some may think (**that**) this is not a big deal, but it affects our daily lives.
▶ think 뒤에 목적어 역할을 하는 명사절을 이끄는 접속사 that이 생략되어 있다.

문제해설

1 위 글의 주제로 가장 알맞은 것은?
① 어떻게 미세먼지가 형성되는가
② 베이징의 날씨 변화
③ 겨울철 유용한 건강 조언
④ 미세먼지의 원인과 영향
⑤ 미세먼지와 가시성은 무엇인가
▶ 미세먼지가 형성되는 원인과 그 결과로 나타나는 부정적인 영향에 관한 글이므로, 글의 주제로는 ④가 적절하다.

2 빈칸에 들어갈 말로 가장 알맞은 것은?
▶ 사역동사 let은 목적격 보어로 동사원형을 쓰므로, ② go가 와야 한다.

내신에 나오는 COMMUNICATION

A 안부 묻고 답하기

p. 17

Check-Up | **1** ⑤ **2** How have you been

문제해설

1 A: 어떻게 지내니?
B: ____________
① 나쁘지 않아. ② 그저 그래.
③ 꽤 잘 지내. ④ 나는 잘 지내, 고마워.
⑤ 괜찮아.
▶ ⑤는 상대방의 사과에 대한 대답으로 쓰는 말이다.

2 대답에서 '잘 지냈어, 고마워.'라고 했으므로, 질문으로는 '어떻게 지냈니?'의 의미인 'How have you been?'이 적절하다.

B 경험 묻고 답하기

p. 18

Check-Up | **1** (1) ⓐ (2) ⓒ (3) ⓑ **2** ④

문제해설

2 A: ____________
B: 응, 나는 그곳에 한 번 가 봤어.
① 어떻게 지냈니?
② 너는 어디 출신이니?
③ 너는 부산에 언제 갈 거니?
④ 너는 부산에 가 본 적이 있니?
⑤ 너는 지난여름에 부산에 어떻게 갔니?

FINAL TEST

pp. 19~21

1 ⑤ **2** (1) Heat (2) hide **3** ② **4** (C)→(B)→(A)→(D) **5** ③ **6** ④ **7** ① **8** ⑤ **9** ④ **10** ④ **11** to **12** ④ **13** The invention made her a millionaire. **14** My dad wanted me to wash my school uniform. **15** ① **16** ④ **17** ① **18** ⑤ **19** call this doll Amber **20** gave her some advice **21** Baker[him] clean his studio **22** He felt something fly[flying] toward him. **23** looked like **24** to have

문제해설

1 ⑤ customer는 '손님'이라는 뜻이다.

2 (1) heat: 뜨겁게[따뜻하게] 만들다
(2) hide: 숨다

3 A: 안녕! 너를 한동안 보지 못했어.
B: 안녕. ____________
A: 잘 지내지 못해. 나는 요즘 꽤 바쁘거든.
▶ 안부를 묻는 상황이므로 빈칸에는 어떻게 지내냐고 묻는 ②가 오는 것이 적절하다.

4 (C) 너는 한국 음식 먹어 본 적 있니?
(B) 응, 나는 김치를 먹어 봤어.
(A) 오! 어땠어?
(D) 약간 매웠지만 맛있었어!

5 ① A: 너는 스케이트를 타 본 적 있니?
B: 아니, 없어.
② A: 어떻게 지냈니?
B: 그저 그래. 나는 아팠어.
④ A: 너는 태국에 가 본 적 있니?
B: 응, 나는 그곳에 두 번 가 봤어.
⑤ A: 어떻게 지내니?
B: 잘 지내. 넌 어때?
▶ ③ 아르바이트를 해 본 적이 있는지 묻는 말에 잘 지낸다고 답하는 것은 어색하다.

6 ④ 동사 expect는 목적격 보어로 to부정사를 쓴다.

7 ① 사역동사 let은 목적격 보어로 동사원형을 쓴다.

8 수여동사 buy가 쓰인 3형식 문장에서는 간접목적어 앞에 전치사 for를 쓴다.
동사 want는 목적격 보어로 to부정사를 쓴다.

9 감각동사의 보어로는 형용사를 써야 하므로 부사 ④ sadly는 적절하지 않다.

10 동사 find는 목적격 보어로 형용사를 쓴다. ④ interest는 명사 또는 동사이다.

11 동사 tell과 show는 3형식 문장에서 간접목적어 앞에 전치사 to를 쓴다.

15 ① 감각동사의 보어로 부사 well이 아닌 형용사 good 등이 와야 한다.

16 ① apologize → to apologize, ② keep → to keep, ③ to sing → sing[singing], ⑤ nervously → nervous로 고쳐야 한다.

17 Jenny는 심한 감기에 걸렸다. 그래서 그녀의 오빠는 그녀가 병원에 가게 했다. 의사는 그녀에게 숨을 깊이 들이쉬도록 했다. 그는 그녀에게 약을 먹고 물을 충분히 마시라고 충고했다. 그는 이것이 그녀를 건강하게 유지시켜 줄 거라고 말했다.
▶ ① 사역의 의미로 쓰이는 get은 목적격 보어로 to부정사를 쓴다.

21 동사 help는 목적격 보어로 to부정사와 동사원형을 모두 쓸 수 있는데 빈칸이 네 개이므로 동사원형인 clean을 써야 한다.

22 지각동사 feel은 목적격 보어로 동사원형 또는 현재분사를 쓴다.

[23-24] 시장에 수박이 있었다. 그 수박은 축구공처럼 보였다. 점원이 내게 그것을 한 조각 먹도록 허락해 주었다.

23 뒤에 명사구 a soccer ball이 이어지므로, looked를 looked like로 고쳐야 한다.

24 동사 allow는 목적격 보어로 to부정사를 쓰므로, have를 to have로 고쳐야 한다.

CHAPTER 02 동사의 시제

GRAMMAR FOCUS ······················· p. 24

A 단순시제와 진행형

1 나는 저녁 여섯 시에 저녁을 먹는다.
지구는 태양 주위를 돈다.

2 Daniel은 어제 중고차를 샀다.
Rachel은 어젯밤에 매우 아팠다.

3 1) 아빠는 평상시처럼 저녁 8시에 집에 도착하실 것이다.
나는 그 여행 계획을 포기하지 않을 것이다.
2) 다음 주에 눈이 올 것이다.
나는 오늘 밤에 나의 집에 친구들을 초대하지 않을 예정이다.

4 1) Lucas가 화장실에서 그의 개를 씻기고 있다.
그들은 Sam을 위한 깜짝 파티를 준비하고 있다.
2) 그들은 서로를 바라보고 있었다.
내가 내 여동생을 보았을 때 그녀는 친구들과 이야기하고 있었다.

| Check-Up | ······································ p. 25

A 1 ate 2 called 3 goes 4 was reading
B 1 are 2 knows 3 swimming 4 travel
C 1 now 2 every day 3 tomorrow 4 yesterday
D 1 booking 2 is 3 ordered 4 will have[is having]

GRAMMAR FOCUS ······················· p. 26

B 현재완료

1 1) Tom과 그의 아내는 하루 종일 그들의 아들을 기다려 왔다.
2) 나는 전에 이 조리법을 시도해 본 적이 없다.
3) A: 너는 런던에 가 본 적이 있니?
B: 응, 가 본 적 있어. / 아니, 가 본 적 없어.

2 1) 우리는 방금 우리의 오래된 물건들을 팔았다.
지하철은 아직 역에 도착하지 않았다.
2) 너는 무지개를 본 적이 있니?
나는 너에게 절대 거짓말을 한 적이 없다.
3) 그녀는 열다섯 살부터 고양이들을 키워 왔다.
Charlie는 6개월 동안 한국어를 공부해 왔다.
4) 나는 내 지갑을 잃어버렸다. (→ 그래서 나는 지금 돈이 하나도 없다.)
나는 이메일 비밀번호를 잊어버렸다. (→ 그래서 나는 지금 이메일에 로그인할 수 없다.)

| Check-Up | ······································ p. 27

A 1 heard 2 has taken 3 finished 4 has been
B 1 경험 2 계속 3 결과
C 1 Have 2 read 3 never been 4 has donated
D 1 has not departed 2 has just repaired 3 have worn

Grammar Practice p. 28

A 1 are 2 go 3 delivered 4 has played 5 was
B 1 canceled 2 has collected 3 is baking 4 have, met 5 am going to take
C 1 leaves 2 has served in the army 3 saw the musical 4 were you doing

문제해설

A 1 현재 시점을 나타내는 today(오늘)가 쓰였으므로 are로 고쳐야 한다.
2 will 뒤에는 동사원형을 써야 한다.
5 when이 이끄는 절이 과거를 나타내고 주어가 3인칭 단수이므로 was를 써서 과거진행형으로 고쳐야 한다.

B 1 과거를 나타내는 last Monday(지난 월요일)가 쓰였으므로 과거시제로 쓴다.
2 '… 동안'의 의미인 for가 쓰였으므로 계속을 나타내는 현재완료를 써야 한다.
5 미래를 나타내는 tomorrow(내일)가 쓰였고 주어가 1인칭 단수이므로 「am going to+동사원형」으로 쓴다.

내신 완성 Grammar Practice p. 29

1 ⑤ 2 ④ 3 ④ 4 have used

문제해설

1 ⑤ 「be going to」 뒤에는 동사원형을 써야 한다.

2 ④ since는 현재완료와 함께 쓰여 계속을 나타낸다.

3 보기와 ④는 계속을 나타내는 현재완료이다. ①과 ⑤는 경험, ②와 ③은 완료를 나타낸다.

서술형에 나오는 WRITING

p. 30

A 1 developed this game five years ago
2 Sue has not eaten anything
3 am going to walk the dog after dinner

B 1 Have, seen a ghost 2 takes place
3 Did, pass the exam 4 is picking fruit

C 1 studied science with Aaron
2 is volunteering at a nursing home
3 will play[is going to play / plays / is playing] badminton at a park

문제해설

B 1 부사 ever(한 번이라도)는 현재완료와 함께 쓰여 경험을 나타낸다.
2 현재에 반복되는 일을 나타내므로 현재시제를 써야 한다.
3 과거를 나타내는 last month(지난달)가 쓰였으므로 과거시제를 써야 한다.
4 right now가 쓰여 지금 일어나고 있는 일을 나타내므로, 현재진행형을 써야 한다.

C 3 미래의 확정된 일정이나 계획을 표현할 때는 미래시제 외에 현재시제나 현재진행형도 쓸 수 있다.

READING WITH GRAMMAR

pp. 31~32

Reading 1 | 1 ④ 2 I have never been to
Words | [1] 밝은

해석 | 너는 다섯 가지 다른 색을 지닌 강을 본 적이 있니? 나는 있어! 지난 휴가 때, 나는 콜롬비아에 가서 Cano Cristales를 방문했어. 그것은 세계에서 가장 아름다운 강들 중 하나야. 현지 사람들은 그것의 색 때문에 그것을 '액체 무지개'라고 불러. 빨간색은 마카레니아 클라비게라라고 불리는 수중 식물로부터 비롯된 거야. 파란색은 물 자체에 의해 만들어져. 그리고 나머지 색상들은 조류, 강의 바닥에 있는 암석, 그리고 반짝이는 노란 모래로부터 비롯되지.

네가 Cano Cristales를 방문할 예정이라면, 가장 좋은 시기는 여름이야. 그때가 내가 갔던 때야! 더운 날씨가 마카레니아 클라비게라를 선홍색으로 만들어! 나는 더 멋진 장소에 가 본 적이 없어!

구문해설

2행 It is **one of the most beautiful rivers** in the world.
▶ one of the+최상급+복수명사: 가장 …한 것들 중 하나

4행 The red comes from an underwater plant **called *Macarenia clavigera***.
▶ called 이하는 명사구 an underwater plant를 수식하는 과거분사구이다.

9행 ... **makes the *Macarenia clavigera* turn** bright red!
▶ make(사역동사)+목적어+동사원형: …를 ~하게 만들다

문제해설

1 ① 세계에서 가장 깊은 강
② Cano Cristales에 있는 다채로운 색의 물고기들
③ 콜롬비아에서 가장 인기 있는 색
④ 콜롬비아에 있는 다섯 가지 색의 강
⑤ Cano Cristales의 수중 관광
▶ 다섯 가지 색을 지닌 콜롬비아의 Cano Cristales 강에 관한 글이므로, ④가 제목으로 가장 적절하다.

2 have never been to: …에 가 본 적이 없다

Reading 2 | 1 ⑤ 2 ③
Words | [1] 공연 [2] 지역; 구역

해석 | 타임스퀘어는 뉴욕시의 중심인 맨해튼에 있는 유명한 교차로이다. 그곳에는 잘 알려진 건물, 거리 공연, 그리고 새해 전야 행사와 같은 관광 명물이 많이 있다. 그러나, 과거에 그곳은 매우 다르게 보였다.

1800년대에, 그곳은 Long Acre Square(롱에이커 스퀘어)라고 불렸으며, 그곳에는 단지 몇 채의 주택들만 있었다. 그 당시, 그곳은 마차 제조업의 중심지였다. 그 후, 1890년대에, 그곳은 큰 극장과 고급 식당들이 있는 지역으로 개발되었다. 1904년, 타임스퀘어는 유명 신문사인 〈뉴욕타임스〉가 근처의 새 사무실로 이전하면서 그 이름을 얻었다. 비록 그 회사는 1913년에 다른 곳으로 이전했지만, '타임스퀘어'라는 이름은 그 이후로도 똑같이 유지되고 있다.

구문해설

1행 Times Square is a famous intersection in **Manhattan**, **the center of New York City**.
▶ Manhattan과 the center of New York City는 동격이다.

5행 In the 1800s, it **was called** Long Acre Square, and there were only a few houses there.
▶ 그곳이 Long Acre Square라 '불렸던' 것이므로 수동태가 쓰였다.

문제해설

1 Times Square에 대해 사실이 아닌 것은?
① 그곳에서 새해 전야 행사가 열린다.
② 그곳은 과거에 다른 이름을 가지고 있었다.
③ 19세기에 대형 극장들이 그곳에 나타났다.
④ 그곳은 신문에서 그 이름을 가져왔다.
⑤ 1913년 이후, 그곳의 이름은 여러 차례 변경되었다.
▶ ⑤ 1913년 〈뉴욕타임즈〉가 회사를 다른 곳으로 이전한 후에도 이름을 유지해 왔다고 했다.

2 (A)와 (B)에 들어갈 어법상 바른 형태를 고르시오.
▶ (A) 과거를 나타내는 부사구 in the past가 쓰였으므로 과거시제인 looked가 적절하다.
(B) since와 함께 쓰여 어떤 상태가 계속됨을 나타내야 하므로 현재완료인 has stayed가 적절하다.

내신에 나오는 COMMUNICATION

A 감정 묻고 답하기

p. 33

Check-Up | 1 ④ 2 (C) → (A) → (B) → (D)

문제해설

1 ④ 기분이 어떠냐는 질문에 '나는 그렇게 느낀다'고 답하는 것은 적절하지 않다.

2 (C) 너는 오늘 기분이 어떠니?
(A) 난 별로 좋지 않아.
(B) 무슨 일 있었니?
(D) 내 여동생이 매우 아파.

B 알고 있는지 묻기

p. 34

Check-Up | 1 ③ 2 Have you heard about the new announcer?

문제해설

1 A: 너는 밖에 비가 오고 있다는 것을 들었니?
B: 응. 우리는 우산을 가지고 가야 해.
▶ ③「Did you hear that ...?」과「Did you know that ...?」은 모두 상대방이 무엇인가에 대해 알고 있는지 묻는 표현이다.

FINAL TEST

pp. 35~37

1 (1) deliver (2) book **2** donate **3** (1) ⓒ (2) ⓐ **4** I am in a good mood **5** ⑤ **6** ③ **7** ② **8** ① **9** ④ **10** ④ **11** has not[never] lost **12** ⑤ **13** ① **14** She is not going to spend much money. **15** ③ **16** ① **17** ④ **18** ① **19** ② **20** Has the singer changed his mind? **21** It has rained since yesterday. **22** She was writing an article about them. **23** didn't[couldn't] finish my report **24** will plant some flowers[am planting some flowers]

문제해설

1 (1) 우체부가 곧 그의 편지를 배달할 것이다.
(2) 너는 발리에 있는 호텔을 예약했니?

3 A: 너는 학교 축제가 있을 거라는 것을 들었니?
B: 아니. 언제야?
A: 다음 주 금요일이야. 나는 장기 자랑 사회를 맡을 거야.
B: 정말? 재밌겠다!

5 ① A: 너는 기분이 어떠니?
B: 나는 우울해.
② A: 너는 오늘 기분이 어떠니?
B: 안 좋아. 나는 시험에 떨어졌어.
③ A: 너는 반 고흐의 작품들을 아니?
B: 응, 알아. 나는 그의 그림들을 좋아해.
④ A: 너는 내일 콘서트에 대해 들었니?
B: 아니. 누가 공연하니?
▶ ⑤ Tim이 컵을 깨뜨린 것을 알고 있었는지 묻는 말에 '아니. 나는 그러지 않았어.'라고 대답하는 것은 자연스럽지 않다.

6 ③ '(과거에) …하고 있었다'의 의미로 과거진행형이 알맞다.

8 ① 변하지 않는 진리를 나타낼 때는 현재시제를 쓴다.

9 will이 쓰였으므로 과거를 나타내는 ④ yesterday(어제)는 알맞지 않다.

10 현재완료(have worked)가 쓰였으므로 과거의 특정 시점을 나타내는 ④ three years ago(3년 전에)는 알맞지 않다.

11 현재완료의 부정은「have[has]+not+v-ed」로 나타내며, not 대신 never를 쓸 수도 있다.

12 ⑤ like와 같이 감정을 나타내는 동사는 진행형으로 쓰지 않는다.

13 보기와 ①은 완료를 나타내는 현재완료이다. ②와 ⑤는 경험, ③은 결과, ④는 계속을 나타낸다.

18 ② is having → has, ③ didn't see → haven't seen, ④ is running → ran, ⑤ I'm going to join → I joined로 고쳐야 한다.

19 ② 문맥상 첫 번째 빈칸에는 '아직'의 의미인 yet이, 두 번째 빈칸에는 '이미'의 의미인 already가 와야 한다.

22 주어가 3인칭 단수인 과거진행형은「was+v-ing」로 나타낸다.

23 현재는 금요일이며, 목요일에는 보고서를 마치지 않았으므로 과거시제의 부정문이 알맞다. didn't 대신 couldn't를 쓸 수도 있다.

24 미래의 계획을 나타낼 때는「will+동사원형」으로 쓰며, 빈칸에 맞게 현재진행형으로 쓸 수도 있다.

CHAPTER 03 수동태

GRAMMAR FOCUS

p. 40

A 수동태의 의미와 형태

1 많은 사람들이 그 노래를 사랑한다.
그 노래는 많은 사람들에 의해 사랑받는다.

2 1) Grayson이 그 낡은 상자들을 발견했다.
→ 그 낡은 상자들은 Grayson에 의해 발견되었다.
2) 학생들은 교실을 청소할 것이다.
→ 교실은 학생들에 의해 청소될 것이다.
3) 기술이 우리의 삶을 변화시키고 있다.

→ 우리의 삶은 기술에 의해 변화되고 있다.
그들은 그 방을 페인트칠하고 있었다.
→ 그 방은 그들에 의해 페인트칠 되고 있었다.

3 1) Hailey는 어제 알람을 맞추지 않았다.
→ 알람은 어제 Hailey에 의해 맞춰지지 않았다.
2) 그가 이 사진들을 찍었나요?
→ 이 사진들은 그에 의해 찍혔나요?

Check-Up

p. 41

A 1 enjoyed 2 be solved 3 was found
4 remembered 5 wasn't written
B 1 reviewed 2 Was 3 were closed
4 be planted
C 1 will be decorated by 2 was not baked by
3 was being prepared by
D 1 Was, finished by 2 is visited by
3 is being spread by

GRAMMAR FOCUS

p. 42

B 주의해야 할 수동태

1 1) 어젯밤에 지진이 일어났다.
큰 글자들이 화면에 나타났다.
2) Jina는 많은 스키 장비를 가지고 있다.
그 아기는 George를 닮았다.

2 나는 그 소식에 놀랐다.
그 백화점은 사람들로 가득 차 있다.

3 Nancy의 가족들은 나의 개를 돌봤다.
→ 나의 개는 Nancy의 가족들에 의해 돌봐졌다.

Check-Up

p. 43

A 1 from 2 run over 3 brought up
4 disappeared 5 resemble
B 1 arrived 2 is known to 3 be thrown away
4 had
C 1 with 2 in 3 at 4 of
D 1 appeared 2 exist 3 will be looked after

Grammar Practice

p. 44

A 1 bitten 2 wasn't[was not] invited
3 appear 4 were satisfied with
B 1 has 2 broken 3 laughed at
4 tested 5 spoken
C 1 Was, changed by 2 is respected by
3 was being repaired by
4 will be employed by
5 were looked down on by

문제해설

A 1 수동태의 의문문은 「be동사+주어+v-ed ...?」이다.
2 수동태의 부정문은 「주어+be동사+not+v-ed ...」이다.
3 appear는 목적어가 필요 없는 동사로, 수동태로 쓰지 않는다.
4 be satisfied with: …에 만족하다

B 1 소유를 나타내는 동사 have는 수동태로 쓰지 않는다.
3 동사구의 수동태는 동사구를 하나의 단어처럼 취급한다.
4 미래시제의 수동태는 「will be+v-ed」이다.

C 3 진행형의 수동태는 「be동사+being+v-ed」이다.
5 look down on: …를 얕보다

내신 완성 Grammar Practice

p. 45

1 ④ 2 ③ 3 ② 4 (1) happened (2) was hit

문제해설

1 ④ 컴퓨터 마우스는 '만들어진' 것이므로, 수동태 was created가 알맞다.

2 be pleased with: …로 즐거워하다
be surprised at: …에 놀라다

3 ② 진행형의 수동태는 「be동사+being+v-ed」이므로, print를 printed로 고쳐야 한다.

4 (1) happen은 수동태로 쓰지 않으므로, 과거시제 happened로 쓴다.
(2) 남자가 자동차에 의해 '치인' 것이므로 동사 hit을 과거시제 수동태 was hit으로 쓴다.

서술형에 나오는 ***WRITING***

p. 46

A 1 The audience is interested in art.
2 Jeff was not raised by them.
3 A subway station is being built by the engineers.
B 1 was played by the orchestra
2 Is, being moved by the children
3 will be graded by computer
C 1 is covered with[in] leaves
2 are filled with water

문제해설

C 1 be covered with/in: …로 덮여 있다
2 be filled with: …로 가득 차다

READING WITH GRAMMAR

pp. 47~48

Reading 1 | 1 ③ 2 ③
Words | [1] 혜택, 이득 [2] 고대의

해석 | 전 세계 사람들이 고추를 좋아하지만, 보통 그것은 건강식품으로 여겨지지는 않는다. 하지만, 그것에는 숨겨진 건강상의 이점들이 있다! 몇몇 종류의 고추는 비타민 C를 오렌지보다 더 많이 함유하고 있다. 그리고 고대 마야인들은 고추를 복통을 위한 약으로 사용했다.

사실, 고추는 오늘날에도 일종의 약으로 쓰인다. 그렇지만 당신은 그것을 먹지 않는다—대신, 그것을 당신의 피부에 바른다. 당신은 고추로 요리한 후에 눈을 만져 본 적이 있는가? 만약 있다면, 당신은 그것이 화끈거리는 느낌을 만들어 낸다는 것을 안다. 이런 이유로, 고추는 흔히 몸의 통증을 위한 크림에서 발견된다. 그것들은 당신의 근육에 열나는 느낌을 만들어 내도록 첨가된다.

구문해설

3행 .... contain **more** vitamin C **than** oranges.
▶ more ... than ~: ~보다 더 많은 …

5행 You don't eat **them**, *though*—instead, you rub **them** on your skin.
▶ them은 앞 문장의 chili peppers를 가리킨다.
▶ though: 그렇지만[하지만]

7행 **Have** you **ever touched** your eyes after cooking with chili peppers?
▶ 현재완료가 부사 ever와 함께 쓰여 경험을 나타낸다.

문제해설

1 (A) 고추는 보통 건강식품으로 여겨지지 않다는 내용 뒤에 고추에는 건강상의 이점이 있다는 상반된 내용이 언급되므로, 빈칸에는 However(하지만)가 적절하다.
(B) 고추가 화끈거리는 느낌을 만들어 내므로 통증을 위한 크림으로 쓰인다는 내용이므로, 빈칸에는 For this reason(이런 이유로)이 적절하다.

2 ③ 고추가 약으로 '쓰여진다'는 의미이므로, 수동태 are used가 알맞다.

Reading 2 | 1 ⑤ 2 ④
Words | [1] 감옥

해석 | 수잔 B. 앤서니는 투표권이 여성들에게 주어지기 전인 1820년에 미국에서 태어났다. 그 당시에는, 남성들만이 투표할 권리를 갖고 있었다. 하지만, 앤서니는 이것이 불공평하다고 생각했다. 그녀는 그것에 관해 강연하기 위해 미국 전역의 소도시들을 방문하기로 결심했다. 많은 여성들이 앤서니의 연설에 감동받았다. 1872년에, 그녀는 심지어 투표를 시도했다! 그녀의 표가 집계되었을까? 아니다. 대신, 그녀는 감옥에 보내졌다. 하지만 앤서니는 이런 어려움들에 의해 멈춰지지 않았다. 그녀는 여성의 권리를 향상시키기 위해 계속 노력했다.

그녀는 여성들이 투표할 권리를 얻기 14년 전인 1906년에 사망했다. 오늘날 앤서니는 여전히 그녀의 노력에 대해 칭송받고 있으며, 그녀의 모습은 미국의 1달러 동전에 있다.

구문해설

3행 However, she believed that **this** was unfair.
▶ this는 앞 문장의 내용을 가리킨다.

4행 She decided to visit towns across the U.S. **to give lectures** about it.
▶ to give lectures는 '강연하기 위해'의 의미로 목적을 나타내는 부사적 용법의 to부정사구이다.

8행 She **kept working** to improve women's rights.
▶ keep v-ing: 계속해서 …하다

10행 She died in **1906**, [fourteen years before women gained the right *to vote*].
▶ 1906년과 fourteen 이하는 동격이다.
▶ to vote는 앞의 명사 the right를 수식하는 형용사적 용법의 to부정사이다.

문제해설

1 위 글의 제목으로 가장 알맞은 것은?
① 미국의 사회적 문제들
② 미국 동전에 있는 유명 인물들
③ 자유롭고 공정한 투표의 중요성
④ 수잔 B. 앤서니의 어려운 어린 시절
⑤ 여성의 권리를 위한 수잔 B. 앤서니의 노력
▶ ⑤ 여성의 투표권을 얻기 위한 수잔 B. 앤서니의 노력에 관한 글이다.

2 어법상 바르지 못한 것은?
▶ ④ 그녀가 감옥에 '보내졌다'는 의미이므로, 수동태 was sent가 알맞다.

내신에 나오는 ***COMMUNICATION***

A 확인 요청하기 p. 49

Check-Up | 1 ③ 2 Did you say you ate salad?

문제해설

1 ③ 상대방의 말을 다시 확인할 때는 「Do you mean ...?」이라고 말할 수 있다.

B 빈도 묻고 답하기 p. 50

Check-Up | 1 How many times
2 (C) → (B) → (D) → (A)

문제해설

2 (C) 너는 얼마나 자주 테니스를 치니?
(B) 나는 이틀에 한 번 테니스를 쳐.
(D) 이틀마다 연습한다는 말이니?
(A) 맞아.

FINAL TEST pp. 51~53

1 ③ 2 employ 3 move 4 ⑤ 5 ⑤ 6 (B) → (A) → (C) → (D) 7 ④ 8 ⑤ 9 ① 10 is looked up to by 11 ④ 12 ④ 13 ⑤ 14 ③ 15 The festival will be held this weekend. 16 ② 17 ⑤ 18 ⑤ 19 Her eyes were filled with tears. 20 ⑤ 21 A man's bag was being checked by the police officer. 22 The old books will be thrown away by Andy. 23 Was the party prepared by them? 24 is being taken care of by the vet

문제해설

1 주어진 영영 풀이는 '어떤 것을 맞게 하다'라는 의미이므로, ③ correct(바로잡다)가 적절하다.

5 A: 너 피곤해 보여. 무슨 일 있었니?
B: 나는 내 방을 청소했어.
A: 너는 일주일에 몇 번 네 방을 청소하니?
B: ____________________
▶ 빈도를 묻는 상황이므로 빈칸에는 ⑤ '한 번이나 두 번.'이 와야 한다.

6 (B) 셔츠 고르는 것 좀 도와주실래요?
(A) 좋아요. 저건 어때요?
(C) 파란색 줄무늬가 있는 셔츠 말입니까?
(D) 맞아요. 저것이 저희의 가장 잘 팔리는 셔츠예요.

7 ④ 집이 '파괴되었다'는 의미의 수동태를 쓴다.

8 ⑤ 박스들이 '실려지고 있다'는 의미의 진행형 수동태를 쓴다.

9 ① 상태를 나타내는 동사인 resemble은 수동태로 쓰지 않는다.

10 동사구를 수동태로 바꿀 때는 동사구를 한 단어로 취급한다.

11 be pleased with: …로 즐거워하다
be made from: …로 만들어지다 (화학적 변화)

12 ④ 수동태의 행위자가 불분명하거나 막연한 일반인일 때는 「by+행위자」를 생략할 수 있다.

16 ② '…로 만들어지다 (물리적 변화)'는 be made of로 나타낸다.

17 ⑤ 미래시제 수동태의 부정문은 「주어+will not be+v-ed ...」이다.

18 ⑤ 목적어가 필요 없는 동사인 disappear는 수동태로 쓰지 않는다.

20 ① didn't → wasn't, ② Two brothers are had by me. → I have two brothers., ③ repair → repaired, ④ a speeding car → by a speeding car로 고쳐야 한다.

23 수동태의 의문문은 「be동사+주어+v-ed ...?」이다.

24 고양이는 수의사에 의해 '돌봐지는' 것이므로 수동태로 써야 하며, 진행형으로 작성하라고 했으므로 is being taken care of by the vet으로 나타낸다.

CHAPTER 04 조동사

GRAMMAR FOCUS p. 56

A 조동사 can, may, will

1 1) 내 남동생은 수영할 수 있다.
나는 그녀처럼 노래를 잘 부를 수 없다.
2) 너는 내 헤어드라이어를 사용해도 된다. 나는 이미 그것을 사용했다.
제가 이 치마를 새것으로 교환해도 되나요?
3) 저에게 물을 좀 가져다주시겠어요?

2 1) Parker 씨는 주말에 사무실에 있을지도 모른다.
그 상점은 내일 문을 열지 않을지도 모른다.
그는 친구들과 문제가 있을지도 모른다.
2) 너는 책 동호회에 언제든지 가입해도 된다.
제가 신분증 없이 건물에 들어가도 될까요?

3 1) 우리 할머니는 내년에 80세가 될 것이다.
나는 너를 더 이상 방해하지 않을게.
2) 에어컨 좀 꺼 주시겠어요?

Check-Up p. 57

A 1 send 2 can 3 can't 4 may
B 1 허가 2 능력 3 요청
C 1 be 2 to pay 3 be able to 4 not use
D 1 will 2 may[might] 3 was not able to

GRAMMAR FOCUS

p. 58

B 조동사 must, should

1 1) 우리는 극장에서 조용히 해야 한다.
나는 갑자기 차를 멈춰야 했다.
우리는 다음 주부터 더 비싼 버스 요금을 내야 할 것이다.
2) William은 너의 거짓말에 놀란 것이 틀림없다.
Jenny가 그녀의 언니일 리가 없다. 그들은 닮지 않았다.

2 우리는 스케이트를 탈 때 무릎 보호대를 착용하는 것이 좋다.
너는 사람들을 그들의 외모로 판단하지 말아야 한다.

C 다양한 조동사 표현

1) 나는 내 생일 파티에 많은 사람들을 초대하고 싶다.
너는 공원에서 운동하고 싶니?
2) 그녀는 피곤해 보인다. 그녀는 일찍 자는 게 낫겠다.
너는 지금 가지 않는 게 낫겠다. 비가 많이 온다.
3) 나는 금요일마다 치킨을 먹곤 했다.
이 식당은 예전에는 교회였다.

Check-Up

p. 59

A 1 used to 2 should 3 don't have to
4 must
B 1 have 2 have to 3 used 4 better not
C 1 don't have to 2 had better
3 must[should] not 4 would like to
5 used to

Grammar Practice

p. 60

A 1 should 2 had better not 3 Can
4 used to
B 1 follow 2 had 3 must not 4 had to
C 1 can[may] sit 2 Would you like to use
3 will stop by 4 will be able to live

문제해설

A 1 문맥상 '수영하기 전에 준비 운동을 해야 한다'는 의미가 되어야 하므로 의무를 나타내는 should가 알맞다.
4 문맥상 '과거에 아이스하키팀의 멤버였다'는 의미가 되어야 하므로 과거의 상태를 나타내는 used to가 알맞다.

B 2 had better: …하는 것이 낫다[좋겠다]
4 과거시제 문장이므로 과거형 had to로 고쳐야 한다.

C 1 허가를 나타낼 때는 조동사 can 또는 may를 쓴다.
2 would like to: …하고 싶다
3 미래의 계획을 나타낼 때는 조동사 will을 쓴다.
4 미래의 가능성을 나타낼 때는 조동사 can의 미래형인 will be able to를 쓴다.

내신 완성 Grammar Practice

p. 61

1 ② 2 ⑤ 3 ④ 4 ①

문제해설

1 ② '…일지도 모른다'라는 의미의 불확실한 추측은 may로 나타낸다.

2 ⑤ 조동사 뒤에는 동사원형이 와야 한다.

3 보기와 ④의 must는 '…임이 틀림없다'라는 추측의 의미이고 나머지는 모두 '…해야 한다'의 의미이다.

4 ① 첫 번째 빈칸에는 '…하는 것이 좋다, …해야 한다'는 의미의 should가, 두 번째 빈칸에는 '…할 수 있다'는 의미의 can이 들어가는 것이 적절하다.

서술형에 나오는 WRITING

p. 62

A 1 Is she able to play the cello?
2 I don't have to wear thick clothes.
3 This factory may harm the environment.
B 1 used to be thin 2 had better recycle
3 would like to ask
C 1 must not speak 2 must throw away

문제해설

B 1 used to: (예전에는) …였다
2 had better: …하는 것이 낫다[좋겠다]
3 would like to: …하고 싶다
ask ... a favor: …에게 부탁을 하다

READING WITH GRAMMAR

pp. 63~64

Reading 1 | 1 ② 2 ②
Words | [1]붓다[따르다] [2]…쪽으로

해석 | 점심으로 맛있는 것을 만들고 싶나요? 그렇다면 당신은 이 오믈렛 조리법을 시도하는 것이 좋겠습니다! 당신은 달걀 5개, 버섯 200g, 양파 한 개, 그리고 약간의 소금이 필요할 거예요. 또한, 당신은 햄이나 베이컨과 같은 고기를 추가해도 됩니다.

달걀, 소금, 그리고 양파를 함께 섞어서 시작하고, 그리고 나서 버섯을 팬에 몇 분간 볶으세요. 달걀 혼합물을 버섯 위에 부으세요. 익지 않은 부분들이 뜨거운 표면에 닿을 수 있도록 혼합물을 팬 중앙 쪽으로 부드럽게 미세요. 오믈렛이 갈색으로 변하기 시작할 때, 당신은 그것을 뒤집어야 합니다. 그것을 좀 더 부치고 나서, 접시에 놓으세요. 그것은 두 사람에게는 충분히 크니, 친구와 그것을 나눠 먹는 것이 좋겠어요!

구문해설

1행 Would you like to make **something delicious** for lunch?
▶ something처럼 -thing으로 끝나는 대명사는 형용사가 뒤에서 수식한다.

4행 Start **by mixing** the eggs, salt, and onion together, and then fry the mushrooms in a pan *for a few minutes*.
▶ by+v-ing: …함으로써
▶ for a few minutes: 몇 분 동안, 잠시

5행 Gently push the mixture toward the center of the pan **so that the *uncooked* parts can reach** the hot surface.
▶ so that+주어+동사: …가 ~하도록
▶ uncooked는 명사 parts를 수식하는 과거분사이다.

문제해설

1 ② 버섯 오믈렛을 조리하는 방법을 설명하는 글이다.

2 본문과 ②의 can은 '허가'를 의미하며 ①, ③, ④는 '능력', ⑤는 '요청'을 의미한다.

Reading 2 | **1** ④ **2** they have to change directions
Words | [1] 보호 [2] 드러내다

해석 | 타조는 날 수 없지만, 그들의 날개는 다른 중요한 일들을 한다. 예를 들어, 타조는 빨리 달려야 할 때 균형을 잡기 위해 날개를 사용한다. 그 새는 넘어지지 않기 위해 날개를 편다. 뿐만 아니라, 타조는 빠르게 방향을 바꿔야 할 때 날개를 배의 키처럼 사용한다.

타조는 보호를 위해서도 날개를 사용한다. 그 새는 주로 아프리카에 사는데, 그곳은 햇빛이 극도로 강하다. 타조는 햇빛이 그들의 새끼들을 아프게 하는 것을 막기 위해 날개를 사용할 수 있다. 그들의 날개의 깃털은 또한 타조의 체온을 조절한다. 밖이 추우면, 날개는 타조의 벌거벗은 위쪽 다리를 덮는다. 반대로, 밖이 너무 더우면, 그 새는 자신을 식히기 위해 맨살을 드러낸다.

구문해설

3행 The birds spread their wings to **keep from falling** over.
▶ keep from v-ing: …하지 않도록 하다

9행 The birds mainly live in Africa**, where** the sun is extremely strong.
▶ where는 Africa에 대한 부연 설명을 하는 계속적 용법의 관계부사이다.

10행 Ostriches can use their wings to **block the sunshine from hurting** their babies.
▶ block A from v-ing: A가 …하지 못하도록 막다[차단하다]

문제해설

1 다음 문장이 들어갈 위치로 가장 알맞은 곳은?
▶ 주어진 문장은 날개의 깃털이 체온을 조절한다는 내용이므로 날씨가 춥고 더울 때 날개가 하는 역할에 대해 설명하는 내용 앞인 ④에 들어가야 한다.

2 괄호 안의 말을 바르게 배열하시오.
▶ 「주어+have to+동사원형」의 어순으로 쓴다.

내신에 나오는 COMMUNICATION

A 소요 시간 묻고 답하기 p. 65

Check-Up | **1** ⑤ **2** How long did it take to reach the top?

문제해설

1 보고서를 끝내는 데 얼마나 걸릴지 묻고 있으므로 네 시간 정도 걸릴 거라고 답하는 ⑤가 알맞다.

B 추측 표현하기 p. 66

Check-Up | **1** (1) ⓒ (2) ⓑ (3) ⓐ **2** ①, ④

문제해설

2 ①, ④ 밑줄 친 문장의 부사 maybe는 '아마'의 의미로 불확실한 추측을 나타내며 조동사 may와 부사 probably가 비슷한 의미로 쓰인다.

FINAL TEST pp. 67~69

1 ⑤ **2** (1) stop (2) fall **3** ① **4** (1) ⓑ (2) ⓐ **5** ③ **6** ④ **7** ③ **8** ② **9** ③ **10** ② **11** ② **12** don't have to follow **13** ④ **14** You had better not take the bus. **15** ⑤ **16** ③ **17** ② **18** was able to drive **19** ⑤ **20** ② **21** used to be a supermarket **22** May[Can] I see your passport? **23** must clean your room **24** must not stay up late at night

문제해설

1 ⑤ gently는 '부드럽게'의 의미이다.

4 (1) A: Paul은 왜 숙제를 안 했니?
B: ⓑ 그는 아마도 그것을 잊었나봐.
(2) A: 새 프로그램을 만드는 데 얼마나 걸릴까?
B: ⓐ 하루 걸릴 거야.

6 have to는 강한 의무를 나타내며, ④ must로 바꿔 쓸 수 있다.

7 ③ 문맥상 과거에 '…할 수 없었다'의 의미인 couldn't가 와야 한다.

8 ② 문맥상 의무나 충고를 나타내는 should가 와야 한다.

9 ③의 may는 '…해도 된다'는 '허가'의 의미이며, 나머지는 '…일지도 모른다'는 '추측'의 의미로 쓰였다.

10 had to: …해야 했다
had better: …하는 게 낫다

11 ② 첫 번째 문장은 미래의 일을, 두 번째 문장은 과거의 습관을 나타내므로 각각 will과 used to가 와야 한다.

14 had better의 부정형은 had better not이다.

16 ① do → to do, ② come not → not come

④ must → have, ⑤ delivered → deliver로 고쳐야 한다.

17 보기와 ②의 can은 '능력'을 나타내며 ①, ③, ⑤는 '허가', ④는 '요청'을 나타낸다.

18 과거의 능력을 나타내는 조동사 could는 was able to로 바꿔 쓸 수 있다.

19 내일 일기예보입니다. 아침에는 매우 춥겠습니다. 따뜻한 옷을 입는 것이 좋겠습니다. 하지만, 여러분은 화창한 오후를 즐길 수 있을 것입니다.
▶ ⑤ 앞에 조동사 will이 있으므로, be able to가 되어야 한다.

20 ② have to의 부정형은 don't have to이다.

22 허가를 나타내는 조동사 may나 can을 이용해 문장을 만든다.

CHAPTER 05 to부정사

GRAMMAR FOCUS
p. 72

A to부정사의 용법
1 1) 로마의 역사를 배우는 것은 재미있다.
클래식 음악을 듣는 것은 나를 안정시킨다.
2) Gerald는 시험에서 높은 점수를 받기를 원한다.
그녀는 에어컨을 끄는 것을 잊었다.
3) 내 계획은 이번 주말에 축제에 가는 것이다.
그의 꿈은 우주 비행사가 되는 것이다.

2 나는 너에게 말할 것이 있다.
사원으로 가는 길을 나에게 알려 줄래?

3 1) 나는 소포를 부치기 위해 우체국에 가야 한다.
2) 우리 할머니는 90세가 되도록 사셨다.
3) Mary는 그녀가 매우 좋아하는 영화배우를 만나서 행복했다.
4) 그런 식으로 말하는 것을 보니 그는 매우 무례하다.
5) 네 전화번호는 기억하기에 쉽다.

Check-Up
p. 73

A 1 목적어 2 주어 3 보어
B 1 ⓒ 2 ⓑ 3 ⓐ 4 ⓓ
C 1 to[in order to] see 2 is 3 to drink
4 to join
D 1 to live in 2 To watch 3 to attend
4 not to cancel

GRAMMAR FOCUS
p. 74

B 가주어와 의미상의 주어
1 결승전 티켓을 구하는 것은 힘들었다.

2 1) 그 기사는 내가 읽기에 지루했다.
우리가 피카소의 그림들을 이해하는 것은 어렵다.
2) 어려움에 처한 사람들을 돕다니 너는 친절하구나.
컵을 또 깼다니 그녀는 조심성이 없었구나.

C to부정사를 활용한 중요 표현
1) Owen은 일찍 일어나기에는 너무 피곤했다.
= Owen은 너무 피곤해서 일찍 일어날 수 없었다.
2) 그녀는 이 무거운 상자들을 옮길 만큼 충분히 힘이 세다.
= 그녀는 힘이 매우 세서 이 무거운 상자들을 옮길 수 있다.
이 가방은 그 책들을 담을 만큼 충분히 크지 않다.

Check-Up
p. 75

A 1 It 2 too 3 enough 4 to go
B 1 for 2 of 3 for
C 1 for him 2 to 3 warm enough 4 so
D 1 important to wear 2 how to play
3 too hot, to 4 not old enough to

Grammar Practice
p. 76

A 1 clean enough 2 to take 3 of 4 too
B 1 to become a photographer
2 to help her mom 3 to win first prize
C 1 Not to run 2 what to do
3 so high, I cannot[can't] reach
4 It, for us to climb

문제해설
A 1 형용사+enough+to-v: ~할 만큼 충분히 …한
2 명사 time을 수식하는 형용사적 용법의 to부정사가 와야 한다.
3 사람의 성격이나 태도를 나타내는 형용사 brave가 있으므로, to부정사의 의미상의 주어로 him 앞에 of를 쓴다.
4 too+형용사+to-v: ~하기에는 너무 …한

B 1 보어 역할을 하는 명사적 용법의 to부정사로 쓴다.
2 목적을 나타내는 부사적 용법으로 쓴다.
3 감정의 원인을 나타내는 부사적 용법으로 쓴다.

C 1 to부정사의 부정형은 「not to-v」 형태로 쓴다.
2 what to-v: 무엇을 …할지
3 so ... that+주어+cannot[can't]: 너무 …해서 ~할 수 없는
4 「It(가주어) ... to-v(진주어)」 구문으로, to부정사 앞에 의미상의 주어 「for+목적격」을 쓴다.

내신 완성 Grammar Practice p. 77

1 ③ 2 ② 3 ③ 4 It, kids to use the machine

문제해설

1 ③ to부정사의 의미상의 주어는 주로 「for+목적격」으로 쓴다.

2 보기와 ②의 to부정사는 앞의 명사를 수식하는 형용사적 용법으로 쓰였다. ①은 목적어 역할을 하는 명사적 용법, ③은 보어 역할을 하는 명사적 용법, ④는 형용사를 수식하는 부사적 용법, ⑤는 목적을 나타내는 부사적 용법으로 쓰였다.

3 ③ winning을 to win으로 고쳐야 한다.

서술형에 나오는 WRITING p. 78

A 1 There is no reason to change our plans.
2 It was easy to become friends with Henry.
3 They talked about how to teach math.

B 1 to[in order to] ride a bicycle
2 when to return[when I should return]
3 to play

C 1 wants[wanted] to be 2 close enough to see

문제해설

B 2 「when to-v」는 '언제 …할지'의 의미이며, 「when+주어+should+동사원형」으로 바꿔 쓸 수 있다.
3 판단의 근거를 나타내는 부사적 용법의 to부정사는 '…하다니, …하는 것을 보니'를 나타낸다.

READING WITH GRAMMAR pp. 79~80

Reading 1 | 1 ② 2 the road is too busy for the penguins to cross
Words | [1] 포함하다

해석 | 뉴질랜드 오아마루에서는, 매일 저녁 쇠푸른펭귄들이 바다를 떠나 그들의 둥지로 걸어간다. 과거에, 그들은 집에 가기 위해 길을 건너야 했다. 불행하게도, 그 길은 펭귄들이 안전하게 건너기에는 너무 붐빈다. 자동차의 불빛이 펭귄들을 눈멀게 했기 때문에 많은 사고가 있었다. 그러나, 이제는 그들이 둥지까지 걸어갈 더 좋은 방법이 있다.

펭귄들을 안전하게 지키기 위해, 마을은 도로 아래에 25m 길이의 터널을 짓기로 했다. 터널은 2016년에 개통되었다. 그것은 펭귄들이 (앞을) 보도록 도와주기 위해 전등을 포함하고 있다. 펭귄들의 터널 이용을 관찰하기 위해 카메라도 보유하고 있다. 이 카메라들은 또한 사람들에게 온라인으로 펭귄 영상을 볼 기회를 제공한다.

구문해설

9행 To **keep the penguins safe**, the town *decided to build* a 25-meter-long tunnel under the road.
▸ keep+목적어+형용사: …를 ~한 상태로 유지하다
▸ 동사 decide는 목적어로 to부정사를 쓴다.

12행 .... **give people the opportunity** to watch videos of the penguins online.
▸ give(수여동사)+간접목적어+직접목적어: …에게 ~를 주다

문제해설

1 ② 눈을 다친 펭귄을 위한 전용 터널이라는 내용은 언급되지 않았다.

2 '~하기에는 너무 …한'을 나타내는 「too+형용사+to-v」의 어순으로 쓴다.

Reading 2 | 1 ① 2 ④
Words | [1] 소리치다

해석 | 어느 금요일, 한 여성이 시청 주차장에 주차를 했다. 그녀의 계획은 빨리 8층을 방문하는 것이었다. 그녀는 엘리베이터에 탔고, 그것은 평상시처럼 움직이기 시작했다. 그러더니 갑자기 그것은 두 층 사이에서 멈췄다. 그녀는 소리쳤고 비상 버튼을 눌렀지만, 아무도 대답하지 않았다. 그녀는 주말 내내 엘리베이터 안에 있어야 했다.

월요일에, 직원들이 와서 그녀를 발견했고, 그녀가 탈출하도록 도와주었다. 하지만 그녀가 주차장을 떠날 때, 한 직원이 그녀의 이야기를 믿지 않았고 그녀에게 주차비로 300달러 이상을 지불하게 했다! 그 여성은 항의하기 위해 법원에 갔다. 법원은 그 직원이 그녀에게 요금을 청구한 것은 잘못되었다고 선언했다. 뿐만 아니라, 시청은 그녀에게 1,000달러를 지불해야 했다. 그날 이후부터, 시청은 그녀가 원할 때는 언제든지 주차장을 무료로 이용하도록 허락했다.

구문해설

5행 On Monday, workers **came**, **found** her, and **helped** her to escape.
▸ 동사 came, found, helped가 접속사 and로 병렬 연결되어 있다.

7행 ..., a worker didn't believe her story and **made her pay** over $300 for parking!
▸ make+목적어+동사원형: …가 ~하게 하다

13행 ..., City Hall **let her use** the parking lot for free anytime [(*when*) she wanted].
▸ let+목적어+동사원형: …가 ~하게 하다
▸ [ ]는 anytime을 수식하는 관계부사절로, she wanted 앞에 관계부사 when이 생략되었다.

문제해설

1 다음 문장이 들어갈 위치로 가장 알맞은 곳은?
▸ ① 주어진 문장은 여자가 주말 내내 엘리베이터에 갇혀 있었다는 내용이므로, 엘리베이터가 멈춰 여자가 소리치고 비상 버튼을 눌렀다는 내용 뒤, 월요일에 직원들이 그녀를 도와주었다는 내용 앞에 오는 것이 자연스럽다.

2 빈칸에 들어갈 말로 가장 알맞은 것은?
▸ ④ 문맥상 '항의하기 위해서'라는 의미가 되어야 하므로, 목적을 나타내는 부사적 용법의 to부정사 to complain이 들어가야 한다.

내신에 나오는 COMMUNICATION

A 여가 활동 묻고 답하기 p. 81

Check-Up | 1 ③ 2 What do you usually do

문제해설

1 한가할 때 무엇을 하는 걸 좋아하는지 묻고 있으므로, 도미노 게임 하는 것을 좋아한다는 ③이 대답으로 적절하다.

B 허락 요청하고 답하기 p. 82

Check-Up | 1 ② 2 (D)→(B)→(C)→(A)

문제해설

1 ② 허락을 요청하는 말에 '그게 좋겠네요.'라고 대답하는 것은 적절하지 않다.

2 (D) 너는 여가 시간이 있을 때 무엇을 하는 걸 좋아하니?
(B) 나는 강을 따라서 조깅하는 것을 좋아해.
(C) 다음번에 내가 너와 함께 해도 될까?
(A) 물론이지.

FINAL TEST pp. 83~85

1 ③ 2 charge 3 ⑤ 4 ⑤ 5 ④ 6 ③ 7 ③
8 ④ 9 My wallet is too big to put in my pocket.
10 when to call 11 rich enough to buy 12 ④
13 ④ 14 not to go out 15 safe to travel around
16 ⑤ 17 ③ 18 ① 19 ⑤ 20 It was difficult for me to find her house. 21 Josh was excited to see her again. 22 to[in order to] read blogs
23 to[in order to] get information

문제해설

3 ⑤ 티셔츠를 입어 봐도 되는지 묻는 말에 동의한다는 대답은 어색하다.

4 시를 쓰는 것을 좋아한다는 대답에 대한 질문으로 ⑤ '너는 한가할 때 무엇을 하는 것을 좋아하니?'가 적절하다.

5 A: 너는 여가 시간에 주로 무엇을 하니?
B: 나는 주로 테니스를 쳐.
A: 정말? 나는 테니스를 배우고 싶어.
B: 그럼 내가 너에게 가르쳐 줄 수 있어.
A: 하지만 나는 테니스 라켓이 없어. 네 것을 빌려도 될까?
B: 물론이야.

6 ③ 결과를 나타내는 부사적 용법의 to부정사가 와야 한다.

7 ③ what to-v: 무엇을 …할지

8 ④ to부정사의 의미상의 주어는 보통 「for+목적격」으로 쓰며, silly와 같이 사람의 성격이나 태도를 나타내는 형용사 뒤에는 「of+목적격」으로 쓴다.

10 「의문사+주어+should+동사원형」은 「의문사+to-v」로 바꿔 쓸 수 있다.

11 「so ... that+주어+can」은 「형용사/부사+enough+to-v」로 바꿔 쓸 수 있다.

12 ① help → to help, ② for → of, ③ so → too, ⑤ play → to play 또는 playing으로 고쳐야 한다.

13 ①, ②, ③, ⑤는 부사적 용법, ④는 형용사적 용법으로 쓰였다.

17 ③ how bake를 how to bake로 고쳐야 한다.

18 보기와 ①은 명사적 용법의 to부정사이다. ②, ③, ④는 부사적 용법, ⑤는 형용사적 용법으로 쓰였다.

19 저희 레스토랑은 3월 3일에 20주년 기념일을 축하하기 위해 이벤트를 열 예정입니다. 저희는 그날 모든 손님들께 무료 음료를 제공할 것입니다. 여러분이 저희 마스코트인 Bambi와 사진을 찍는 것도 무료일 것입니다. 저희는 여러분께 서비스를 제공하게 되어 매우 기쁩니다.
▸ ⑤ 문맥상 목적을 나타내는 in order to serve가 아닌 감정의 원인을 나타내는 to serve가 와야 한다.

22, 23 목적을 나타내는 부사적 용법의 to부정사로 나타낸다.

CHAPTER 06 동명사

GRAMMAR FOCUS p. 88

A 동명사의 역할과 주요 표현

1 1) 자연의 사진을 찍는 것은 내가 가장 좋아하는 활동이다.
기부를 하는 것은 가난한 아이들을 도울 수 있다.
2) 그녀는 오늘 아침 그 책을 읽는 것을 끝마쳤다.
이 공장은 초콜릿을 생산하는 것으로 알려져 있다.
3) 그의 버릇들 중 하나는 밤늦게 먹는 것이다.

2 나는 너와 언쟁하고 싶지 않다.
그 드라마는 다시 볼 가치가 있다.
미래에 대해서 걱정해도 소용없다.

Check-Up p. 89

A 1 주어 2 전치사의 목적어 3 보어
B 1 washing 2 making 3 not calling 4 having
C 1 becoming[to become] 2 going 3 posting
D 1 look forward to 2 kept on 3 are busy

GRAMMAR FOCUS

p. 90

B 동명사와 to부정사

1 나는 월요일마다 쿠키와 빵 굽는 것을 연습한다.
그녀는 그 수학 문제를 푸는 것을 포기했다.

2 그들은 장래에 의사가 되기를 원한다.
Michael은 그의 공부 습관을 바꾸기로 결정했다.

3 1) 나는 만화 그리는 것을 좋아한다.
그 꽃들은 봄에 피기 시작한다.
2) ① 나는 어렸을 때 고양이를 키웠던 것을 기억한다.
내일 너의 여권을 가져올 것을 기억해라.
② 그녀는 새끼 사자들을 만졌던 것을 절대 잊지 못할 것이다.
오늘 저녁까지 네 방을 청소할 것을 잊지 마.
③ Kelly는 하얀 코트를 산 것을 후회했다.
내가 너를 실망시키게 되어서 유감이다.
④ 나는 (시험 삼아) 그 수프에 소금을 더 넣어 보았다.
그는 그 벌레를 죽이려고 노력했지만, 못했다.

Check-Up

p. 91

A 1 teaching 2 to go 3 playing 4 to find
B 1 to leave 2 eating 3 turning 4 to send
5 contact
C 1 to visit 2 changing[to change] 3 selling
D 1 to set 2 drawing 3 seeing

Grammar Practice

p. 92

A 1 to keep 2 laughing[to laugh] 3 getting
4 continuing
B 1 going 2 running 3 to ask
C 1 eating 2 coming 3 playing[to play]
4 winning[to win]
D 1 was worth trying 2 feel like working
3 cannot[can't] help accepting

문제해설

A 1 promise는 to부정사를 목적어로 취한다.
2 start는 동명사와 to부정사 둘 다 목적어로 취한다.
3 have a hard time v-ing: …하는 데 어려움을 겪다
4 look forward to v-ing: …하기를 기대하다

B 2 forget v-ing: (과거에) …했던 것을 잊다
3 stop to-v: …하기 위해 멈추다

C 1 be used to v-ing: …하는 데 익숙하다
2 전치사의 목적어로 동명사가 와야 한다.
3 love는 동명사와 to부정사 둘 다 목적어로 취한다.
4 보어 자리에는 동명사 또는 to부정사가 올 수 있다.

D 1 be worth v-ing: …할 가치가 있다
2 feel like v-ing: …하고 싶다
3 cannot[can't] help v-ing: …하지 않을 수 없다

내신 완성 Grammar Practice

p. 93

1 ③ 2 ① 3 ⑤ 4 ③

문제해설

2 ① choose는 목적어로 to부정사를 취한다.

3 ⑤는 진행형을 만드는 현재분사이고 나머지는 모두 동명사이다.

4 Jackson은 그의 누나의 헤드폰을 망가뜨렸고 그녀에게 말할 것을 잊었다. 그의 누나가 이것을 알았을 때, 그녀는 매우 화가 나서 그에게 계속 소리 질렀다.
▸ forget to-v: (미래에) …할 것을 잊다
keep (on) v-ing: 계속 …하다

서술형에 나오는 WRITING

p. 94

A 1 She is good at taking care of animals.
2 Not having close friends made him sad.
B 1 passing the bottle 2 doing your homework
C 1 want to share 2 enjoy playing

문제해설

B 1 mind는 동명사를 목적어로 취한다.
2 put off는 동명사를 목적어로 취한다.

C 신문 수업
신문을 좋아하나요? 반 친구들과 정보를 공유하고 싶은가요? 그렇다면 이 수업을 들어 보세요.
밴드 수업
함께 무대 위에서 악기 연주를 즐기는 건 어떤가요? 그것은 새로운 경험이 될 거예요!
afterclass@neschool.com으로 이메일을 보내 주세요.
▸ 1 want는 to부정사를 목적어로 취한다.
2 enjoy는 동명사를 목적어로 취한다.

READING WITH GRAMMAR

pp. 95~96

Reading 1 | 1 ② 2 (A) shooting (B) telling
Words | [1] 연습하다 [2] 자랑스럽게

해석 | 한 남자와 황제가 몇몇 병사들을 보고 있었다. 병사들은 화살 쏘는 것을 연습하고 있었다. 남자는 황제에게 깊은 인상을 주고 싶어서, 거짓말을 했다. 그는 "어렸을 때, 저는 화살을 매우 잘 쏘았습니다."라고 말했다. "그렇다면, 자네의 실력을 보여주시오."라고 황제가 말했다. 남자는 거짓말했던 것을 즉시 후회했다. 황제에게 거짓말하는 것은 죄였기 때문에 그는 두려움에 떨기 시작했다!

황제는 남자에게 세 개의 화살을 주었다. 남자는 첫 번째 화살을 쏘았지만, 그것은 목표물에서 멀리 떨어졌다. "저것은 폐하의 병사들이 쏘는 방식입니다."라고 남자는 재빠르게 말했다. 다음 화살은 조금 더 (목표물에) 가까웠다. "저것은 폐하의 장군들이 쏘는 방식입니다." 마

침내, 세 번째 화살이 목표물을 맞혔다. "그리고 저것은 제가 쏘는 방식입니다."라고 남자는 자랑스럽게 말했다.

구문해설

7행 The emperor **gave the man three arrows**.
▶ give+간접목적어+직접목적어: …에게 ~를 주다

8행 "That is **how** your soldiers shoot," the man said quickly.
▶ how는 방법을 나타내는 관계부사로, '…하는 방법'의 의미이다.

문제해설

1 ② 황제에게 거짓말하는 것은 죄이며 남자는 거짓말한 것을 후회했다고 했으므로, 그가 두려움에 떨었다고 하는 것이 알맞다.

2 (A) be good at은 '…를 잘하다'의 의미로, 전치사 at의 목적어로 동명사가 와야 한다.
(B) 문맥상 '(과거에) …했던 것을 후회하다'의 의미가 되어야 하므로, 동명사 telling이 와야 한다.

Reading 2 | 1 ④ 2 to work
Words | [1] 병 [2] 나타내다, 표현하다

해석 | 1841년에, 미국인 화가 존 랜드는 유화 튜브 물감을 발명했다. 이 발명 전에는, 화가들은 물감을 갈아서 기름과 섞어야 했다. 그들이 야외에서 작업하기를 택했을 때, 그들은 깨지기 쉬운 유리병에 물감을 챙겨야만 했다. 반면에, 튜브 물감은 가지고 다니기 쉬웠다.

한 젊은 화가인 클로드 모네는 튜브 물감에 기꺼이 많은 돈을 썼다. 모네와 그의 친구 르누아르는 튜브 물감으로 야외에서 그림 그리는 것을 정말 좋아했다. 그들은 빛과 색의 순간을 포착하여 그것들을 캔버스에 표현했다. 이것은 인상주의라고 불리는 새로운 화풍이었다. 르누아르는 수년 후에 "튜브 안 물감이 없다면, 인상주의는 없을 것이다."라고 말했다.

구문해설

4행 On the other hand, paint tubes were easy **to carry** around.
▶ to carry는 형용사 easy를 수식하는 부사적 용법의 to부정사로, '가지고 다니기에'의 의미이다.

5행 One young artist, Claude Monet, **was willing to spend** a lot of money on paint tubes.
▶ be willing to-v: 기꺼이 …하다

12행 ..., "**Without** paint in tubes, there **would be** no Impressionism."
▶ 「Without[But for] ..., 주어+would+동사원형」 형태의 가정법 과거로 '…이 없다면, ~할 텐데'라는 의미이다.

문제해설

1 위 글의 제목으로 가장 알맞은 것은?
① 모네 그림들의 특징
② 언제 유화 튜브 물감이 발명되었나
③ 두 젊은 화가들의 영리한 발명품
④ 튜브 물감이 인상주의에 미친 영향
⑤ 모네와 르누아르: 누가 더 위대한 화가였나?
▶ ④ 튜브 물감의 발명이 인상주의라는 새로운 화풍에 영향을 주었다는 내용의 글이다.

2 밑줄 친 단어를 바르게 고치시오.
▶ choose는 목적어로 to부정사를 취한다.

내신에 나오는 COMMUNICATION

A 관심에 대해 묻고 답하기 p. 97

Check-Up | 1 ② 2 he has much interest in space

문제해설

1 밑줄 친 문장은 자신의 관심사를 표현한 것으로, ②(나는 내 방을 꾸미는 것에 빠져 있어.)로 바꿔 쓸 수 있다.

B 증상 묻고 답하기 p. 98

Check-Up | 1 ③ 2 ②

문제해설

1 ③ 무슨 일이냐고 묻는 말에 안됐다고 대답하는 것은 적절하지 않다.

FINAL TEST pp. 99~101

1 ④ 2 invent 3 keep[stay] in touch 4 ④ 5 ③ 6 ① 7 ③ 8 ③ 9 ④ 10 ④ 11 I couldn't [could not] help laughing at his jokes. 12 She gave up drawing a picture of herself. 13 ② 14 ④ 15 ③ 16 ⑤ 17 ③ 18 ⑤ 19 I am used to sleeping on a bed. 20 ③ 21 finished answering 22 The book is not worth buying. 23 to feed the fish twice a day 24 giving too much food

문제해설

1 ④ crowded는 '붐비는'의 뜻이다.

4 아파 보인다며 증상을 묻는 말에 대한 답으로 적절한 것은 ④(나는 독감에 걸렸어.)이다.

6 ② A: 무슨 일이니?
B: 나는 발목에 통증이 느껴져.
③ A: 너는 무엇에 관심이 있니?
B: 나는 첼로를 연주하는 게 재밌다고 생각해.
④ A: 너는 역사에 관심이 있니?
B: 아니. 나는 역사에 별로 관심이 없어.
⑤ A: 네 아버지는 요리에 관심이 많으시니?
B: 응, 아빠는 그것에 매우 관심이 많으셔.
▶ ① 무슨 일인지 묻는 말에 이보다 더 좋을 순 없다고 대답하는

것은 어색하다.

7 ③ practice는 목적어로 동명사를 취한다.

8 ③ remember v-ing: (과거에) …했던 것을 기억하다

9 ④ decide는 목적어로 to부정사를 취한다.

10 ④ hope는 목적어로 to부정사를 취한다.

11 cannot help v-ing: …하지 않을 수 없다

12 give up은 목적어로 동명사를 취한다.

13 ① began to bleeding → began to bleed 또는 began bleeding, ③ go → going, ④ make → making[to make], ⑤ Wearing not → Not wearing으로 고쳐야 한다.

14 ④ on v-ing: …하자마자

15 ③ 전치사의 목적어로 동명사가 쓰이며 부정어 not은 동명사 앞에 온다.

16 빨리 먹는 것은 당신의 건강에 안 좋은 습관이다. 그것은 당신이 배부르다고 느껴지지 않아서 많이 먹게 만든다. 그것은 위장병을 유발할 수 있다. 지금부터, 천천히 먹도록 노력하라.
▸ ⑤ '…하려고 노력하다'의 의미는 「try to-v」이므로 to eat이 적절하다.

17 ③ have a hard time v-ing: …하는 데 어려움을 겪다

18 ⑤ keep (on) v-ing: 계속 …하다

20 ③ promise는 목적어로 to부정사를 취한다.

21 finish는 목적어로 동명사를 취한다.

22 be worth v-ing: …할 가치가 있다

23 문맥상 물고기에게 매일 두 번씩 먹이를 주는 것을 잊지 말라고 해야 하므로 「forget to-v」((미래에) …할 것을 잊다)를 쓴다.

24 문맥상 너무 많은 먹이를 주는 것을 피하라고 해야 하므로 「avoid v-ing」(…하는 것을 피하다)를 쓴다.

CHAPTER 07 분사

GRAMMAR FOCUS ························ p. 104

A 현재분사와 과거분사

1 1) 놀라운 이야기 날고 있는 새
2) 다림질된 셔츠 떨어진 나뭇잎들

2 1) 소리치고 있는 남자는 매우 화가 나 보인다.
나는 리어왕이라고 불리는 연극을 보았다.
2) Bentley는 피곤해 보인다.
그녀는 나를 한 시간 동안 기다리게 했다.

3 내 성적은 실망스러웠다.
나는 내 성적에 실망했다.

Check-Up ··· p. 105

A 1 chopped 2 living 3 amazing 4 excited
B 1 made 2 sleeping 3 dancing 4 shocking
C 1 bored 2 interesting 3 leaving 4 pleased
D 1 painted 2 called 3 broken

GRAMMAR FOCUS ························ p. 106

B 분사구문

1 카드를 받았을 때, 그는 행복했다.
그 소식을 듣는 동안, 그녀는 아무 말도 할 수 없었다.

2 1) 일과를 마친 후에, 그는 차를 한 잔 마셨다.
2) 친절한 사람이기 때문에, Gary는 모두에게 사랑받는다.
3) 오른쪽으로 돌면, 너는 역을 찾을 것이다.
4) 창문 밖을 바라보면서, 나는 나의 가족에 대해 생각했다.
5) 안전한 곳에 숨었음에도 불구하고, 그들은 여전히 두려움을 느꼈다.

Check-Up ··· p. 107

A 1 Cooking 2 Being 3 Waving 4 Not having
B 1 Being 2 Drinking 3 Reading
C 1 Taking 2 Being 3 Visiting 4 Living
D 1 그녀의 집으로 걸어가는 동안[걸어가고 있을 때]
2 할 일이 많았기 때문에

Grammar Practice p. 108

A 1 cut 2 buried 3 Being 4 Answering
B 1 worn 2 sitting 3 raising 4 surprised 5 held
C 1 humming[hum] 2 added 3 thrilling
D 1 Finishing her bath 2 Not being busy 3 Arriving in New York

문제해설

A 1 분사가 사역동사의 목적격 보어로 쓰일 때, 목적어와 분사와의 관계가 수동이면 과거분사를 쓴다.
2 명사 treasure를 수식하는 분사로 '숨겨진'이라는 수동의 의미인 과거분사가 와야 한다.
3, 4 분사구문은 부사절의 동사를 v-ing 형태로 고쳐서 만든다.

B 1 '해진'이라는 완료의 의미를 나타내는 과거분사가 와야 한다.
2 '앉아 있는'이라는 진행의 의미를 나타내는 현재분사가 와야 한다.
3 '팔을 들고 있는'이라는 진행의 의미를 나타내는 현재분사가 와야 한다.
5 '열린'이라는 수동의 의미를 나타내는 과거분사가 와야 한다.

D 1 부사절에서 접속사 After와 주어 she를 생략한 후, 동사 finished를 Finishing으로 고친다.
2 부사절에서 접속사 Because와 주어 he를 생략한 후, 부정의 분사구문을 만들기 위해 동사 wasn't를 Not being으로 고친다.
3 부사절에서 접속사 When과 주어 I를 생략한 후, 동사 arrived를 Arriving으로 고친다.

내신 완성 Grammar Practice

p. 109

1 ② 2 ③ 3 ③ 4 (1) Opening the refrigerator, you will see some orange juice. (2) Driving the car, she listened to music.

문제해설

1 ② '사인된'이라는 수동의 의미를 나타내는 과거분사가 와야 한다.

2 ③ 문맥상 '…할 때'를 의미하는 부사절로 바꿔 쓸 수 있다.

3 ③ 주어가 감정을 일으키는 원인이므로 현재분사인 amazing으로 써야 한다.

4 (1) 접속사 If와 주어 you를 생략한 후, 동사 open을 Opening으로 고친다.
(2) 접속사 While과 주어 she를 생략한 후, 동사 drove를 Driving으로 고친다.

서술형에 나오는 WRITING

p. 110

A 1 Who is the man wearing
2 She found a box covered with
3 Not understanding the question, I asked for
B 1 seemed excited 2 had his car repaired
C 1 Arriving at the meeting place
2 being too late

문제해설

B 1 주어가 감정을 느끼는 주체이므로 보어로 과거분사 excited가 와야 한다.
2 '수리되게 했다'라는 수동의 의미를 나타내기 위해 목적격 보어로 과거분사가 와야 한다.

C 내 친구 Jack과 나는 뮤지컬을 보기로 계획했다. 내가 약속 장소에 도착했을 때, 나는 그를 찾을 수 없었다. 그는 마침내 삼십 분 뒤에 도착했다. 하지만, 우리가 너무 늦었기 때문에, 우리는 극장에 들어갈 수 없었다.
▶ 부사절에서 접속사와 주어를 생략한 후, 동사를 v-ing 형태로 고친다.

READING WITH GRAMMAR

pp. 111~112

Reading 1 | 1 ② 2 Wanting a prettier tree
Words | [1] 전통 [2] 모이다

해석 | 우크라이나에서, 사람들은 크리스마스트리에 거미 모양의 장식을 놓는다. 이 전통은 한 가난한 가족에 관한 전설에서 비롯된다. 그들은 크리스마스트리를 가지고 있었지만, 그것을 장식할 여유가 없었다. 더 예쁜 트리를 원했기 때문에, 그 가족의 아이들은 크리스마스이브에 울기 시작했다. 이 슬픈 소리를 들은 후에, 집에 있는 몇몇 거미들이 계획을 세웠다. 가족이 잘 때, 거미들은 크리스마스트리에 모였다. 그들은 나무를 아름답게 만들면서 나뭇가지를 거쳐 흰 거미줄을 쳤다. (그들은 밤사이 먹이를 잡기 위해 거미줄을 지었다.)
크리스마스 아침, 가족이 깨서 커튼을 열었다. 아침 햇살이 거미줄을 은빛과 금빛으로 변하게 하면서 나무 위의 거미줄에 쏟아졌다! 이것이 당신이 크리스마스트리에서 거미 장식품을 자주 볼 수 있는 이유이다.

구문해설

6행 They put their white webs across the branches, **making the tree beautiful**.
▶ make+목적어+형용사: …를 ~하게 만들다

7행 They built them **to catch** their prey overnight.
▶ to catch는 목적을 나타내는 부사적 용법 to부정사이다.

문제해설

1 크리스마스트리를 장식하지 못한 한 가난한 가족을 위해 거미들이 트리를 장식해 주었다는 내용의 글이므로, 거미가 먹이를 잡기 위해 거미줄을 쳤다는 내용인 ②는 흐름과 관계없다.

2 밑줄 친 부분은 부사절 As[Because] the children of the family wanted a prettier tree로 나타낼 수 있으며, 이를 분사구문으로 바꿀 때 접속사와 주어를 생략하고, 동사를 현재분사 Wanting으로 고쳐서 만들 수 있다.

Reading 2 | 1 ② 2 ⑤
Words | [1] 들어 올리다

해석 | 오늘 나는 부모님과 함께 토드 강에서 신나는 보트 경주에 참가했다. 하지만, 그것은 우리의 예상과 많이 달랐다. 토드 강은 자주 (물이) 말라서, 사람들은 물 대신 모래 위에서 재미있는 보트 경주를 한다. 우리가 그곳에 도착했을 때, 보트 경주들 중 하나가 막 시작했다. 그 보트는 바닥이 없어서, 보트 안에 서 있는 사람들이 보트를 들고 달렸다! 결승선에 맨 먼저 도착한 팀이 우승자였다. 이후에, 해군, 해적, 그리고 바이킹이라고 불리는 큰 보트 세 척이 서로 싸웠다. 그 팀들은 물총을 사용하고 '밀가루 폭탄'이라고 불리는 밀가루 주머니를 다른 보트에 던지며 싸웠다. 우리는 그 행동을 보면서 정말 즐거운 시간을 보냈다!

구문해설

2행 However, it **was** much **different from** our expectations.

▶ be different from: …와 다르다

6행 The team [**who** reached the finish line first] was the winner.

▶ who ... first는 선행사 The team을 수식하는 주격 관계대명사절이다.

8행 The teams fought **using** water guns and **tossing** bags of flour ....

▶ using과 tossing은 '…하면서'라는 의미의 동시동작을 나타내는 분사구문으로, 등위 접속사 and로 병렬 연결되어 있다.

문제해설

1 위 글의 제목으로 가장 알맞은 것은?

① Todd 강 경주의 기원
② 마른 강에서의 색다른 보트 경주
③ 전설적인 전투: 해적 대 바이킹
④ 물 위에서의 흥미로운 보트 경주
⑤ Todd 강 경주에 대한 몇 가지 주의 사항

▶ 마른 Todd 강에서 펼쳐지는 독특한 보트 경주들에 관한 글이므로, 글의 제목으로는 ②가 알맞다.

2 어법상 바르지 못한 것은?

▶ ⑤ 문맥상 '보면서'의 의미를 나타내는 분사구문이 와야 하므로, 현재분사인 watching으로 고쳐야 한다.

내신에 나오는 COMMUNICATION

A 걱정·두려움 표현하기 p. 113

Check-Up | 1 ③ 2 I am afraid of traveling alone.

문제해설

1 A: 너 안 좋아 보여. 무슨 일이니?
B: 나는 내일 오디션이 걱정돼.
A: 괜찮아. 다 잘될 거야.
① 화난 ② 미안한 ③ 걱정되는 ④ 기쁜 ⑤ 궁금한
▶ ③ 문맥상 걱정을 나타내는 표현이 와야 한다.

B 기억 묻고 답하기 p. 114

Check-Up | 1 ① 2 I forgot

문제해설

1 ① remember의 목적어로 to부정사가 오는 경우는 '(앞으로) …할 것을 기억하다'의 의미이므로, 문맥상 적절하지 않다.

FINAL TEST pp. 115~117

1 ② 2 afford 3 ④ 4 ④ 5 am anxious about
6 ② 7 ④ 8 ② 9 bored 10 ③ 11 ③ 12 ⑤
13 studying at the library 14 (1) Coming (2) tired
15 ③ 16 wrapped in beautiful paper 17 ⑤
18 The ducks swimming in the lake 19 Believing he was right 20 Putting some coins in the machine, you will get a drink.
21 decorating → decorated 22 break → broken
23 had her hair permed

문제해설

1 ② toss는 '던지다'라는 뜻이다.

2 afford: (…를 살[할]) 여유가 되다

3 A: 너 걱정 있어 보여. 무슨 문제가 있니?
B: 새 학기가 곧 시작돼.
나는 새 친구들을 만나는 게 두려워.
▶ ④ 걱정이나 두려움을 표현하는 「I'm afraid of ...」는 「I'm scared of ...」로 바꿔 쓸 수 있다.

6 ② '잠긴'이라는 수동의 의미를 나타내는 과거분사가 와야 한다.

7 ④ '스키 타고 있는'이라는 진행의 의미를 나타내는 현재분사가 와야 한다.

8 ② '만들어진'이라는 수동의 의미를 나타내는 과거분사가 와야 한다.

10 첫 번째 빈칸에는 '쓰인'이라는 수동의 의미를 나타내는 과거분사 written이 와야 한다.
두 번째 빈칸에는 목적어 someone과 능동 관계를 나타내는 현재분사 touching이 와야 한다.

11 ③은 전치사의 목적어로 쓰인 동명사이고, 나머지는 현재분사이다.

12 ⑤ 분사구문의 부정형은 분사 앞에 부정어를 붙여서 나타내므로, Having not any money를 Not having any money로 고쳐야 한다.

13 「지각동사+목적어+목적격 보어」의 어순으로 쓰며, 목적어와 목적격 보어가 능동 관계이므로 현재분사 studying을 쓴다.

14 Keira의 엄마는 병원에서 일하신다. 엄마는 어젯밤 늦게까지 일하셨다. 집에 오셨을 때, 엄마는 지쳐 보였다. 그래서 Keira는 엄마의 집안일을 도와드렸다.
▶ (1) 분사구문이 되도록 현재분사 Coming으로 써야 한다.
(2) 주어 she가 감정을 느끼는 주체이므로 과거분사가 와야 한다.

16 명사 a present를 수식하는 과거분사구 wrapped in beautiful paper를 뒤에 써서 문장을 완성한다.

17 ① exciting → excited, ② amazed → amazing, ③ surprising → surprised, ④ confused → confusing으로 고쳐야 한다.

20 부사절에서 접속사 If와 주어 you를 생략하고, 동사 put을 Putting으로 고친다.

[21-22] 나는 온라인에서 꽃무늬로 장식된 접시를 주문했다. 하지만 그 접시를 받았을 때, 나는 그것이 깨진 것을 발견했다.

21 '장식된'이라는 수동의 의미를 나타내는 과거분사 decorated로 고쳐야 한다.

22 '깨진'이라는 수동의 의미를 나타내는 과거분사 broken으로 고쳐야 한다.

23 「사역동사+목적어+목적격 보어」의 어순으로 쓰며, 목적어와 목적격 보어가 수동 관계이므로 과거분사 permed를 쓴다.

CHAPTER 08 형용사와 부사

GRAMMAR FOCUS ························ p. 120

A 수량형용사

많은 사람들이 그 연설을 듣기 위해 모였다.
나는 그 책에서 많은 정보를 얻을 수 없었다.
팬케이크를 만들기 위해서, 나는 약간의 달걀과 약간의 우유가 필요하다.
이것은 어려운 주제라서, 이해하는 학생들이 거의 없다.
튜브에 치약이 거의 없다. 우리는 새것을 사야 한다.

B 형용사의 위치

1) 그 차에는 잘못된 것이 아무것도 없다.
나는 네게 말할 중요한 것이 있어.
2) 모든 학생들이 오늘 현장 학습을 떠났다.
나는 이 모든 만화책들을 이미 읽었다.
3) 나는 그만큼 아름다운 일몰을 한 번도 본 적이 없다.

| Check-Up | ·· p. 121

A 1 like 2 few 3 much 4 something cold
B 1 ③ 2 ② 3 ② 4 ③
C 1 much 2 call[are calling]
3 anything good 4 little
D 1 A lot of people 2 such a fun activity
3 nothing new 4 All her students

GRAMMAR FOCUS ························ p. 122

C 「동사+부사」

1 너는 다음 주에 언제든지 내 자전거를 돌려줘도 된다.
이번 주 수요일까지 숙제를 제출하세요.
Amelia는 고기를 구운 직후에 환풍기를 켰니?

2 1) 내 남동생의 울음이 나의 가족을 깨웠다.
추웠기 때문에 그녀는 재킷을 입었다.
2) 그가 그의 짐을 떨어뜨려서, 나는 그를 위해 그것을 주웠다.

| Check-Up | ·· p. 123

A 1 put the meeting 2 it off 3 them up
B 1 fill it out 2 took her scarf
3 put them down
C 1 Hurry up 2 throw away 3 find out
D 1 try on 2 turned up 3 give, back

Grammar Practice p. 124

A 1 funny a story 2 something light
3 Many[A lot of/Lots of] 4 picked it up
B 1 lots of goals 2 such a great
3 a few coins
C 1 turn it down 2 put out 3 get on
D 1 We had little rain 2 all her money on a backpack

문제해설

A 1 so+형용사+a(n)+명사: 그만큼[매우] …한 ~
2 -thing으로 끝나는 대명사는 형용사가 뒤에서 수식한다.
3 teenagers는 셀 수 있는 명사이므로 Many나 A lot of, Lots of를 써야 한다.
4 동사구의 목적어가 대명사이므로 동사와 부사 사이에 it이 온다.

B 2 such+a(n)+형용사+명사: 그만큼[매우] …한 ~
3 문맥상 주머니에 동전이 조금 있었다는 내용이므로 a few를 써야 하며, 뒤에는 복수명사 coins가 와야 한다.

내신 완성 Grammar Practice p. 125

1 ④ 2 ⑤ 3 (1) broke down (2) get up
4 (1) such a charming picture (2) buy lots of juice

문제해설

1 ④ a little은 셀 수 없는 명사를 수식하는 수량형용사이다.

3 (1) break down: 고장 나다
(2) get up: 일어나다

4 (1) 「so+형용사+a(n)+명사」는 「such+a(n)+형용사+명사」로 바꿔 쓸 수 있다.
(2) much는 lots of로 바꿔 쓸 수 있다.

서술형에 나오는 WRITING p. 126

A 1 We have enough toy cars for all those children.
2 Can you put a little pepper in my soup?
3 I didn't say anything bad about him.
B 1 Most drivers like 2 Few people
3 turned off his smartphone[turned his smartphone off]
C 1 a lot of good things 2 such a low price

문제해설

B 3 동사구의 목적어가 명사일 때 목적어는 부사 뒤 또는 동사와 부사 사이에 올 수 있다.

C 저희 벼룩시장에 오세요
벼룩시장에서, 여러분은 신발부터 책까지 많은 좋은 물건들을 살 수 있습니다. 대부분의 물건들이 중고여서, 당신은 그것들을 매우 낮은 가격에 살 수 있습니다. 싸게 살 수 있는 물건들이 많을 것이며, 모두 환영합니다!

READING WITH GRAMMAR pp. 127~128

Reading 1 | **1** ④ 2 Michelangelo thought of something clever
Words | [1] 영리한, 똑똑한 [2] 재주, 재능

해석 | 미켈란젤로는 역대 가장 위대한 예술가들 중 한 명이다. 그러나 그가 젊었을 때는, 돈을 벌기 위해 고군분투했다. 그는 후원자를 찾으면서, 이탈리아를 돌아다녔다. 불행히도, 대부분의 사람들은 새로운 예술가들에 의해 만들어진 조각품을 원치 않았다. 그들은 고대 로마 예술가들에 의해 만들어진 오래된 조각품을 선호했다. 그래서 미켈란젤로는 영리한 것을 생각해냈다—그는 오래된 것들처럼 보이는 새 조각품들을 만들 수 있었다!
그는 *Sleeping Cupid*라고 불리는 조각품을 만들었다. 그런 다음 그는 그것을 집어 들고, 던지고, 흙에 굴렸다. 한 부유한 남자가 *Sleeping Cupid*를 구입했다. 그는 그것이 고대 예술 작품이라고 생각했다. 그러나 이후에, 미켈란젤로가 실수로 진실을 말했다. 처음에 남자는 매우 화가 났지만, 그때 그는 미켈란젤로의 재능을 인정했다. 그는 미켈란젤로를 용서하고 그의 새로운 후원자가 되었다.

구문해설

1행 Michelangelo is **one of the greatest artists** *of all time*.
▶ one of the+최상급+복수명사: 가장 …한 것들 중 하나
▶ of all time: 역대[지금껏]

3행 Unfortunately, most people didn't want statues [**made** by new artists].
▶ made 이하는 statues를 수식하는 과거분사구이다.

5행 ...—he could make new statues [**that** looked like old *ones*]!
▶ that 이하는 선행사인 new statues를 수식하는 주격 관계대명사절이다.
▶ ones는 앞에 나온 명사(statues)와 같은 종류의 사물을 가리키는 부정대명사이다.

문제해설

1 ④ 당시 사람들은 새로운 예술가들이 만든 조각품보다는 고대 로마 예술가들이 만든 오래된 조각품을 선호했기 때문에, 미켈란젤로는 오래되어 보이도록 하는 것을 생각해 냈다고 했다.

2 something처럼 -thing으로 끝나는 대명사는 형용사가 뒤에서 수식하므로, clever something을 something clever로 고쳐야 한다.

Reading 2 | **1** ⑤ **2** ④
Words | [1] 약 [2] 격려하다, 용기를 북돋우다

해석 | Brian은 암을 앓고 있는 중학생이었다. 그는 많은 특수한 약을 먹어야 했고 매주 많은 진료를 받아야 했다. 많은 치료 때문에, 그는 자신이 점점 더 적은 머리카락을 갖게 되는 것을 발견했다. 마침내, 그는 "저는 머리카락이 거의 없어서 학교에 가고 싶지 않아요."라고 엄마에게 말했다. 그는 친구들이 자신을 비웃을까 봐 두려웠다. 하지만 그의 엄마는 그가 학교에 가도록 격려했다.
며칠 후에, Brian은 학교에 가서 놀라운 것을 보았다. 그의 모든 반 친구들이 그들의 머리를 민 것이었다! 그것은 매우 의미 있는 뜻밖의 일이었다. 그들 중 한 명이 그에게 "학교를 그만두지 마. 이제 머리카락이 없는 사람은 너 혼자만이 아니야."라고 말했다.

구문해설

3행 Because of the many treatments, he found **that** he had *less and less* hair.
▶ that은 found의 목적어 역할을 하는 명사절을 이끄는 접속사이다.
▶ less and less: 점점 더 적은

5행 But his mother **encouraged him to go** to school.
▶ encourage+목적어+to-v: …가 ~하도록 격려하다

문제해설

1 글의 마지막에 Brian이 느꼈을 감정은?
▶ ⑤ 병으로 머리카락이 빠져 친구들이 놀릴까 봐 학교에 갈 용기가 없었던 자신을 위해 반 친구들이 모두 머리를 민 것을 보고 Brian은 고마움을 느꼈을 것이다.

2 어법상 바르지 못한 것은?
▶ ④ all이 명사를 수식할 때는 소유격 앞에 위치해야 하므로 All his classmates가 되어야 한다.

내신에 나오는 COMMUNICATION

A 상기시켜 주기 p. 129

Check-Up | **1** forget, won't **2** ⓐ, ⓑ

문제해설

1 A: 우리 캠핑 여행을 위해 준비할 것이 있니?

B: 음… 따뜻한 옷을 챙길 것을 잊지 마.
A: 알겠어, 잊지 않을게.
▶ 상대방에게 어떤 일을 상기시킬 때는 「Don't forget to-v …」를 쓸 수 있다. 이에 대해 Okay, I won't. 등으로 대답할 수 있다.

B 확신 여부 묻고 답하기

p. 130

Check-Up | 1 ④ 2 ①

문제해설

1 A: 너 Emily가 유럽에서 돌아온 것을 알았니?
B: ______________
A: 물론이지. 내가 어제 그녀를 봤어.

2 밑줄 친 문장은 확신한다는 의미이므로, 이와 바꿔 쓸 수 있는 것은 ① '물론이지.'이다.

FINAL TEST

pp. 131~133

1 ② 2 (1) quit (2) hire 3 (B)→(C)→(A)→(D)
4 ① 5 I have no doubt that you will succeed.
6 ④ 7 ① 8 try on 9 got on 10 ③ 11 ④
12 put off the appointment[put the appointment off]
13 take off 14 ④ 15 ① 16 ② 17 Nothing new happened 18 ④ 19 few 20 ⑤ 21 The all members → All the members 22 Much → Many[A lot of/Lots of] 23 such a great vacation
24 someone diligent and positive

문제해설

1 clever는 '영리한, 똑똑한'의 의미로, ② smart(영리한, 똑똑한)와 바꿔 쓸 수 있다.

2 (1) 너는 왜 그 일을 그만두었니?
(2) 그 회사는 프로젝트 관리자를 고용할 것이다.

3 (B) 저녁으로 이탈리아 음식을 먹는 게 어때?
(C) 좋아. 근처에 좋은 장소가 있니?
(A) 은행 옆에 유명한 곳이 있어.
(D) 아, 기억나. 그럼 테이블을 예약할 것을 잊지 마.

4 ①은 '이 동아리에 가입하는 게 어때?'라는 권유를 나타내는 표현이다. 나머지는 모두 '너 이 동아리에 가입하고 싶은 게 확실하니?'라는 뜻으로 확신 여부를 묻는 표현이다.

6 셀 수 있는 명사(weeks)를 수식하는 수량형용사는 ④ a few이다.

7 ① water는 셀 수 없는 명사이며, many는 셀 수 있는 명사를 수식하는 수량형용사이다.

8 try on: (옷 등을) 입어 보다

9 get on: (버스 등에) 타다

10 ③ a lot of는 셀 수 있는 명사와 셀 수 없는 명사 앞에 모두 올 수 있다.

11 turn up: (라디오 등의) 소리를 크게 하다
turn on: (전기·가스·수도 등을) 켜다

14 ④ most는 뒤에 나오는 명사의 수에 동사의 수를 일치시키므로 is를 are로 고쳐야 한다.

18 ① a lot → a lot of, ② wake up me → wake me up, ③ many → much[a lot of/lots of], ⑤ threw away it → threw it away로 고쳐야 한다.

19 문맥상 셀 수 있는 명사를 수식하면서 부정의 의미를 지니는 few(거의 없는)가 알맞다.

20 ⑤ 동사구의 목적어가 대명사(it)인 경우에는 동사와 부사 사이에 목적어가 와야 하며, '너에게'라는 의미는 to you로 나타낸다.

21 all은 명사를 수식할 때 정관사 the 앞에 위치한다.

22 셀 수 있는 명사를 수식하는 '많은'이라는 의미의 수량형용사는 many, a lot of, lots of이다.

23 such+a(n)+형용사+명사: 그만큼[매우] …한 ~

24 저희와 함께 일합시다!
저희는 직원이 필요합니다. 그/그녀는 부지런해야 합니다. 또한 저희는 그/그녀가 긍정적이기를 바랍니다.
▶ -one으로 끝나는 대명사는 형용사가 뒤에서 수식한다.

CHAPTER 09 전치사(구)

GRAMMAR FOCUS

p. 136

A 전치사의 목적어와 전치사구의 역할

1 나는 네 옆에 앉고 싶다.
한 무리의 새들이 하늘에서 날고 있다.
당신은 이 버튼을 눌러서 프로그램을 시작할 수 있습니다.

2 1) 네 티셔츠에 있는 것은 무엇이니?
호랑이에 관한 다큐멘터리를 보자.
2) Chris는 꽃가게에서 튤립을 조금 샀다.
몇몇 학생들은 시험에 대해 걱정한다.

Check-Up

p. 137

A 1 belongs 2 the cup 3 eats out
4 The food
B 1 of 2 for 3 after 4 leaving
C 1 me 2 with 3 visiting 4 for
D 1 laughed at 2 are fond of 3 is famous for
4 was different from

GRAMMAR FOCUS
p. 138

B 주요 전치사의 의미 차이

1 이번 주 목요일까지 숙제를 제출해라.
그가 정오까지 기다렸지만, 그녀는 오지 않았다.

2 그 축제는 5월 5일부터 7일까지 열린다.
그들은 작년 이래로 서로 알고 지냈다.

3 Melissa와 그녀의 팀원들은 두 시간 동안 요가를 했다.
나는 겨울방학 동안 스키 타는 것을 배웠다.

4 해변을 따라서 산책하자.
그 개는 거리를 가로질러 뛰어갔다.
뜨거운 물이 파이프를 통해 흘렀다.

5 학생들은 박물관에 버스로 갈 것이다.
그는 파란색 펜을 사용하여 그의 이름을 썼다.

Check-Up
p. 139

A 1 with 2 during 3 in 4 until
B 1 with 2 along 3 during 4 since
C 1 by 2 for 3 from
D 1 for 2 through 3 by 4 across

Grammar Practice
p. 140

A 1 her 2 to 3 with 4 using
B 1 asked for 2 are[were] proud of
3 is ready for
C 1 Those socks on the floor
2 am not sure of the exact title
3 in the parking lot looks
D 1 since last Wednesday 2 for Paris
3 through the emergency exit

문제해설

A 1 전치사의 목적어로 대명사가 올 경우 목적격을 쓴다.
2 belong to: …에 속하다
3 be filled with: …로 가득 차다
4 be good at은 '…하는 데 능숙하다'의 의미이며, 전치사 at의 목적어로 동명사 using을 써야 한다.

B 1 ask for: …를 요청하다
2 be proud of: …를 자랑스러워하다
3 be ready for: …에 준비가 되다

C 1 on the floor는 명사를 뒤에서 수식하는 형용사 역할을 한다.
2 be sure of: …를 확신하다
3 in the parking lot은 명사를 뒤에서 수식하는 형용사 역할을 한다.

D 1 '… 이래로'의 의미로 전치사 since를 사용한다.
2 '…를 향하여'의 의미로 전치사 for를 사용한다.
3 '…를 통하여'의 의미로 전치사 through를 사용한다.

내신 완성 Grammar Practice
p. 141

1 ④ 2 ⑤ 3 ② 4 (1) look after
(2) belonged to (3) be absent from

문제해설

1 ④ '…부터'의 의미로 전치사 from을 쓴다.

2 ⑤는 명사를 뒤에서 수식하는 형용사 역할이고, 나머지는 동사를 수식하는 부사 역할이다.

3 ② listen to: …를 듣다

4 (1) look after: …를 돌보다
(2) belong to: …에 속하다[…의 소유이다]
(3) be absent from: …에 결석하다

서술형에 나오는 WRITING
p. 142

A 1 chopped onions with a knife
2 praised Lisa for helping other students
B 1 slept for eight hours 2 begin in an hour
3 don't agree with your opinion
C 1 waiting for a bus
2 famous for its night views

문제해설

B 1 '…동안'의 의미로 전치사 for를 사용한다.
2 '…후에'의 의미로 전치사 in을 사용한다.
3 agree with: …에 동의하다

C 1 wait for: …를 기다리다
2 be famous for: …로 유명하다

READING WITH GRAMMAR
pp. 143~144

Reading 1 | 1 (A) break down (B) swim 2 ③
Words | [1] 위, 배 [2] 무게, 체중

해석 | 악어에 대해 무엇이든지 물어보세요!—악어 사냥꾼
Q: 저는 어젯밤 인터넷에서 악어에 관한 기사를 읽었어요. 기사에는 악어가 돌을 먹는다고 쓰여 있었어요. 이게 사실인가요?
A: 육식을 하는 포식 동물이 돌을 먹는다는 것이 이상하게 들릴 수도 있지만, 그것은 사실입니다. 악어는 평균적으로 위(배) 속에 10~15파운드의 돌들을 가지고 있습니다. 이 돌들은 중요한 기능을 합니다. 악어는 대개 먹이를 씹지 않습니다. 대신, 그들은 그것을 통째로 삼킵니다. 위 속의 돌들은 그들이 음식, 특히 딱딱한 껍질과 단단한 뼈를 가진 동물들을 분해하는 것을 도와줍니다. 돌들은 또한 악어의 몸에 무게를 더해 줍니다. 이것은 그들이 물속 깊은 곳에서 헤엄치는 것을 가능하게 합니다.

구문해설

4행 **It** may sound strange [**that** meat-eating predators eat rocks], but it is ture.

▶ It은 가주어이고 that ... rocks가 진주어이다.

8행 The rocks in their stomach **help them break down** the food, ...

▶ help+목적어+동사원형: …가 ~하는 것을 돕다

11행 This makes **it** possible **for them to swim** in deep parts of the water.

▶ it은 가목적어, for them은 to부정사의 의미상의 주어, to swim 이하가 진목적어이다.

문제해설

1 악어는 위 속의 음식물을 분해하고 그들이 물속 깊이 헤엄치기 위해 돌을 삼킨다.

2 밑줄 친 about crocodiles와 ③은 명사를 수식하는 형용사 역할의 전치사구이며, 나머지는 모두 부사 역할을 하는 전치사구이다.

Reading 2 | 1 ③ 2 blamed the man for spreading it

Words | ¹ 도둑

해석 | 한 남자가 거짓 소문을 퍼트렸다. "내 이웃은 도둑이에요."라고 그가 말했다. 이후에, 이웃은 그 소문 때문에 절도를 이유로 체포되었다. 법정에서, 그 이웃은 그것(소문)을 퍼트린 것을 이유로 남자를 비난했다. 판사가 이것에 관해 남자에게 물었을 때, 그는 그것을 인정했다. "하지만 그건 단지 말이었어요. 저는 아무도 해치지 않았어요."라고 그는 말했다. 판사가 남자에게 말했다. "당신이 이웃에 관해 말했던 모든 것을 적으세요. 그 종이를 작은 조각으로 자르고, 그것들을 공중에 버리세요. 그리고 내일 다시 오세요." 남자는 그가 들은 대로 했다.

다음 날, 판사는 "이제 그 조각들을 찾아서 다시 합치세요."라고 말했다. "그건 불가능해요!" 남자는 외쳤다. "맞습니다. 손상된 평판을 바로잡을 방법 또한 없습니다."라고 판사가 말했다. 마침내 남자는 자신의 실수를 깨닫고 이웃에게 사과했다.

구문해설

1행 Later, the neighbor **was arrested** for a theft *because of* the rumor.

▶ 이웃이 '체포되는' 것이므로, 수동태 was arrested가 쓰였다.

▶ because of: …때문에

5행 Write down everything [(**that**) you said about your neighbor].

▶ everything 뒤에 목적격 관계대명사 that이 생략되었다.

7행 The man did **as** he was told.

▶ as는 '…대로'의 의미를 나타내는 접속사이다.

11행 There is also no way **to fix** a damaged reputation, ...

▶ to fix는 앞의 명사 way를 수식하는 형용사적 용법의 to부정사이다.

문제해설

1 위 글의 주제로 알맞은 것은?

① 참을성이 있다면, 좋은 일이 일어날 수 있다.
② 외모로만 누군가를 판단하지 마라.
③ 한 번 내뱉어진 말은 쉽게 돌이킬 수 없다.
④ 동시에 너무 많은 일을 하려고 하지 마라.
⑤ 더 많이 무언가를 할수록, 그것을 더 잘하게 될 것이다.

▶ ③ 자신이 퍼트린 소문 때문에 이웃의 평판을 손상하고 나중에 이것을 뉘우친 내용에 관한 글이다.

2 괄호 안의 단어를 바르게 배열하시오.

▶ '…를 ~의 이유로 탓하다'를 나타내는 「blame ... for ~」 구문에서 for는 전치사이므로 뒤에 목적어(spreading it)가 와야 한다.

내신에 나오는 COMMUNICATION

A 기대 표현하기 p. 145

Check-Up | 1 ③ 2 looking forward to

문제해설

1 ③ 「look forward to v-ing」는 「can't wait to-v」로 바꿔 쓸 수 있다.

B 도움 요청하고 답하기 p. 146

Check-Up | 1 ⑤ 2 (A)→(C)→(D)→(B)

문제해설

1 ⑤ 가방 나르는 것을 도와줄 수 있는지 요청하는 말에 '나는 네 도움은 필요 없어.'라고 대답하는 것은 어색하다.

2 (A) 제가 부탁 하나 해도 될까요?
(C) 네. 무엇을 도와드릴까요?
(D) 제 휴대 전화를 찾을 수 없어요. 당신 것을 써도 될까요?
(B) 물론이죠. 여기 있어요.

FINAL TEST pp. 147~149

1 ② 2 (1) reply (2) swallow 3 ① 4 ②, ⑤ 5 ② 6 ④ 7 ⑤ 8 ⑤ 9 are not ready for 10 ① 11 ② 12 ⑤ 13 Katie is walking across the road. 14 ④ 15 ① 16 ① 17 is busy with 18 along the street 19 ① 20 is fond of 21 for 22 The car does not belong to him. 23 goes to school by bicycle

문제해설

1 주어진 영영 풀이는 '모든 세부 사항이 완전하게 올바른'이라는 의미이므로, ② exact(정확한)가 적절하다.

3 A: 너는 방학에 무슨 계획이 있니?
B: 아니, 없어. 네가 방학 동안 해외여행을 갈 거라고 들었어!
A: 응, ______________________.
▶ 문맥상 빈칸에는 ①(나는 내 여행이 기다려져.)이 들어가는 것이 자연스럽다.

4 ②와 ⑤는 상대방에게 부탁할 때 쓰는 표현이다.

5 ① A: 내가 너에게 부탁 하나 해도 될까?
B: 물론이지. 내가 뭘 도와줄까?
③ A: 제가 부탁 하나 해도 될까요?
B: 물론이죠.
④ A: Lena가 파티에 올 거야.
B: 정말? 나는 빨리 그녀를 보고 싶어.
⑤ A: 내가 설거지하는 것 좀 도와줄 수 있니?
B: 물론이지.
▶ ② 영화가 내일 개봉한다는 말에 그것을 찾고 있다는 대답은 어색하다.

6 for: … 동안 (기간의 길이)

7 until: …까지 (동작·상태의 계속)

8 during: … 동안 (특정 기간)

10 be sure of: …를 확신하다
be different from: …와 다르다

11 be famous for: …로 유명하다
by: …까지 (완료 기한)

12 laugh at: …를 비웃다
be good at: …하는 데 능숙하다

16 ①은 '…후에'의 의미로 시간의 경과를 나타내며, 나머지는 모두 '…안에'의 의미로 장소를 나타낸다.

19 ①에는 be proud of의 of가, 나머지에는 모두 전치사 for가 와야 한다.

[20-21] Ron은 농구를 좋아한다. 어느 날 그는 경기 중에 다쳤다. 그는 통증 때문에 일주일 동안 걸을 수 없었다.

20 be fond of: …를 좋아하다

21 a week는 기간의 길이를 나타내는 말이므로 for가 와야 한다.

22 belong to: …에 속하다[…의 소유이다]

23 by: …로 (교통 수단)

CHAPTER 10 관계사

GRAMMAR FOCUS
p. 152

A 관계대명사 who, whom, whose, which
너는 지금 노래 부르고 있는 소녀를 아니?

1 1) Carl과 축구하고 있는 소년은 내 남동생이다.
2) Ariana와 David는 9년간 알아온 오랜 친구가 있다.
3) 경찰은 자전거를 도난당한 소년을 도와주었다.

2 1) 우리는 요즘 인기 있는 운동화를 사고 싶다.
그녀는 그녀가 일주일 전에 그린 그림을 팔았다.
2) 나는 창문이 깨진 집을 보았다.

Check-Up
p. 153

A 1 who 2 which 3 which 4 who
B 1 a restaurant 2 a movie 3 the sweater 4 My cousin
C 1 whose 2 which[that] 3 who[that] 4 which[that]
D 1 whose 2 who[that] 3 which[that] 4 whom[who/that]

GRAMMAR FOCUS
p. 154

B 관계대명사 that, what

1 저쪽에 서 있는 아이들은 Jack의 친구들이다.
나는 선생님께서 추천해 주신 책을 즐겨 읽었다.

2 우리가 점심으로 만든 것은 버섯 피자였다.
소음 때문에 그들은 그녀가 말한 것을 들을 수 없었다.
우주를 탐험하는 것이 내가 미래에 하고 싶은 것이다.

Check-Up
p. 155

A 1 that 2 what 3 that 4 that 5 whose
B 1 that 2 that were 3 which
C 1 that[which] 2 O 3 that[which] 4 O
D 1 what 2 that 3 that 4 What

GRAMMAR FOCUS
p. 156

C 관계부사

1 우리 가족은 Oliver가 일하는 체육관에서 운동한다.

2 1) 나는 우리 팀이 우승한 날을 잊지 않을 것이다.
2) 그녀는 그녀가 한 달에 한 번 봉사 활동을 했던 마을을 방문했다.
3) 이것이 Mike가 떠난 이유이다.

4) 기술은 학생들이 공부하는 방식을 변화시켜 왔다.

| Check-Up | .... p. 157

A 1 why 2 where 3 how 4 when
B 1 (the city) 2 (the reason) 3 (a time) 4 (an island)
C 1 when 2 why 3 where
D 1 how 2 where 3 why 4 when

Grammar Practice p. 158

A 1 whose 2 who[that]
3 where[at which / in which]
B 1 whom you're talking about
2 when our vacation starts
3 why he seems nervous
4 how she practices dancing
C 1 why 2 where 3 when 4 how
D 1 who[that] live in this town
2 which[that] I bought last month
3 what[the thing which / the thing that] I told them

문제해설

A 1 선행사가 관계사절 안에서 수식하는 명사의 소유격 역할을 하므로 소유격 관계대명사 whose가 알맞다.
2 선행사가 사람이므로 주격 관계대명사 who[that]가 알맞다.
3 장소를 나타내는 명사 a place가 선행사이므로 관계부사 where 또는 at which[in which]가 알맞다.

D 1 선행사인 The fishermen을 수식하는 주격 관계대명사 who[that]를 써서 문장을 완성한다.
2 선행사 The cell phone을 수식하는 목적격 관계대명사 which[that]를 써서 문장을 완성한다.

내신 완성 Grammar Practice p. 159

1 ③ 2 ④ 3 ① 4 (1) which[that] she bought during her trip (2) which we slept last night

문제해설

1 ③ 선행사가 시간을 나타내므로 관계부사 when이 알맞다.
2 ④ 선행사 the way와 관계부사 how는 함께 쓸 수 없다.
3 ①은 목적격 관계대명사이고 나머지는 모두 주격 관계대명사이다.
4 (2) 장소를 나타내는 the tent를 선행사로 하는 관계부사 where 대신 「전치사+관계대명사」 형태인 in which로 나타낼 수 있다.

서술형에 나오는 WRITING p. 160

A 1 I am thinking about what you told me.
2 The girl who wrote the song graduated from this school.
3 Jake drew a house whose roof was covered with snow.
B 1 (whom[who/that]) many students respect
2 the way (in which) people lived
3 (which[that]) the doctor has
C 1 which[that] was built
2 who[that] painted

문제해설

B 1 사람을 선행사로 하는 목적격 관계대명사 who(m) 또는 that을 이용한다. 목적격 관계대명사는 생략할 수 있다.
2 방식을 나타내는 선행사 the way (in which)를 이용한다.
3 사물을 선행사로 하는 목적격 관계대명사 which[that]를 이용한다. 목적격 관계대명사는 생략할 수 있다.

C 1 사물을 선행사로 하는 주격 관계대명사 which[that]를 이용한다.
2 사람을 선행사로 하는 주격 관계대명사 who[that]를 이용한다.

READING WITH GRAMMAR pp. 161~162

Reading 1 | 1 ⑤ 2 (A) where (B) what
Words | [1]손상, 피해 [2]구하다

해석 | 우리는 불가사리가 산호를 죽이는 것을 어떻게 막을 수 있을까? 과학자들은 해답을 발견했다고 생각한다—바로 불가사리를 죽이는 로봇이다. 그 로봇은 COTSbot이라고 불린다. 이것은 "악마 불가사리 로봇"의 약자이다. 악마 불가사리는 뾰족한 가시가 있는 커다란 불가사리다. 그것은 산호를 먹는 것을 정말 좋아한다. 그것은 세계에서 가장 큰 산호초 지대인 Great Barrier Reef에 큰 피해를 입혀 왔다. 과학자들은 산호초를 구하고 싶어 한다. 이것이 바로 그들이 COTSbot을 발명한 이유이다.

그것은 악마 불가사리가 사는 장소들 주변을 헤엄쳐 다닌다. 이 불가사리들의 가시가 그것(COTSbot)이 찾는 것이다. 그것이 불가사리들을 발견하면, 그것들을 죽이기 위해 독을 사용한다. 과학자들은 COTSbot이 곧 Great Barrier Reef를 보호하기를 희망한다.

구문해설

1행 How can we **stop starfish from killing** coral?
▸ stop A from v-ing: A가 …하는 것을 막다

4행 It has done a lot of damage to **the Great Barrier Reef, the biggest coral reef in the world**.
▸ the Great Barrier Reef와 the biggest coral reef in the world는 동격이다.

9행 When it finds starfish, it uses poison **to kill** them.
▸ to kill은 목적을 나타내는 부사적 용법의 to부정사이다.

문제해설

1 ⑤ COTSbot은 독을 사용해 악마 불가사리를 죽인다고 했다.

2 (A) 선행사가 장소를 나타내는 places이므로 관계부사 where가 알맞다.
(B) 선행사가 없으므로 선행사를 포함하는 관계대명사 what이 알맞다.

Reading 2 | 1 ③ 2 ③
Words | [1]양 [2]환경

해석 | 당신은 무료 저녁 식사를 위해 자전거를 타 본 적이 있는가? 당신은 덴마크에 있는 한 호텔에서 그것을 할 수 있다. 그곳에 묵는 손님들은 호텔을 위한 전기를 만들어 내는 특별한 운동용 자전거를 탈 수 있다. 당신이 자전거를 더 많이 탈수록, 더 많은 전기를 만들어 낸다. 각 자전거에는 당신이 만들어 내는 에너지의 양을 보여주는 화면이 있다. 당신이 만드는 에너지는 배터리에 저장된다. 이후에, 그 에너지는 호텔에서 전기를 관리하기 위해 사용하는 공간으로 이동된다.
손님들은 대략 10와트의 전기를 만들어 낼 때마다 무료 저녁 식사 쿠폰을 받는다. 이것은 15분 정도의 페달 밟기가 걸린다. 이 재미있는 생각은 호텔이 환경과 그곳의 손님들을 동시에 돕는 방법이다.

구문해설

6행 **The more** you ride the bikes, **the more** electricity you make.
▶ the+비교급 ..., the+비교급 ~: …하면 할수록 더욱 ~하다

8행 Each bike has a screen which[that] shows the amount of energy [(**which**[**that**]) you create].
▶ you 앞에 energy를 선행사로 하는 목적격 관계대명사 which[that]가 생략되었다.

문제해설

1 위 글의 제목으로 가장 알맞은 것은?
① 호텔에서의 전기 이용
② 덴마크에 있는 한 호텔의 특별한 행사들
③ 한 호텔의 환경친화적인 방침
④ 덴마크에 있는 한 호텔 주변의 자전거 도로
⑤ 자전거로 운동하는 것의 장점들
▶ 이 글은 덴마크의 한 호텔이 환경과 손님들을 동시에 돕기 위해 손님이 특별한 운동용 자전거로 전기를 생산하면 무료 저녁 식사를 제공한다는 내용이므로, ③이 제목으로 가장 적절하다.

2 어법상 바르지 못한 것은?
▶ ③ 선행사가 a screen이고 관계사절에서 주어 역할을 하므로 주격 관계대명사 which 또는 that이 와야 한다.

내신에 나오는 COMMUNICATION

A 시간 약속 정하기

p. 163

Check-Up | 1 ⑤ 2 Are you free

문제해설

1 5시에 만날 수 있는지 물었으므로 ⑤(미안하지만, 못 만나. 우리 나중에 언젠가 만날 수 있니?)가 대답으로 적절하다.

B 의견 묻고 답하기

p. 164

Check-Up | 1 ①, ④ 2 What do you think of[about]

문제해설

1 A: ______________
B: 나는 멜로디가 환상적이라고 생각해.
① 너는 그 음악에 대해 어떻게 생각하니?
② 너는 음악 듣는 것을 좋아하니?
③ 너는 어떤 종류의 음악을 좋아하니?
④ 너는 그 음악에 대해 어떻게 생각하니?
⑤ 너는 왜 음악 듣는 것을 즐기니?
▶ ①, ④ 상대방의 의견을 물을 때는 「How do you like ...?」, 「How do you feel about ...?」 등의 표현을 쓸 수 있다.

FINAL TEST

pp. 165~167

1 ② 2 electricity 3 (C)→(A)→(D)→(B) 4 ① 5 ③ 6 ③ 7 ⑤ 8 ③ 9 ② 10 ③ 11 when 12 ⑤ 13 ⑤ 14 that 15 the reason why 16 ④ 17 ① 18 where 19 ③ 20 The way he talks makes me upset. 21 I cut the potatoes which[that] I grew. 22 That→What[The thing which/The thing that] 23 who[that]

문제해설

1 ② poison은 '독'이라는 뜻이다.

3 (C) 너는 이 사진에 대해 어떻게 생각하니? 내가 어제 찍었어.
(A) 나는 그것이 놀랍다고 생각해. 네가 찍은 다른 사진들을 볼 수 있을까?
(D) 미안하지만, 그것들은 집에 있어. 내가 내일 가져올게.
(B) 좋아! 그것들을 보기를 기대할게.

4 ① 이번 주말에 시간 있는지 묻는 말에 왜 시간이 되는지 되묻는 것은 어색하다.

5 ① A: 우리 다음 주 금요일에 만날까?
B: 미안하지만, 나는 그날 다른 계획들이 있어.
② A: 오늘 밤에 만나는 게 어때?
B: 오늘은 안 돼.
④ A: Brown 선생님의 수업에 대해 어떻게 생각하니?
B: 나는 그의 수업이 매우 흥미롭다고 생각해.
⑤ A: 너 이번 주 토요일에 한가하니?
B: 미안해. 나는 그날 바빠.
▶ ③ 이 소설에 대한 의견을 묻는 말에 언젠간 소설을 쓰고 싶다는 대답은 어색하다.

6 ③ 선행사가 동물이고 관계사절 안에서 주어 역할을 하므로 주격 관계대명사 which가 알맞다.

7 ⑤ 선행사가 사람이고 관계사절 안에서 동사의 목적어 역할을 하므로 목적격 관계대명사 whom이 알맞다.

8 ③의 빈칸에는 소유격 관계대명사 whose가 와야 한다.

9 ② 선행사 the way, 관계부사 how, the way in which 중 하나가 쓰인 문장인 ②가 알맞다.

11 선행사가 시간을 나타내므로 관계부사 when을 써야 한다.

12 ① who → which[that], ② that → what, ③ why → when[on which], ④ what → which[that]로 고쳐야 한다.

14 첫 번째 빈칸에는 주격 관계대명사 who나 that이, 두 번째 빈칸에는 목적격 관계대명사 which나 that이 와야 하므로 공통으로 들어갈 말은 that이다.

16 ④ 주격 관계대명사는 생략할 수 없다.

17 ①은 목적격 관계대명사, 나머지는 모두 주격 관계대명사이다.

19 ③ 선행사가 관계사절 안에서 수식하는 명사의 소유격으로 쓰이므로 빈칸에는 소유격 관계대명사 whose가 와야 한다.

21 선행사가 사물인 the potatoes이므로 목적격 관계대명사 which나 that을 써서 문장을 완성한다.

23 Jim: 나는 미술 동아리에 가입하고 싶은데, 그림을 잘 못 그려.
Sue: 걱정하지 마. 그리기에 관심이 있는 누구든 미술 동아리에 가입할 수 있어.
Jim: 정말? 그럼 가입해야겠다.
▸ 사람인 선행사를 수식하는 주격 관계대명사 who나 that을 써야 한다.

CHAPTER 11 접속사

GRAMMAR FOCUS

p. 170

A 부사절을 이끄는 접속사

1 1) 나는 우리 할아버지가 돌아가셨을 때 많이 울었다.
2) Ethan은 그의 여동생이 버스에 탈 때 그녀를 보았다.
3) 내가 자고 있는 동안에, 누군가가 나에게 담요를 덮어 주었다.
4) 우리 운동을 시작하기 전에 준비 운동을 하자.
Joe는 Nancy가 떠난 후에 탁자 위에서 그녀의 휴대 전화를 발견했다.
5) 그가 올 때까지 여기에서 기다리세요.

2 내가 그녀의 이름을 잊어버려서 그녀는 내게 화가 났다.
나는 비밀번호를 모르기 때문에, 컴퓨터에 로그인 할 수 없다.
날씨가 안 좋았기 때문에 우리의 항공편은 취소되었다.

3 비록 그는 배가 고팠지만, 아무것도 먹지 않았다.
비록 그녀는 수영을 잘 못했을지라도, 최선을 다했다.

4 1) 만약 당신이 일정을 변경하고 싶다면, 저에게 알려 주세요.
2) 네가 바쁘지 않으면 지금 이야기하자.

Check-Up

p. 171

A 1 While 2 after 3 although 4 because
B 1 Unless, are 2 If, not 3 Unless, study
C 1 as 2 When 3 Though 4 until

GRAMMAR FOCUS

p. 172

B 명사절을 이끄는 접속사

1 1) 그가 해고되었다는 것은 사실이다.
2) 나는 그 책이 도움이 된다고 생각한다.
3) 문제는 그들은 충분한 돈을 갖고 있지 않다는 것이다.

2 우리는 그녀가 영어로 말할 수 있는지 궁금하다.
나는 그 수업에 등록해야 할지 (말아야 할지) 모르겠다.

C 짝으로 이루어진 접속사

1) 그와 그의 형은 둘 다 축구 팬이다.
2) 내가 너에게 문자 메시지를 보내거나 전화할게.
3) 그녀는 울지도 웃지도 않았다.
4) 그 다큐멘터리는 교육적일 뿐만 아니라 흥미롭다.
5) 그 소설은 2018년이 아니라 2010년에 쓰였다.

Check-Up

p. 173

A 1 but 2 whether 3 It 4 neither 5 Both
B 1 are 2 how I can get to 3 that 4 but 5 or
C 1 that 2 if[whether] 3 as well as 4 either, or 5 not, but

Grammar Practice

p. 174

A 1 that 2 are 3 see 4 because of
B 1 before 2 whether 3 Since 4 even though 5 Unless
C 1 both, and 2 either, or take a walk 3 not only, but also 4 when the library closes

문제해설

A 1 think의 목적어 역할을 하는 명사절을 이끄는 접속사 that이 와야 한다.
2 「both A and B」는 복수 취급한다.
3 조건을 나타내는 접속사가 이끄는 부사절에서는 미래의 일이라도 현재시제로 나타낸다.
4 뒤에 명사구(the strong wind)가 나왔으므로, 접속사 because가 아닌 전치사 because of가 와야 한다.

B 1 before: … 전에
2 whether ... or not: …인지 아닌지
3 since: … 때문에
4 even though: 비록 …일지라도
5 unless: (만약) …하지 않으면

C 1 both A and B: A와 B 둘 다
2 either A or B: A나 B 중 하나
3 not only A but also B: A뿐만 아니라 B도
4 간접의문문의 어순은 「의문사+주어+동사」이다.

내신 완성 *Grammar Practice* p. 175

1 ② 2 ④ 3 ⑤ 4 (1) until the rain stops
(2) Jake as well as Jane likes

문제해설

1 첫 번째 빈칸에는 '…하면서'의 의미를, 두 번째 빈칸에는 '… 대로'의 의미를 나타내는 접속사가 와야 하므로, 공통으로 들어갈 말은 ② as이다.

2 ① 저는 당신이 휴가를 즐기시길 바랍니다.
② Carter는 모두가 그를 좋아한다고 생각한다.
③ 그녀는 그녀에게 열쇠가 없다는 것을 깨달았다.
④ 내가 일주일 전에 산 자전거가 고장 났다.
⑤ 우리는 축구팀이 최선을 다했다는 것을 안다.
▶ ④의 that은 목적격 관계대명사이며, 나머지는 모두 목적어 역할을 하는 명사절을 이끄는 접속사이다.

3 ⑤ 시간을 나타내는 접속사가 이끄는 부사절에서는 미래의 일이라도 현재시제로 나타내므로 will go를 go로 고쳐야 한다.

서술형에 나오는 *WRITING* p. 176

A 1 Nobody knows whether he left
2 We asked Emma where she wanted to go
3 I listened carefully as she told me
B 1 heart broke when she heard the news
2 tried bungee jumping even though I was a little afraid
3 always takes notes since he often forgets things
C 1 both, and 2 neither, nor

문제해설

B 1 Olivia는 가슴이 아팠다. 그녀는 소식을 들었다.
→ Olivia는 소식을 들었을 때 가슴이 아팠다.
2 나는 번지점프를 했다. 나는 조금 무서웠다.
→ 비록 나는 조금 무서웠지만 번지점프를 했다.
3 Tom은 항상 메모를 한다. 그는 자주 잊어버린다.
→ Tom은 자주 잊어버리기 때문에 항상 메모를 한다.

C 1 우유와 오렌지 주스 둘 다 있으므로, 「both A and B」를 써야 한다.
2 의자 위에 있는 가방이 파란색도 갈색도 아니므로, 「neither A nor B」를 써야 한다.

READING WITH GRAMMAR pp. 177~178

Reading 1 | 1 ② 2 ③
Words | ¹금속 ²비슷한

해석 | 우주는 어떤 냄새가 날까? 우주는 진공 상태이기 때문에, 대부분의 사람은 그것이 아무 냄새도 나지 않는다고 생각한다. 그러나, 많은 우주 비행사들은 이것이 사실이 아니라고 말한다. 물론, 그들은 우주 냄새를 직접 맡을 수 없다. 그러나 그들이 우주를 탐험한 후에 우주선 안으로 돌아가면, 그들의 우주 헬멧과 우주복에서 우주의 냄새를 맡을 수 있다.
한 우주 비행사는 그것이 불에 탄 금속 같은 냄새가 난다고 말했다. 다른 사람들은 그 냄새를 불에 탄 고기와 비슷하다고 묘사했다. 한 우주 관광객은 심지어 그것이 불에 탄 아몬드 쿠키 같은 냄새가 난다고 기록했다! 비록 사람들이 냄새를 다른 방식으로 묘사할지라도, 우주는 특별한 냄새를 가지고 있다는 것이 분명하다. 과학자들은 무엇이 이 냄새를 야기하는지 알아내려고 여전히 애쓰고 있다!

구문해설

3행 However, many astronauts say (**that**) *this* isn't true.
▶ say 뒤에 목적어 역할을 하는 명사절을 이끄는 접속사 that이 생략되었다.
▶ this는 앞 문장의 it doesn't smell like anything을 가리킨다.

11행 ..., **it**'s clear [**that** space *does* have a special smell].
▶ it은 가주어이고 that 이하가 진주어이다.
▶ does는 뒤에 나오는 동사 have를 강조하는 조동사이다.

문제해설

1 ① 우주 냄새를 맡는 것은 불가능하다
② 우주는 특별한 냄새를 가지고 있다
③ 우주 비행사들은 우주복을 착용해야 한다
④ 우주 비행사들은 우주의 냄새를 좋아한다
⑤ 그 냄새는 탄 음식에 의해 야기된다
▶ 사람들마다 다르지만 우주에서 어떤 특정한 냄새를 맡았다고 했으므로, 빈칸에는 ②가 들어가는 것이 적절하다.

2 ③의 that은 목적격 관계대명사이며, 본문과 나머지의 that은 모두 명사절을 이끄는 접속사로 쓰였다.

Reading 2 | 1 ③ 2 but also because
Words | ¹자원봉사자

해석 | 벽이 수리가 필요할 때 그것을 고치는 많은 방법들이 있다. 독일인 예술가인 Jan Vormann의 방법은 창의적이고 아름답다. 대부분의 수리공은 낡은 벽을 수리하기 위해 페인트와 회반죽을 사용하지만, Vormann은 (낡은 벽의) 틈과 구멍을 선명한 빛깔의 레고 블록

으로 채운다. (레고 블록은 Ole Kirk Christiansen이라는 한 목수에 의해 처음으로 만들어졌다.) Vormann은 로마에서 그의 첫 번째 벽을 작업한 후에, 그의 기법을 사용하기 위해 전 세계 곳곳으로 초대를 받기 시작했다. 오늘날, 자원봉사자 팀들과 함께, 그는 여전히 흥미로운 레고 예술 작품을 만든다. Vormann이 이 기법을 선택한 것은 그것이 재미있을 뿐만 아니라, 그것은 시선을 끌 수 있는 아주 좋은 방법이기도 하기 때문이다. 지나가던 사람들도 그 재미를 즐기고 싶어서, 종종 멈춰 서서 Vormann과 함께 동참하기도 한다.

구문해설

6행 ..., Vormann began to get invited to places all around the world **to use** his technique.
▶ to use는 목적을 나타내는 부사적 용법의 to부정사이다.

10행 People **passing by** often stop and join in with Vormann, *as* they want to enjoy the fun, too.
▶ passing by는 명사 People을 수식하는 현재분사구이다.
▶ as는 '… 때문에'의 의미로 이유를 나타내는 접속사로 쓰였다.

문제해설

1 위 글에서 필요하지 않은 문장은?
▶ 낡은 벽을 수리하는 데 레고 블록을 사용하는 독일인 예술가에 관한 글이므로, 레고 블록이 누구에 의해 처음 만들어졌는지에 대한 내용인 ③은 흐름과 관계없다.

2 밑줄 친 부분과 같은 의미가 되도록 빈칸을 채우시오.
▶ not only A but also B: A뿐만 아니라 B도
because: … 때문에

내신에 나오는 COMMUNICATION

A 장래 희망 묻고 답하기 p. 179

Check-Up | 1 ② 2 What are you going to be

문제해설

1 미래에 무엇이 되고 싶은지 물었으므로, 요리사가 되고 싶다는 ②가 대답으로 적절하다.

B 제안하기 p. 180

Check-Up | 1 ② 2 why don't you write a letter

문제해설

1 ②는 '우리는 왜 저녁으로 스테이크를 먹니?'의 의미이고, 나머지는 모두 저녁으로 스테이크를 먹자는 제안의 의미이다.

FINAL TEST pp. 181~183

1 ③ 2 (1) cause (2) sweat 3 ⑤ 4 (D)→(B)→(C)→(A) 5 What do you want to be 6 ② 7 ④ 8 ③ 9 either a bus or 10 ③ 11 ① 12 ③ 13 Ann is not only smart but also kind. 14 ① 15 when she opened the gift 16 ⑤ 17 (A) that (B) until 18 ① 19 ③ 20 because → because of 21 Although he was sad, he smiled. 22 Both, are carrying a bag 23 Neither, is wearing glasses

문제해설

1 그 이야기는 매우 재미있다.
① 슬픈 ② 무서운 ③ 재미있는 ④ 전통의 ⑤ 창의적인

2 (1) 빠르게 운전하는 것은 사고를 야기할 수 있다.
(2) 나는 매운 음식을 먹을 때 땀을 많이 흘린다.

3 ⑤ 제안하는 물음에 '신경 쓰지 마. 난 괜찮아.'라고 대답하는 것은 어색하다.

4 (D) 너는 미래에 무엇이 될 거니?
(B) 나는 베스트셀러 작가가 되고 싶어.
(C) 멋지다! 너는 소설을 쓰고 싶니?
(A) 응. 나는 판타지 소설을 쓰고 싶어.

6 문맥상 ② '…할 때'의 의미인 접속사 when이 와야 한다.

7 문맥상 ④ '(만약) …하지 않으면'의 의미인 접속사 unless가 와야 한다.

8 문맥상 ③ '… 때문에'의 의미인 접속사 because가 와야 한다.

9 either A or B: A나 B 중 하나

11 ①「neither A nor B」는 B에 동사의 수를 일치시킨다.

12 ③ 문맥상 '비록 …이지만'의 의미인 접속사 though 또는 although가 와야 자연스럽다.

14 A: 너 콘서트가 언제 시작하는지 아니?
B: 5분이나 10분 후에 시작할 거야.
A: 곧 내가 제일 좋아하는 가수를 볼 수 있다니 믿을 수가 없어.
▶ ① 간접의문문은「의문사+주어+동사」의 어순이므로, the concert starts로 고쳐야 한다.

16 ⑤ 문맥상 '비록 …이지만'의 의미인 접속사 Although가 와야 한다.

17 (A) 보어 역할을 하는 명사절을 이끄는 접속사 that이 와야 한다.
(B) '…할 때까지'의 의미를 나타내는 접속사 until이 와야 한다.

18 첫 번째 빈칸에는 '…이기 때문에', 두 번째 빈칸에는 '…하고 있을 때'를 나타내는 접속사가 와야 하므로, 공통으로 들어갈 말은 ① as이다.

19 ③의 if는 '…인지'의 의미이며, 나머지는 모두 '(만일) …라면'의 의미이다.

20 지난주에, 나의 사촌은 야구장에 가고 싶어 했다. 하지만, 비 때문에 경기가 취소되어서, 그는 집에 머물러야 했다.

▶ 뒤에 명사 rain이 왔으므로, 접속사 because 대신 전치사 because of를 써야 한다.

22 both A and B: A와 B 둘 다

23 neither A nor B: A도 B도 아닌

CHAPTER 12 대명사가 만드는 중요 구문

GRAMMAR FOCUS ······ p. 186

A 부정대명사

1 A: 이 근처에 슈퍼마켓이 있나요?
B: 제과점 건너편에 하나 있어요.
이 신발은 제게 커요. 더 작은 것이 있나요?

2 나는 이미 애플파이 한 조각을 먹었고 또 하나 주문했다.

3 모두가 긴 여행 후에 지쳤다.
요즘 모든 것이 잘되어 간다.
그 호텔에 있는 모든 방이 예약되었다.
모든 돈이 상환되었다.

4 Ron과 Teresa는 우주 비행사가 되고 싶어 한다. 둘 다 우주에 관심이 있다.
두 과학자 다 연구 결과에 만족했다.

5 각각의 사람은 카드 세 장을 받는다.
각각의 배우들은 다른 영화로 유명해졌다.
모든 학생은 열흘 내에 도서관 책을 반납해야 한다.

Check-Up ······ p. 187

A 1 Each 2 are 3 both 4 ones
B 1 every 2 all 3 Both 4 another
C 1 has 2 it 3 item
D 1 Each 2 one 3 Every 4 another

GRAMMAR FOCUS ······ p. 188

B 부정대명사 구문

나는 두 마리의 애완동물이 있다. 하나는 앵무새이고, 나머지 하나는 원숭이이다.
차 세 대가 있다. 하나는 파란색, 다른 하나는 빨간색, 나머지 하나는 검은색이다.
어떤 관광객들은 호텔에서 쉬었고, 다른 어떤 관광객들은 쇼핑을 갔다.
쿠키 일부는 여기 있는데, 나머지 전부는 어디 있니?
Jim과 Chloe는 서로 이야기하고 있다.
농구 선수들이 서로에게 공을 패스하고 있다.

C 재귀대명사

1 어떤 사람들은 그들의 옷을 통해 자신을 표현한다.
Amy는 거울 속에 있는 자신의 모습을 봤다.

2 나는 직접 전구를 교체했다.
너는 디자인 자체를 바꿀 순 없다.

Check-Up ······ p. 189

A 1 us 2 herself 3 One 4 the other 5 each
B 1 O 2 X 3 X 4 O
C 1 themselves 2 another 3 the other
D 1 yourself 2 Some, others 3 One, the other

Grammar Practice p. 190

A 1 myself 2 it 3 ones 4 were
B 1 one 2 each 3 the other 4 Some
C 1 by himself 2 herself 3 Some, others 4 One, another, the other

문제해설

A 1 목적어가 주어와 동일하므로 재귀대명사를 써야 한다.
3 앞에 나온 명사(socks)와 같은 종류의 사물을 가리키고 복수형이므로 ones가 되어야 한다.
4 「all (of)+명사」 뒤에 나오는 동사는 명사의 수에 일치시킨다.

B 2 '매년'이라는 의미를 나타내기 위해 each가 와야 한다.
3 one ... the other ~: (둘 중의) 하나는 …, 나머지 하나는 ~
4 some ... the others ~: 어떤 것[사람]들은 …, 나머지 전부는 ~

C 1 by oneself: 혼자서
3 some ... others ~: 어떤 것[사람]들은 …, 다른 어떤 것[사람]들은 ~
4 one ... another ~ the other ~: 하나는 …, 다른 하나는 ~, 나머지 하나는 ~

내신 완성 Grammar Practice p. 191

1 ④ 2 ① 3 ⑤ 4 (1) helped one another (2) make yourselves at home

문제해설

1 앞에 나온 명사와 같은 종류의 사물을 추가적으로 나타낼 때는 ④ another를 쓴다.

2 ① 「each+단수명사」는 단수 취급하므로 have를 has로 고쳐야 한다.

3 ⑤ 강조 용법의 재귀대명사는 생략 가능하다. 나머지는 동사나 전치사의 목적어 역할을 하는 재귀 용법으로 쓰였다.

4 (1) one another: 서로
(2) make oneself at home: 편안하게 지내다

서술형에 나오는 WRITING p. 192

A 1 All of the members write greeting cards
2 Both of my aunts are planning to move
3 I will buy another pair

B 1 Each of the passengers has to
2 She imagined herself
3 helped ourselves to

C 1 One, the other
2 One, another, the other

문제해설

B 3 help oneself to: …를 마음껏 먹다

C 1 너는 어느 공을 원하니? 하나는 야구공이고, 나머지 하나는 축구공이야.
▸ one ... the other ~: (둘 중의) 하나는 …, 나머지 하나는 ~

2 세 명의 소년이 있다. 한 사람은 주황색 셔츠를 입고 있고, 다른 한 사람은 줄무늬 셔츠를 입고 있고, 나머지 한 사람은 검은색 셔츠를 입고 있다.
▸ one ... another ~ the other ~: 하나는 …, 다른 하나는 ~, 나머지 하나는 ~

READING WITH GRAMMAR pp. 193~194

Reading 1 | 1 ① 2 ③
Words | [1] 깊은 [2] 포기하다

해석 | 어느 날, 개구리 두 마리가 구덩이에 빠졌다. 그들은 밖으로 뛰어나오려고 애썼지만, 그 구덩이는 너무 깊었다. 다른 모든 개구리들이 구덩이 주위로 모여서 그 운 나쁜 한 쌍을 내려다보았다. "이건 정말 끔찍하구나!"라고 그들은 말했다. "저 구덩이는 정말 깊어. 너희들은 절대로 저기에서 나오지 못할 거야!" 이것을 듣고, 개구리들 중 한 마리는 포기하고 구덩이에서 뛰쳐나오길 시도하는 것을 멈췄다. 하지만 나머지 한 마리는 계속해서 점점 더 높이 뛰었다. 마침내, 그 개구리는 그 끔찍한 구덩이에서 탈출할 수 있었다.

지켜보고 있던 몇몇 개구리들이 그에게 왜 포기하지 않았는지 물어보았지만, 그는 대답하지 않았다. 사실, 그는 귀가 들리지 않았고 나머지 개구리들이 자신을 응원하고 있다고 생각했다.

구문해설

4행 **Hearing this**, one of the frogs gave up and stopped trying ....
▸ Hearing this는 분사구문으로, After one of the frogs heard this로 바꿔 쓸 수 있다.

5행 But the other **kept jumping** *higher and higher*.
▸ keep+v-ing: 계속 …하다
▸ 비교급+and+비교급: 점점 더 …한[하게]

8행 Some frogs [**who** were watching] asked him [*why* he didn't give up], ...
▸ who were watching은 선행사 Some frogs를 수식하는 주격 관계대명사절이다.
▸ why 이하는 asked의 직접목적어 역할을 한다.

문제해설

1 ①은 구덩이에서 나오기를 포기한 개구리를, 나머지는 모두 나오기 위해 노력한 개구리를 가리킨다.

2 구덩이에 빠진 두 마리 중 나오기를 포기한 개구리 외에 '나머지 한 마리'를 가리키는 말이 와야 하므로, ③ the other가 적절하다.

Reading 2 | 1 ③ 2 itself
Words | [1] 흡수하다 [2] 보이지 않는

해석 | 탁 트인 물속에서는 숨을 곳이 아무 데도 없다. 하지만, 어떤 상어들은 이 문제를 극복했다. 바다에서 가장 작은 상어들 중 하나인 랜턴상어는 특별한 방법으로 자신을 숨길 수 있다. 이 상어는 태양으로부터 빛을 흡수해서 빛을 다시 만들어 내는 장기들을 가지고 있다. 이것들은 랜턴상어가 그것의 이름이 시사하는 것처럼 빛나게 해 준다.

하지만 이것이 어떻게 상어를 숨겨 줄까? 화창한 날에 포식자나 먹잇감이 상어 밑에서 헤엄치고 있다고 상상해 봐라. 보통, 그들은 햇빛 아래에서 상어의 윤곽을 볼 수 있다. 하지만, 랜턴상어가 빛을 낼 때, 그것은 그저 물속의 햇빛 그 자체처럼 보일 뿐이다. 이것은 랜턴상어를 안 보이게 함으로써 포식자와 먹잇감 둘 다 랜턴상어를 발견하지 못하게 한다.

구문해설

2행 **The lantern shark**, **one of the smallest sharks in the ocean**, can hide ....
▸ The lantern shark와 one ... in the ocean은 동격이다.

3행 The shark has organs [**that** *absorb* light from the sun and *reproduce* it].
▸ that 이하는 선행사 organs를 수식하는 주격 관계대명사절이다.
▸ 관계사절 안에서 동사 absorb와 reproduce가 접속사 and로 병렬 연결되어 있다.

11행 This **keeps** *both* predators *and* prey **from finding** the lantern shark by making it "invisible."
▸ keep+목적어+from v-ing: …가 ~하지 못하게 하다
▸ both A and B: A와 B 둘 다
▸ it은 the lantern shark를 가리킨다.

문제해설

1 아래 요약문을 읽고 빈칸 (A)와 (B)에 들어갈 말이 바르게 짝지어

진 것을 고르시오.

▶ ③ 랜턴상어는 자신의 장기로 빛을 내서 자신을 보호한다고 하였으므로, 빈칸에는 light(빛)와 organs(장기들)가 와야 한다.

2 밑줄 친 단어를 바르게 고치시오.

▶ 문장의 주어가 The lantern shark이므로, 재귀대명사로 themselves가 아닌 itself가 와야 한다.

내신에 나오는 COMMUNICATION

A 이해 점검하기 p. 195

Check-Up | 1 ①, ③ 2 Do you understand

문제해설

1 A: 시청역에서 2호선으로 갈아타세요. 제 말 이해하시겠어요?

B: ____________

▶ 이해했는지 물었을 때는 ①(그렇지 않아요.)이나 ③(죄송하지만, 이해가 안 돼요.)과 같이 대답할 수 있다.

B 조언 구하고 답하기 p. 196

Check-Up | 1 ⑤ 2 I think you should apologize to him.

문제해설

1 A: 나 감기에 걸렸어. 내가 무엇을 해야 할까?

B: ____________

▶ 감기에 걸려서 조언을 구하는 말에 대한 대답으로 적절한 것은 ⑤ '진찰을 받는 게 어때?'이다.

FINAL TEST pp. 197~199

1 ⑤ 2 pair 3 (B) → (D) → (C) → (A) 4 ③ 5 ④ 6 ② 7 ① 8 ① 9 themselves 10 beside himself 11 ⑤ 12 ② 13 ④ 14 ④ 15 ③ 16 ② 17 ⑤ 18 ③ 19 by yourself 20 were → was 21 was → were 22 The three men encouraged one another. 23 some, the others

문제해설

1 ⑤ overcome은 '극복하다'의 의미이다.

3 (B) 너 걱정 있어 보여. 무슨 일이니?

(D) 나는 지하철에 열쇠를 놓고 내렸어. 내가 무엇을 해야 할까?

(C) 내 생각에 너는 분실물 취급소에 가 봐야 해.

(A) 알겠어. 그렇게 해 볼게.

4 A: ____________

B: 아니요. 다시 설명해 주시겠어요?

① 어떻게 그렇게 말하실 수 있죠?

② 그것이 마음에 드나요?

③ 제 말 이해하시겠어요?

④ 그것을 다시 한 번 말해 주시겠어요?

⑤ 제가 뭘 해야 한다고 생각하시나요?

▶ 문맥상 빈칸에는 이해를 점검하는 표현인 ③이 와야 한다.

5 A: 토마토 스파게티는 어떻게 만들면 될까?

B: 먼저, 면을 9분 정도 삶아.

A: 응. 그다음엔?

B: 그러고 나서, 토마토를 조금 썰고 그것들을 약간의 채소, 소스, 소금 조금과 섞어. 다 이해하니?

A: 응, 이해해.

▶ 주어진 문장은 상대방이 이해했는지 확인하는 표현으로 '이해해.'라는 대답 바로 전인 ④에 들어가는 것이 적절하다.

6 ② every + 기간: …마다

7 ① 뒤에 동사 were가 쓰인 것으로 보아, 복수 취급하는 부정대명사 All이 와야 한다.

8 ①의 myself는 강조 용법으로 쓰인 재귀대명사이고, 나머지는 모두 재귀 용법으로 쓰였다.

10 beside oneself: 제정신이 아닌

11 ⑤ 문맥상 앞에 나온 명사와 같은 종류의 사물을 추가적으로 나타내는 것이므로, another를 쓴다.

12 All of 뒤에 복수명사 my friends가 왔으므로, 첫 번째 빈칸에는 like가 와야 한다.

「each of + 복수명사」는 단수 취급하므로, 두 번째 빈칸에는 wants가 와야 한다.

13 ④ 「every + 단수명사」는 단수 취급하므로, were를 was로 고쳐야 한다.

16 첫 번째 빈칸에는 앞의 명사와 같은 종류의 사물 중에 불특정한 것을 가리키는 one이 와야 한다.

두 번째 빈칸에는 '(둘 중의) 하나는 …, 나머지 하나는 ~'의 의미인 「one ... the other ~」 구문의 One이 와야 한다.

17 사진에 세 명의 소녀가 있다. 그들은 서로 손을 잡고 있다. 한 명은 청바지를 입고 있고, 다른 한 명은 치마를 입고 있고, 나머지 한 명은 교복을 입고 있다.

▶ ⑤ '하나는 …, 다른 하나는 ~, 나머지 하나는 ~'은 「one ... another ~ the other ~」로 나타낸다.

18 ③에는 앞에 나온 명사와 같은 종류의 사물을 가리킬 때 쓰는 부정대명사 one이 알맞다. 나머지에는 모두 앞에 나온 명사를 다시 가리키는 it이 와야 한다.

19 by oneself: 혼자서, 혼자 힘으로

[20-21] 모든 배우가 무대 뒤에 있었다. 그들 모두는 공연 전에 연습을 하고 있었다.

20 「every + 단수명사」는 단수 취급한다.

21 「all of + 대명사」는 동사의 수를 대명사에 일치시킨다.

22 one another: 서로

23 Grace의 반에서, 어떤 학생들은 테니스를 좋아하고 나머지 전부는 배구를 좋아한다.

▶ some ... the others ~: 어떤 사람들은 …, 나머지 전부는 ~

CHAPTER 13 비교 구문

GRAMMAR FOCUS ········· p. 202

A 비교 구문의 형태

1 그는 그의 아버지만큼 다정하다.
Jane은 Sammy만큼 피아노를 잘 친다.
오늘은 어제만큼 춥지 않다.

2 둥근 탁자가 오래된 램프보다 더 저렴하다.
이 티셔츠는 저것보다 더 편안하다.
Wilson은 고기보다 생선을 더 좋아한다.

3 건강이 가장 중요한 것이다.
1) 그 판다는 그 동물원에서 가장 인기 있는 동물이다.
2) Bill은 그의 형제들 중에서 가장 키가 크다.

Check-Up ········· p. 203

A 1 hotter, hottest 2 better, best 3 wiser, wisest 4 more beautiful, most beautiful
B 1 much 2 most 3 high 4 than
C 1 dark 2 prettier 3 less 4 the most diligent
D 1 far later than 2 the largest 3 as white as 4 the most difficult

GRAMMAR FOCUS ········· p. 204

B 주요 비교 표현

1 1) 그녀는 가능한 한 크게 소리쳤다.
= 그녀는 그녀가 할 수 있는 한 크게 소리쳤다.
2) 이 책은 저것보다 네 배 더 두껍다.
발리까지의 비행은 홍콩까지의 비행보다 두 배 더 오래 걸린다.

2 1) 점점 더 많은 사람들이 해외로 여행을 가고 있다.
겨울이 시작되면 낮이 점점 더 짧아진다.
2) 우리가 더 높이 올라갈수록, 공기는 더 희박해진다.
그녀를 더 오래 기다릴수록, 그는 더 화가 났다.
3) 너는 피자와 치킨 중에서 어느 것을 더 좋아하니?
Brad와 Charles 중에서 누가 더 잘생겼니?

3 1) 부산은 한국에서 가장 큰 도시들 중 하나이다.
그녀는 역대 가장 위대한 시인들 중 한 명이다.
2) 그것은 내가 지금까지 본 것 중 가장 무서운 영화이다.
너는 우리가 지금까지 들어 본 것 중 가장 아름다운 목소리를 가지고 있다.

Check-Up ········· p. 205

A 1 the kindest 2 soon 3 four times 4 pianists
B 1 quickly 2 bigger than 3 more, more
C 1 worse and worse 2 or 3 colder
D 1 as often as possible 2 the most unique, have ever 3 one of the smartest

Grammar Practice p. 206

A 1 not as[so] sour 2 farther 3 longest 4 happier
B 1 more fluently 2 warmer, warmer 3 brief 4 most famous
C 1 heavier than 2 as fast as 3 the tallest 4 three times more expensive

문제해설

A 1 not as[so]+형용사의 원급+as: …만큼 ~하지 않은
3 the+최상급+명사+(that)+주어+have ever v-ed: …가 지금까지 ~한 것 중 가장 …한 (명사)

B 1 비교급+than: …보다 더 ~한[하게]
2 비교급+and+비교급: 점점 더 …한[하게]
3 as+원급+as possible: 가능한 한 …한[하게]
4 the+최상급+in+장소/범위: …에서 가장 ~한[하게]

C 3 the+형용사의 최상급: 가장 …한
4 배수사+비교급+than: …보다 몇 배로 ~한[하게]

내신 완성 Grammar Practice p. 207

1 ④ 2 ⑤ 3 ②, ⑤ 4 (1) is more convenient than (2) more and more excited

문제해설

2 첫 번째 빈칸에는 문맥상 '(정도가) 더 나아간'의 의미인 further가 와야 한다.
두 번째 빈칸 앞에 the, 뒤에 「of+복수명사」가 왔으므로, 빈칸에는 최상급 least가 와야 한다.

3 William의 가게는 우리 동네에서 가장 저렴한 가게이다. 그곳의 대부분의 제품들은 다른 상점들의 것보다 훨씬 더 저렴하다. 하지만 그곳의 제품들이 동네에서 가장 안 좋기 때문에 그 가게는 가장 인기 있지는 않다.
▶ ② 부사 very는 비교급을 수식할 수 없다.
⑤ 형용사 bad의 최상급은 worst이므로, the worst가 되어야 한다.

서술형에 나오는 WRITING p. 208

A 1 This is the largest museum he has ever visited.
2 The harder you study, the better your grades will be.
B 1 Which is smaller, or 2 the deepest lakes
3 much more attractive than
C 1 as old as 2 the most
3 more expensive than

문제해설

B 3 비교급을 강조하는 부사(much)는 비교급 앞에 온다.

C 1 Hills 호텔은 Star 호텔만큼 오래되었으므로 원급 비교 구문인 as old as를 써야 한다.
2 Beachside 호텔은 세 호텔들 중 가장 객실이 많으므로 최상급인 the most를 써야 한다.
3 Star 호텔은 Hills 호텔보다 더 비싸므로 비교급 비교 구문인 more expensive than을 써야 한다.

READING WITH GRAMMAR pp. 209~210

Reading 1 | 1 ② 2 10 billion times greater than
Words | ¹ 성공적인

해석 | 이 숫자를 보아라: 10,000,000,000,000,000,000,000,000,000,000,000,000,000,000,000,000,000,000,000,000,000,000,000,000,000,000,000,000,000,000,000,000,000,000,000,000,000,000. 그것은 당신이 지금까지 본 것 중 가장 큰 숫자인가? 그것은 무엇인가? 1조? 아니, 그렇지 않다. 100개의 0이 있으므로, 그것은 1조보다 훨씬 더 크다.

1938년에 수학자 Edward Kasner가 그것을 적었다. 그러고 나서 그는 조카에게 그 숫자의 이름을 생각해 보라고 했다. 9살짜리 소년은 "구골"이라고 결정했다. 그러면, 구골은 얼마나 클까? 우주에 얼마나 많은 모래 알갱이가 들어갈 수 있는지 상상해 보아라. 구골은 그것보다 100억 배 더 크다. 그것은 또한 세계에서 가장 성공적인 기술 기업들 중 하나의 이름에 영감을 주었다. 맞다—구글(Google)은 구골(googol)의 틀린 철자이다! 그 회사는 자신들의 검색 엔진이 정말 많은 정보를 찾을 수 있음을 보여주기 위해 그 이름을 선택했다.

구문해설

7행 **Having 100 zeros**, it's much bigger than a trillion.
▸ Having 100 zeros는 이유를 나타내는 분사구문이다.

9행 Mathematician Dr. Edward Kasner **wrote it down** in 1938.
▸ 동사구(wrote down)의 목적어가 대명사(it)이므로 목적어가 동사와 부사 사이에 왔다.

14행 That company chose the name **to show** *that* their search engine can find lots and lots of information.
▸ to show는 목적을 나타내는 부사적 용법의 to부정사이다.
▸ that은 동사 show의 목적어 역할을 하는 명사절을 이끄는 접속사이다.

문제해설

1 ① 우주의 크기
② Googol: 100개의 0을 가진 숫자
③ 역사상 가장 위대한 수학자
④ 수학 천재였던 9살 소년
⑤ Google은 어떻게 성공적인 기업이 되었나
▸ 100개의 0을 가진 숫자인 googol의 탄생 일화와 그것이 얼마나 큰 숫자인지 설명한 글이므로, ②가 제목으로 가장 적절하다.

2 '…보다 몇 배로 ~한'을 나타내는 「배수사+비교급+than」의 어순으로 쓴다.

Reading 2 | 1 match 2 ③
Words | ¹ 가구 ² 표현

해석 | 당신은 멋진 셔츠를 사지만, 그것에 어울리는 바지를 갖고 있지 않다. 그래서 당신은 새 바지를 사고 어울리는 신발이 필요하다고 결정한다. 계속해서, 당신은 나가서 당신이 이미 가진 것에 어울리는 새로운 물건을 산다. 이것은 '디드로 효과'라고 불린다.

18세기, Denis Diderot라는 한 남자는 아름다운 가운을 받았다. 이 가운과 비교하여, 그의 집의 나머지 것들이 덜 매력적으로 보였다. 그는 벽에 걸 더 많은 미술 작품과 방에 놓을 더 좋은 가구가 필요하다고 생각했다. 그는 그 특별한 가운에 맞추기 위해 가장 좋고 최신의 물건들을 사기 시작했다. 그가 더 많이 사면 살수록, 그는 새 물건을 더 많이 원했다. Diderot가 이 이야기를 에세이에서 언급한 이후로, 사람들은 비슷한 상황을 묘사하기 위해 '디드로 효과'라는 표현을 사용해 왔다.

구문해설

3행 ..., you go out and buy new stuff to match [**what** you already own].
▸ what은 선행사를 포함하는 관계대명사로, 동사 match의 목적어 역할을 하는 관계사절을 이끈다.

9행 He started to buy the best and newest things **in order to match** the special gown.
▸ in order to-v: …하기 위해서

12행 ..., people **have used** the expression ....
▸ have used는 계속을 나타내는 현재완료이다.

문제해설

1 본문에서 쓰인 단어를 이용하여 빈칸을 채우시오.
디드로 효과는 당신이 이미 가진 것들과 맞추기 위해 새로운 물건을 계속 사는 것을 의미한다.
▸ 본인에게 새로 생긴 가운과 맞추기 위해 새로운 물건들을 계속해서 샀던 Diderot의 이야기에서 기원이 된 '디드로 효과'를 설명한 글이다.

2 빈칸 (A)와 (B)에 들어갈 말이 바르게 짝지어진 것은?
▸ the+비교급, the+비교급: …하면 할수록, 더 ~하다

내신에 나오는 COMMUNICATION

A 비교하기 p. 211

Check-Up | 1 ② 2 more interesting, or

문제해설

1 A: 이 영화는 우리가 지난번에 본 것보다 더 기니?
B: ____________________
① 모르겠는데, 아마 아닐 거야.
② 나는 이전에 영화를 본 적이 없어.
③ 아니, 이 영화는 그것보다 훨씬 더 짧아.
④ 이 영화는 그것보다 20분 더 길어.
⑤ 이 영화는 우리가 지난번에 본 것만큼 길어.
▶ ② 영화가 지난번에 본 것보다 더 긴지 묻는 말에 영화를 본 적이 없다고 대답하는 것은 어색하다.

2 A: 너는 수학과 과학 중 어떤 과목이 더 흥미롭다고 생각해?
B: 나는 과학이 더 흥미로운 것 같아.

B 경고하기 p. 212

Check-Up | 1 ③ 2 Be sure not to make the same mistake again.

문제해설

1 ③은 '떠들도록 해라.'는 의미로, 주어진 그림과 어울리지 않는다. ①과 ②(조용히 하도록 해라.), ④(떠들지 않도록 조심해라.), ⑤(떠들지 않도록 해라.)는 모두 상대방에게 조용히 하라는 경고 표현이다.

FINAL TEST pp. 213~215

1 ⑤ 2 convenient 3 ① 4 (B)→(D)→(A)→(C) 5 ④ 6 ③ 7 ② 8 ④ 9 ④ 10 ③ 11 ④ 12 is far larger than mine 13 one of the most famous 14 ⑤ 15 ⑤ 16 ④ 17 ②, ③ 18 warmer than 19 most 20 as 21 younger than 22 as heavy as 23 the tallest of

문제해설

1 ⑤ valuable은 '소중한'이라는 뜻이다.

3 A: 이 두 가지가 가장 잘 팔리는 재킷입니다.
B: 전 두 개 다 좋아요. ____________________
A: 흰 것이 검은 것보다 더 저렴합니다.
▶ 빈칸 뒤에서 어느 것이 더 저렴한지 대답하고 있으므로, 빈칸에는 ① '어느 것이 더 저렴한가요?'가 오는 것이 가장 자연스럽다.

4 (B) 나는 네가 휴일에 해외여행을 갈 거라고 들었어.
(D) 맞아. 이번이 내 첫 번째 해외여행이 될 거야. 네가 조언을 좀 해줄래?
(A) 위장약을 챙기도록 해.
(C) 알겠어. 미리 좀 살게.

5 A: 나는 테니스 경기를 보러 코트에 갈 거야.
B: 재미있겠다! 하지만 경기 중에는 자리를 지키도록 해.
A: 아, 명심하도록 할게.
▶ ④의 「be careful not to-v」는 밑줄 친 부분의 「make sure to-v」와 반대되는 표현이다.

6 ③ the+최상급+in+장소: …에서 가장 ~한[하게]

7 ② 형용사의 비교급+than: …보다 더 ~한

8 ④ the+비교급, the+비교급: …하면 할수록, 더 ~하다

9 ④ 부사 very는 비교급을 수식할 수 없다.

10 「not as[so]+형용사의 원급+as」는 '…만큼 ~하지 않은'의 의미로 ③ 형용사 bad의 비교급 worse는 빈칸에 들어갈 말로 적절하지 않다.

11 ④ 형용사 important와 intelligent는 3음절 이상의 단어로, 원급 앞에 more를 붙여 비교급을 만든다.

14 ⑤ 「the+최상급+명사+that+주어+have ever v-ed」 구문이 쓰인 문장이므로, hotter를 the hottest로 고쳐야 한다.

15 ① harder → the harder, ② much → many, ③ good → better, ④ little → less로 고쳐야 한다.

17 ②, ③ 배수사를 이용한 비교 표현은 「배수사+as+원급+as」 또는 「배수사+비교급+than」으로 나타낼 수 있다.

18 내일은 오늘보다 더 따뜻하므로, warmer than이 와야 한다.

[19-20] 이 꽃병은 우리 가게에서 가장 비싼 제품이다. 우리는 그것을 옮길 때 우리가 할 수 있는 한 조심하려고 노력한다.

19 the+최상급+in+장소/범위: …에서 가장 ~한[하게]

20 as+원급+as+주어+can: ~가 할 수 있는 한 …한[하게]

21 Andy는 Patrick보다 더 어리다.

22 Tim은 Andy만큼 무겁다.

23 Patrick은 셋 중 가장 키가 크다.

CHAPTER 14 가정법

GRAMMAR FOCUS p. 218

A 가정법의 의미와 형태

2 2) 그들이 로마에 있다면, 콜로세움을 둘러볼 수 있을 텐데.
(← 그들은 로마에 없어서, 콜로세움을 둘러볼 수 없다.)
내가 축구를 잘한다면, 축구팀에 가입할 수 있을 텐데.
(← 나는 축구를 잘하지 않아서, 축구팀에 가입할 수 없다.)

3 2) Abby가 기차를 탔었다면, 수업에 늦지 않았을 텐데.
(← Abby가 기차를 타지 않아서, 수업에 늦었다.)
비가 오지 않았다면, 우리는 소풍을 갈 수 있었을 텐데.
(← 비가 와서, 우리는 소풍을 갈 수 없었다.)

Check-Up p. 219

A 1 had 2 turn 3 had run 4 would
B 1 could drive 2 would have bought
3 rains 4 didn't have
C 1 were[was] 2 had come 3 have waited
D 1 didn't have, could join
2 hadn't thrown away, could have exchanged

GRAMMAR FOCUS p. 220

B I wish 가정법

1 2) 내가 유명한 모델이면 좋을 텐데.
(← 내가 유명한 모델이 아니어서 유감이다.)
내가 너와 시간을 더 보내면 좋을 텐데.
(← 내가 너와 시간을 더 보내지 않아서 유감이다.)
내가 청중들 앞에서 말을 잘할 수 있으면 좋을 텐데.
(← 내가 청중들 앞에서 말을 잘하지 못해서 유감이다.)

2 2) 내가 그 물품을 발명했더라면 좋았을 텐데.
(← 내가 그 물품을 발명하지 않아서 유감이다.)
내가 시험 공부를 열심히 했더라면 좋았을 텐데.
(← 내가 시험 공부를 열심히 하지 않아서 유감이다.)
나는 문을 열 수 없어. 내가 열쇠를 잃어버리지 않았더라면 좋았을 텐데.
(← 내가 열쇠를 잃어버려서 유감이다.)

Check-Up p. 221

A 1 hope 2 were 3 could 4 had bought
B 1 could record 2 were[was] 3 had come
4 had brought
C 1 hadn't stayed 2 had 3 were[was]
D 1 had worn 2 hadn't spent 3 had

Grammar Practice p. 222

A 1 hadn't[had not] quit 2 were[was] 3 were
4 hadn't[had not] watched
B 1 were[was] 2 had learned[learnt]
3 have won 4 could paint
C 1 were[was] close 2 knew, could call
3 hadn't had, have stayed 4 didn't see

문제해설

A 1 뒤에 과거를 나타내는 표현 last year가 있으므로, 과거 사실과 반대되는 소망을 나타내는 I wish 가정법 과거완료로 쓴다.
2 「If+주어+동사의 과거형, 주어+could+동사원형」은 '만약 …라면, ~할 수 있을 텐데'라는 의미의 가정법 과거로, if절의 be동사는 were 또는 was를 쓴다.
3 뒤에 현재를 나타내는 표현 now가 있으므로, 현재에 이루기 힘든 소망을 나타내는 I wish 가정법 과거로 쓴다.
4 If+주어+had v-ed, 주어+could+have v-ed: 만약 …했다면, ~할 수 있었을 텐데

내신 완성 Grammar Practice p. 223

1 ④ 2 ⑤ 3 ③ 4 (1) had taken your advice
(2) didn't[did not] have, could eat

문제해설

1 ④ last week가 쓰인 것으로 보아 과거 사실에 반대되는 소망을 나타내는 I wish 가정법 과거완료가 와야 하므로, had attended가 알맞다.
2 Ben은 다리를 다쳐서, 스키를 타러 갈 수 없었다.
▶ ⑤ 가정법 과거완료는 과거 사실과 반대되는 상황을 가정한다.
3 ③ 현재 사실과 반대되는 상황을 가정하는 가정법 과거이므로 if절의 be동사는 과거형 were가 되어야 한다.

서술형에 나오는 WRITING p. 224

A 1 I wish I could stay longer.
2 If Bill had not driven, the accident wouldn't have happened.
3 I wish I had bought the chair in another color.
B 1 I hadn't[had not] forgotten about my sister's birthday
2 had known your address, I would[could] have picked you up
3 had enough apples, you could make an apple pie
C 1 could[would] go there
2 could have conversations

문제해설

B 1 I wish 가정법 과거완료 구문이다.
2 가정법 과거완료 구문이다.
3 가정법 과거 구문이다.

C 안녕, Charles! 네가 시카고로 돌아간 지 1년이 되었구나. 우리 함께 미술 수업을 듣던 때가 그리워. 시립 미술관에서 클림트 전시회가 열릴 거야. 네가 여기 있다면, 우리는 함께 그곳에 갈 수 있을 텐데[갈 텐데]. 너와 그의 그림에 대한 대화를 할 수 있으면 좋을 텐데. 언젠가 너를 만날 것을 기대하고 있을게.

READING WITH GRAMMAR

pp. 225~226

Reading 1 | 1 ② 2 were[was]
Words | [1] 귀찮게 하다 [2] 대답하다

해석 | 두 젊은 여성이 고급 식당에서 식사를 하고 있을 때, 한 부인이 그들의 테이블로 와서 그중 한 명에게 말했다. "귀찮게 해서 미안하지만, 당신은 꼭 제 딸처럼 생겼네요. 그 애는 작년에 죽었어요. 내가 그 애를 마지막으로 한 번 볼 수 있으면 좋을 텐데. 내가 당신에게 부탁 하나 해도 될까요? 내가 떠날 때, 당신이 내게 손을 흔들며 '잘 가세요, 엄마.'라고 말해 주겠어요?" 그 여자는 그 부인이 안쓰러워서, 그녀가 부탁했던 대로 하기로 했다. 하지만 그 부인이 떠나기 전에, 그 젊은 여성은 일어서서 그 부인의 식사 비용을 내겠다고 제안했다. 그녀의 친구가 왜 그러냐고 묻자, 그녀는 대답했다. "지금 이 순간, 그 분은 내가 그분의 딸이라고 생각하고 있어. 그분의 딸이 살아 있다면, 그녀는 (나와) 똑같이 할 텐데."

구문해설

5행 ..., so she agreed to do **as** the lady *had asked*.
▶ 접속사 as는 '…대로'의 의미로 쓰였다.
▶ 부인이 부탁한 시점이 그녀(젊은 여성)가 요청 받은 대로 하기로 했던 때보다 앞에 있어났으므로, 과거완료 had asked가 쓰였다.

8행 ..., she thinks (**that**) I am her daughter.
▶ think 뒤에 목적어 역할을 하는 명사절을 이끄는 접속사 that이 생략되었다.

문제해설

1 ②는 부인의 딸을 가리키며, 나머지는 모두 부인을 가리킨다.

2 현재 사실과 반대되는 상황을 가정하는 가정법 과거 문장이므로 if절의 동사는 과거형으로 쓴다.

Reading 2 | 1 ④ 2 I wish my car had wings
Words | [1] 개발하다 [2] 기능

해석 | 여러분은 '내 차에 날개가 있어서 내가 차량들 위로 날아갈 수 있으면 좋을 텐데.'라고 생각해 본 적이 있는가? 미국의 한 회사가 여러분의 꿈을 실현시켜 줄 수도 있는 차를 개발했다. 그것은 두 개의 좌석, 네 개의 바퀴, 그리고 접을 수 있는 날개가 있다. 날개를 펼치기 위해, 여러분은 그저 버튼만 누르면 된다. 그러면 차는 단 30초 만에 비행기로 변할 것이다! 그것은 약 800킬로미터의 거리를 최대 시속 185km의 속도로 날 수 있다. 그것의 비행 기능 때문에, 그것은 이륙하기 위해 활주로가 필요하고, 운전자들은 조종사 면허증이 필요하다. 그것은 마치 다른 비행기들과 같은 것처럼 들리지만, 그것은 궂은 날씨에도 성공적으로 착륙해서 도로 위를 달릴 수 있다.

그 차를 만든 회사는 그것이 곧 판매될 것이라고 믿는다. 이제, 여러분이 이 놀라운 차를 갖는다면 어떨지 상상해 봐라. 정말 멋질 텐데!

구문해설

11행 Now, imagine what **it would be** like **if you had** this amazing car.
▶ If+주어+동사의 과거형, 주어+would+동사원형: 만약 …라면, ~할 텐데

13행 How wonderful it **would** be!
▶ 문맥상 would는 앞 문장에 나온 가정법 과거의 연장으로, be 뒤에 if you had this amazing car가 생략되었다.

문제해설

1 날아다니는 차에 대해 사실이 아닌 것은?
① 그것은 접히고 펼쳐질 수 있는 날개가 있다.
② 그것은 차와 비행기 둘 다로 사용될 수 있다.
③ 그것은 공중에서 시속 185km의 속도에 이를 수 있다.
④ 그것은 활주로 없이 이륙할 수 있다.
⑤ 그것을 운전하기 위해, 소유자들은 조종사 면허증이 있어야 한다.
▶ ④ 날아다니는 차는 이륙하기 위해 활주로가 필요하다고 했다.

2 괄호 안의 단어를 바르게 배열하시오.
▶ '…라면 좋을 텐데'라는 의미를 나타내는 「I wish+주어+동사의 과거형」의 어순으로 작성한다.

내신에 나오는 COMMUNICATION

A 기원하기

p. 227

Check-Up | 1 ③ 2 ③

문제해설

1 ③은 '나는 네가 매우 운이 좋다고 생각해.'라는 의미인 반면, 나머지는 모두 상대방에게 행운을 빌어 줄 때 쓰는 표현이다.

B 반복 요청하기

p. 228

Check-Up | 1 ③ 2 I beg your pardon

문제해설

1 ③은 '내 말을 따라해 줄래?'의 의미로, 문맥상 적절하지 않다.

FINAL TEST

pp. 229~231

1 ⑤ 2 distance 3 ⑤ 4 keep my fingers crossed 5 ④ 6 ② 7 ④ 8 ④ 9 ① 10 have participated 11 had come 12 ⑤ 13 ④ 14 If I had been careful 15 I were[was] as tall as Tom 16 ② 17 ① 18 ④ 19 ④ 20 If I had gone to Arizona, I could have visited the Grand Canyon. 21 I wish I had discussed the matter with you. 22 I would fly in the sky 23 I would talk with animals

문제해설

1 그들은 바다 근처의 값비싼 호텔에 머물렀다.
① 큰 ② 조용한 ③ 살아 있는 ④ 접을 수 있는 ⑤ 비싼

3 ⑤ 내일 역사 시험을 본다는 말에 '네가 시험을 잘 봤더라면 좋았을 텐데.'라고 대답하는 것은 적절하지 않다.

5 A: 그 차를 달게 만들려면, 설탕을 넣고 약한 불에서 5분간 저으세요.
B: 다시 말해 줄래요?
▶ 밑줄 친 문장은 상대방의 말을 반복해 주길 요청하는 표현이다. ④는 '왜 내게 그것을 말했니?'의 의미이다.

6 나에게 지금 쉴 시간이 있다면 좋을 텐데.
▶ ② 현재를 나타내는 now가 쓰였으므로 I wish 가정법 과거가 되어야 한다.

7 네가 우산을 가져왔다면, 너는 젖지 않았을 텐데.
▶ 과거 사실과 반대되는 상황을 가정하는 가정법 과거 완료가 되어야 하므로, ④ had brought가 적절하다.

8 • 우리가 해변에 있다면 좋을 텐데.
• 내가 너라면, 그런 비싼 차를 사지 않을 텐데.
▶ ④ I wish 가정법 과거와 가정법 과거의 if절에서 be동사는 과거형을 쓴다.

9 ① 가정법 과거 「If+주어+동사의 과거형, 주어+could+동사원형」 구문이 쓰였다.

10 가정법 과거완료 「If+주어+had v-ed, 주어+could+have v-ed」 구문이 쓰였으므로, have participated가 알맞다.

11 과거를 나타내는 표현인 last night가 쓰였으므로, I wish 가정법 과거완료로 쓴다.

12 A: 복권에 당첨된다면 너는 무엇을 하겠니?
B: 내가 복권에 당첨된다면, 그 돈을 자선 단체에 기부할 텐데.
▶ ⑤ 가정법 과거 구문이므로, 빈칸에 「주어+would/should/could/might+동사원형」이 와야 한다.

14 내가 주의하지 않아서, 나는 다쳤다.
▶ 과거 사실과 반대되는 가정법 과거완료를 쓴다.

15 내가 Tom만큼 키가 크지 않아서 유감이다.
▶ 현재 이루기 힘든 소망을 나타내는 I wish 가정법 과거를 쓴다.

17 ① 과거를 나타내는 표현인 at that time이 쓰였으므로, I wish 가정법 과거완료 「I wish+주어+had v-ed」가 되어야 한다. 따라서 are를 had been으로 고쳐야 한다.

19 나는 어제 밤늦게까지 게임을 했다. 그래서 오늘 아침 늦잠을 잤고 학교에 늦었다. 내가 일찍 일어났더라면, 늦지 않았을 텐데.
▶ ④ 가정법 과거완료에서 if절의 동사는 「had v-ed」를 쓰므로, get up을 had gotten[got] up으로 고쳐야 한다.

20 내가 Arizona에 가지 않았기 때문에, 나는 그랜드 캐니언을 방문할 수 없었다.

[22-23] Q: 너에게 초능력이 있다면 너는 무엇을 할 거니?

22 Joan: 나에게 초능력이 있다면, 나는 하늘을 날 텐데.

23 Eric: 나에게 초능력이 있다면, 나는 동물들과 이야기할 텐데.
▶ 현재 또는 미래에 실현 가능성이 희박한 일을 상상할 때는 가정법 과거를 쓴다. 또한, 질문에 조동사 would가 있으므로, 대답할 때도 would를 쓰는 것이 적절하다.